SINATRA

THE ENTERTAINER

FRANK DID IT HIS WAY
DORIS IS FOLLOWING SUIT
DON'T LET HER EASY MANNER
DECEIVE YOU

BENEATH LIES A
MALEMUTE.

SHE DIDN'T ᴱᵃˢⁱˡʸ GET THE JOB SHE HAS
SENDING COMPETITORS TO ROUT
DON'T MISTAKE HER FOR A
POLLYANNA
OR SHE'LL KNOCK YOUR
STUPID BRAINS OUT.

G J HARRINGTON
STAMFORD
1985

SINATRA
THE ENTERTAINER

by
ARNOLD SHAW

with
TED ALLAN
Photographic Consultant

Designed by
ED CARAEFF

DELILAH BOOKS
Distributed by
The Putnam Publishing Group
N E W   Y O R K

A Delilah Book
Delilah Communications Ltd.
118 E. 25 Street
New York, New York 10010

ISBN: 0-933328-43-5
Library of Congress Catalog Card
Number: 82-71724

Manufactured in the U.S.A.
First printing 1982

Special thanks to Stephanie Bennett,
Amit Shah, Una Fahy, Richard Schatzberg,
Virginia Rubel, Sharon Kapnick, and
Kathryn Greene.

BOOK DESIGN: ED CARAEFF

TED ALLAN

For thoughtful discussions and/or comments on the manuscript, I wish to express my indebtedness to Bill Willard of *Daily Variety;* Jim Seagrave of the Frontier Hotel and formerly of Caesars Palace; Forrest Duke, Pete Mikla of the *Las Vegas Review-Journal;* Elliot Krane and Joe Delaney of the *Las Vegas Sun;* Jeannie Sakol of Delilah Communications; Peter Lind Hayes and Mary Healy; film producer Walter Shenson; photographer Ted Allan; music executive Sam Trust without whom this book might have remained in manuscript; and most of all, to my wife, Ghita Milgrom Shaw.

The text itself names others who were the source of valuable insights and information.

CONTENTS

In March 1982, a group of dedicated fans of Francis Albert Sinatra flew from Belgium to Nepal and Tibet in the Himalayas. Equipped with mountaineering paraphernalia—cleated boots, pitons, ice axes, climbing ropes, oxygen tanks and sun glasses—they embarked on the ascent of the highest mountain in the world, Mt. Everest. Defying the thin, rarefied air, falling rocks, concealed crevasses, the blinding glare of the sun, the extreme heat of the day and the freezing temperatures at night, and the danger of high winds, sudden snow falls and avalanches, they slowly made their way upward. After days of exhausting and treacherous climbing, they reached an altitude of 16,000 feet. There, on the summit of rugged Kala Pattar peak, they embedded an ice pick with a flag bearing the name and insignia of the Sinatra Society of Belgium!

Of the numerous tributes that have been paid to Sinatra, his golden tonsils and artistry, this surely was one of the most daring and imaginative, a testimonial that embodied a legendary symbolism.

Waving on a wind-swept peak, the flag is an appropriate and colorful emblem of the man who has been feted as the Entertainer of the Century by his peers and characterized as the Washington Monument of Entertainers by a President of the United States. Sinatra stands today on a pinnacle of the entertainment world as he has for four decades, an artist who has surpassed in longevity, scope, humanity, and appeal, the achievements of every other popular singer of our time.

Not too long ago, Las Vegas columnist Forrest Duke observed: "Sinatra opens a one-week engagement at Caesars Palace. It's four weeks off. But every night is a sellout as of now. And when Sinatra is in town, he sells out not only Caesars Palace but the town."

About a week later, syndicated columnist Earl Wilson noted: "Sinatra opens for one week at the Royal Festival Hall in London. Four hours after seats went on sale, the house was sold out. There were over 20,000 requests for the 4,000 seater."

The sellout phenomenon repeats itself whether he performs at Carnegie Hall in New York City, the Newport Jazz Festival in Rhode Island, the Universal Amphitheatre near Los Angeles, the Marcãna Stadium in Brazil, the Sun City Hotel in the South African Republic of Bophuthatswana, or the Pyramids near Cairo. Ol' Blue Eyes' microphone is still a magic wand, weaving a spell for people everywhere.

But even when he is just a sound and not a presence, his audience and appeal persist. The longest-running radio show in this country reportedly emanates from a suburb of Philadelphia. Titled *Friday with Frank,* devoted entirely to Sinatra recordings, it has been continuously on the air since the year that Elvis Presley exploded on the record scene. Sid Mark, its emcee, is one of a number of disc jockeys around the country with a Sinatra-focussed format. In 1974, Mark found the audience for his program growing at such a pace that he added a four-hour *Sunday with Frank* to his celebration of the Sinatra discography.

As for the ladies, the love affair that had its beginnings in the early '40s shows no sign of abatement. I cannot forget a concert at the Forest Hills Stadium not too long ago when a middle-aged Manhattan matron went charging down the aisle, and in the middle of a number, put her arms around Frank for a moment of bliss. Hardly had she returned to her chair when another well-dressed woman left her husband's side and rushed to the front of the outdoor arena to plant a delicate kiss on Frank's cheek. Startled security guards were now running from different corners of the stadium to establish a barrier between the singer and the audience. But a third woman, also middle-aged and evening-gowned, got to Sinatra, took his hand, and held it tenderly to her cheek, if she did not kiss it.

There were singers, of course, before Sinatra with undeniable appeal to the ladies—Al Jolson, whose dynamic style magnetized even a rocker like Jerry Lee Lewis (who saw him only on the screen); Rudy Vallee, the Vagabond Lover, after whom a chichi Manhattan night spot (later the Copa) was named; Bing Crosby, whose enormous record sales built the fledgling Decca Record company and was still the Number One hitmaker when the Voice made his early volcanic appearances at the New York Paramount.

But none of these swept the females off their feet as Sinatra did and left them moaning, sobbing, panting, or screaming ecstatically. The hysteria generated by the thin singer became a subject for speculation and analysis by critics and psychologists, many of whom traced the phenomenon to the female mothering instinct. But it was one of the teenagers, writing as a middle-aged contributor to *The New York Times,* who laughed the mother explanation out of court.

"What yo-yo's!" wrote Martha Weinman Lear . "Whatever Sinatra stirred beneath our barely budding breasts, it wasn't motherly. The thing we had going with Frankie was sexy."

Truth to speak, what Sinatra brought into popular singing, apart from his masterful handling of lyrics and fine taste in the choice of songs, was quite simply sex. None of the singers who preceded him, nor many who have followed, have made so blatant a use of songs as an instrument for making love. Sinatra never just sang; he seduced.

However, it was not the kind of sex that made an object of the woman, as the Rolling Stones and other rock groups have done. In Sinatra's style, sex was allied to deep feeling. And he was a tender lover as well as a vulnerable one. When he suffered because "no one cares," as he titled one of his albums, or he was "a fool to want her" in the wee hours of the morning, his anguish was so palpable that they wept with him and for him.

In short, it was not just on the levels of ecstasy and heartache that he grabbed his listeners. The pitch of his singing was equally intense when he was buoyant and sang "Come Fly with Me" or "New York, New York." Singing was an unabashed expression of sheer emotion.

And he lived his life with the abandon, the extravagance, and the recklessness of the romanticist whether he was pursuing a passionate love affair while still married, belting an unfriendly columnist in the jaw, or walking off a movie set, despite a binding contract. Some termed it arrogance. Others attributed his conduct to an uncontrollable temper. Whatever the explanation, he had no fear of fighting tough odds even when his career was at stake, and he did not back down when he faced formidable enemies in the media. For that matter, he faced even tougher odds when he staged the greatest comeback in entertainment history in the mid-'50s. He had guts as well as talent.

The image of the man who challenged and rose above the human condition has become blurred in recent years. But for much of his remarkable career and life, he was the incurable Romantic, an artist who strove insistently to extend his reach and, as a singer, to scale the summits of expressiveness.

In 1982 the voice is not what it was, nor can it be. Admittedly, the willowy, wraithlike figure has developed a midriff bulge. Admittedly, the youthful crooner of World War II is now a senior citizen whose joking reference to Geritol at a concert brought an offer of a sizable stipend if the "aside" could be used in the company's advertising. Then how does one explain his continued hold on audiences?

The Sinatra spell is a product not only of his gemlike artistry but of several other factors that make him a mythic figure of our time. From the beginning, he had magnetism and electricity. His appearance on stage is awaited even today with hushed anticipation, and his entry evokes gasps and gurgles of excitement. Despite changes in his career and life, he possesses a mystique that is a disparate combination of tenderness and toughness, of vulnerability

and violence, of compassion and coarseness whose dialectical interplay adds a dazzling dimension to his work. Heightened by artful showmanship, these elements attract audiences that were not part of the swooning syndrome, or privy to his thunderous emergence in popular music.

Nor can the nostalgic factor be discounted. His recordings, in Peter Bogdanovich's memorable phrase, "are not only his autobiography but ours as well." He excites a remembrance of things past because he has freighted events so forcefully and irrevocably with his singing. But the songs work their necromancy in a kind of imagined nostalgia on those whose lives and loves and memories were not part of his biography. This includes writers even on the rock publication, *Rolling Stone*, one of whom observed in 1980: "When Sinatra left the stage, we realized we might never witness artistry that big and that provocative again."

Regardless of where he stands today—and the man has changed as inevitably as his voice—he remains the embodiment and summation of an era. The Swing era was the era of the Big Bands, the Big Ballads, and of the Saturday night *Hit Parade*, a coast-to-coast radio show on which he starred in the '40s. It was also the era of a worldwide war against racism whose idealism stirred a young Sinatra to take time from his work to address young people around the country on tolerance and to make a film short that brought him his first Oscar.

The walls of Sinatra's Rancho Mirage home in California are a mosaic of framed awards, many of them in recognition for his devotion to the welfare of others. He might have received these honors had he never stepped before a microphone, walked into a recording studio, performed on a showroom stage, or appeared before a motion picture camera. But they were made possible and his efforts have yielded such gigantic returns because the preeminent romantic vocalist of our time is also a business giant.

Having carved out for himself a sky-high place in the entertainment history of the 20th century, he insists on calling himself a "saloon singer." But he was always a singer's singer, an entertainer who raised popular singing to the highest level of creativity. From a cultural and historical standpoint, he—more than any other entertainer of our time—forced the public, musicians, songwriters, and critics to recognize that the popular song can be a form of art and popular singing, an expressive and evocative art form.

This book is not a biography, not a life story, but a retrospective cameo. It is *deja vu*, a glance down the corridors of time at the work of one of the great entertainers and the foremost popular singer of the century.

—— Arnold Shaw
Las Vegas
May 27, 1982

I

The 40th Anniversary Party

DECEMBER 12, 1979

DECEMBER IS TRADITIONALLY A DULL MONTH IN Las Vegas. From Thanksgiving until New Year's, hotel executives expect room occupancy and gaming revenues to dip perceptibly. But 1979, beginning with the weekend December 8th, presented a vastly different picture. The town crackled with unwonted expectancy.

Planes landing at McCarran Airport were packed and disgorged an unusually large complement of celebrities. A surprising number of private jets zoomed in to disembark other luminaries. Taxis sped back and forth from the Strip to the airport as impatient tourists queued up in a long waiting line. Luxury limousines were in demand for the more important arrivals.

By Monday, December 10, it was evident that something big was happening. Strip traffic on what should have been a slow Monday was bumper to bumper. The apex of the action was at Caesars Palace, where a massive sidewalk marquee, mounted on four tall Roman columns, bore the legend: "SINATRA, His first 40 years." But it gave no real indication of what was creating the electricity in the town.

On the curving facade of the casinotel, above the main entrance beyond the fountains, hung two huge oil paintings. They were reportedly, as future editions of the *Guinness Book of World Records* would verify, the largest oils ever produced. Nine stories high, measuring 80-feet long by 45-feet wide, one depicted a slender Sinatra in a gray suit and polka-dot bow tie as he looked in 1939; the other, in full color, displayed the more rotund Sinatra of 1979 in a tuxedo and black bow tie. Commissioned by Caesars Palace, the giant-size paintings were the work of two brothers, David and Doug Brega. Doug Brega was the winner, with a portrait of Diana Ross, of the previous summer's Paint-the-Fence Art Festival at Caesars. The brothers labored over a five-week period, using up 16 gallons of paint and working in a large, open area of the city's Convention Center on their one-piece canvases. (After the festivities were over, the hotel could not find an area large enough to store the two portraits without rolling them and injuring them.)

Inside the bustling casino lobby, at the foot of the wide staircase leading to the Circus Maximus, the main showroom, a large gilt frame on a brass stand carried a reproduction of the two king-size paintings. It bore the legend "All Hail Frank Sinatra on the occasion of his 40th year in show business, December 12, 1979," which happened also to be his 64th birthday.

The 12th was a Wednesday, and the source of the city's excitement was revealed in Las Vegas's two major newspapers. Both ran editorials congratulating Caesars Palace on hosting a celebration the evening of the Hoboken superstar's 40th year in the entertainment field. The *Las Vegas Sun* memorialized the occasion by placing its editorial on its front page, a place, as it explained, "usually reserved for public matters of great significance, or the memorialization of momentous historic events." Heading its testimonial "Double Magic: Sinatra and Las Vegas," it hailed the man "with the golden voice and magnetic personality [as one who had] survived all the mood changes of a fickle public" and "almost single-handedly" put Vegas on the international map.

The excitement over Sinatra's double anniversary and what was soon known as the biggest party in Vegas history was not limited to Las Vegas. It carried over to Los Angeles where the *Herald-Examiner* devoted almost a full page to an article of reminiscences by columnist James Bacon, who was described as "the only columnist still around who goes back 40 years with Sinatra." It could have added that the 40-year relationship was a friendly one.

Of Sinatra, whom he had heard for the first time with the Harry James Band at the College Inn in Chicago's Hotel Sherman in 1939, Bacon said simply: "He's okay in my book." When people ask him how he remains on such good terms with the man "who has the shortest press list in town," he replies jestingly "Easy, I treat him like any other god."

In a more analytical vein, Bacon explained; "The secret of dealing with Frank is to be professional. I have never seen Frank be anything but professional with the press when they are professional." It was Bacon's contention that there are "aggressive city editors, out to get the scowling picture," who do not hesitate to play "dirty pool."

Bacon indicated that he was himself able to print items like: "Frank is going to Rome where the Pope will make him a cardinal. That way we will only have to kiss his ring." Or when Sinatra got into a hassle at the Sands Hotel in Vegas with casino boss Carl Cohen and was belted in the mouth — it was right after Israel won the Six Days' War in 1967 — Bacon wired Sinatra: "Frank, if I have told you once, I have told you a thousand times. Don't fight Jews in the desert." An item like this will "horrify Frank's friends." But with his "terrific sense of humor," Bacon wrote, "Frank loved it."

Several years before the 40th anniversary, Sinatra had told Bacon: "I have a Sicilian temper, but over the years, I have always admired people with restraint. I guess I've always wanted to be more like them. I feel now that I have mellowed." By 1979 Suzy, a New York columnist who was also a good friend of Sinatra's, felt that he had changed: "Frank is getting older," she wrote. "He has mellowed and he has suddenly become more religious."

The mellowing process had begun, perhaps, with the passing of his father in 1969. It had gained momentum with the unfortunate death of his mother in a plane crash in 1977, a shock that had admittedly taken him time to overcome. Of his marriage to Barbara Marx in 1976, an uncle had said: "She has changed Frank completely. She has turned him right around. Frank has grown up a lot."

At 64 Sinatra was back in the fold of the Catholic church, having had his first marriage annulled, reportedly in Rome. Under the guidance of his mother, Barbara Marx had converted to Catholicism, and their civil marriage ceremony had been sanctified at some unspecified date by an exchange of vows in church. As early as 1977 Sinatra had told an interviewer: "I was an altar boy. I still practice my religion dutifully. I go regularly to Mass." On Columbus Day, two months before the Caesars Palace party, he had, in fact, attended Mass at St. Patrick's Cathedral in New York and had been photographed receiving communion. It was the point at which the world became aware of Sinatra's active return to the faith of his parents.

The morning of the anniversary party the switchboard at Caesars Palace was in an uproar. Calls from people clamoring for tickets were coming in like bullets from an automatic rifle. But there were no tickets. It was strictly a party hosted by Caesars Palace, and only invited guests could come. Apart from tourists, there were many locals, all too many, who felt that they should be invited.

"Getting a part in *Chorus Line* or interviewing Garbo," reported the *Hollywood Reporter*, " is a snap compared to what it is like in Vegas, trying to get on the list of invitees to Sinatra's history-making 64th birthday and 40th year in show business celebration. Local bigwigs, politicians, society Turks and stars from around the world are jockeying, cajoling for tickets." The invitation list had been made up by Sinatra, his press people, and executives of Caesars Palace, and invites had been sent by Western Union telegrams. The chosen people numbered 1,200 movie and TV stars, film producers, sports celebrities, hit songwriters, music people associated with Sinatra, and personal friends.

Before the beginning of the evening's festivities, a beaming Sinatra met with reporters, photographers, and broadcasters for a brief interview-photo session. The following day's papers featured pictures showing him in an exuberant mood with, among others, comic Rich Little, actors Glenn Ford, Milton Berle, Dean Martin, Cary Grant, and Sinatra's wife, Barbara.

It was a nostalgic evening, as well it should have been. One area in the hotel lobby contained a replica of the marquee of the New York Paramount Theatre, where Sinatra appearances had sparked bobby-sox hysteria and a near riot. Attendants in this area were dressed in the regalia of Paramount usherettes. The three-hour show in the Circus Maximus, taped for a shorter airing on NBC-TV on January 3, 1980, opened with the Harry James Band playing "One O'Clock Jump." The remembrance of things past brought Nancy Jr. and Frank Jr. onstage with a medley of songs like "I'll Never Smile Again," songs that Frank had sung and recorded during his days as a band vocalist with the James and Tommy Dorsey orchestras.

The Sinatra family—wife Barbara and his three children—occupied a raised table in the center of the large room—the so-called Snake Pit. Tributes were given by many luminaries, including Orson Welles, who adapted Shakespeare for his panegyric and who introduced two distinguished envoys. The Consul General of Israel read a cablegram from Menachem Begin: "You are one of the best friends Israel has, and you have proved your sentiments for our land with your deeds. We are proud to have the Frank Sinatra International Student Center on Mt. Scopus and the Frank Sinatra Brotherhood Youth Center in Nazareth." The Ambassador from Egypt voiced Anwar Sadat's sentiments: "We are still talking about your trip to Cairo a few weeks ago. Your concert is an unforgettable experience that raised $500,000. The moments that you and I shared were all too brief." (When Sadat was assassinated in 1981 Sinatra released a statement: "He was my brother, the bravest man I ever knew. He put his life on the line in his eternal search for peace in the Middle East. Now life has been savagely torn from him and he has died as no man should die. I knew Anwar Sadat and I loved him.")

A wire from President Jimmy Carter, read at the banquet, was a fuller and more analytical expression of sentiment: "The sound of your voice has long been a part of my life—as it was for all Americans and for much of the rest of the world. Over the years you have given us all many memories on record and on film. When we recall the great events of our time or the important moments of our individual lives, it is always with the accompaniment of a song—done your way."

During breaks in the taping of the show, Sinatra was the recipient of five different awards. Representing ASCAP (American Society of Composers, Authors and Publishers), Jule Styne, who had composed many of Frank's hits between 1953 and 1960, presented the first Pied Piper Award. NARAS (National Academy of Recording Arts and Sciences) proffered a special Trustee's Award "for his lifetime devotion to the highest standards of recording artistry." In behalf of the Variety Clubs, Monty Hall delivered a "Humanitarian of the Year, 1980" award. Milton Berle announced that Caesars Palace had named a new fountain after him, the coins of which would be contributed in his name to the John Wayne Memorial Cancer Foundation of UCLA; Berle presented an initial contribution from Caesars Palace of $50,000.

It was Dean Martin who produced an award that was apparently a surprise to Sinatra and that really shook him up. It was a diploma from Hoboken High School, which Frank had left during his sophomore year. He had never stopped regretting that he was a dropout. "My only sorrow," he said at one point during the evening, "is that my father and mother didn't live to see what happened to their Italian son."

By her spontaneous and tremulous reaction, Lillian Carter, the former President's mother, reminded all of the continuing spell of the singer's persona: "I always wanted to meet Frank Sinatra," she gushed, as she grasped his hand. She added: "Frank and I have two things in common. We both get misquoted in the press and we're both Dodger fans."

James Bacon reported: "They tried to locate the doctor who brought Frank into the world 64 years ago. But they discovered that when the doctor spanked Frank at birth, Jilly Rizzo hit the doctor and he hasn't been heard from since."

The film and TV stars who came to celebrate included Lucille Ball, Peter Falk, Glenn Ford, Cary Grant, Rita Hayworth, Louis Jourdan, Gene Kelly, Jack Klugman, Robert Mitchum, Dinah Shore, and Orson Welles, so that the guest list read like a *Who's Who* of Hollywood. Friends and admirers from the world of song included Paul Anka, Tony Bennett, Mac Davis, Lola Falana, Robert Merrill, Wayne Newton, Lou Rawls, Donna Summer,

Dionne Warwick, Henry Mancini, and Andy Williams, among others. Also present were the arranger-conductors with whom Sinatra had worked through the years (Don Costa, Gordon Jenkins, Quincy Jones, Billy May, Sy Oliver), songwriters Jimmy Van Heusen and Sammy Cahn, and Sarge Weiss, a man who had served as his music coordinator for close to 40 years.

There was a bevy of the country's foremost comics, including Milton Berle, Red Buttons, Charlie Callas, Pat Henry, Rich Little, Don Rickles, and Red Skelton, as well as the manager of the Los Angeles Dodgers, Tommy Lasorda, and best-selling novelist Harold Robbins.

"Spiro Agnew, Frank's old pal, was there," Bacon reported, "but kept a low profile. Frank has that old Sicilian loyalty to friends, no matter how much trouble they get into. Agnew, however, was not on the guest list and was not given a name tag."

In closing the evening's entertainment, after he had recovered from the shock of receiving his high school diploma, Frank sang for his supper. He dedicated "I've Got You Under My Skin" to the audience, observing that he had seldom found himself in a room so full of love. As many hoped he would, he concluded his stint with his "anthem," as he called it, "New York, New York." Sinatra scintillated among all the bright stars.

The cost of the shindig to Caesars Palace was reported at a staggering $750,000, perhaps not surprising since it included not only the expenses of dining, wining, and structuring the evening but also advertising abroad as well as nationally. The citizens of fifteen foreign countries, including Japan, France, England, and Australia, were all advised of Sinatra's 40th year in show business—the *first* 40, as the Caesars Palace marquee read.

For a number of guests, forty-eight to be exact, the evening did not end with Caesars's dinner show, which ostensibly stretched into the wee hours of breakfast in your tux. In his private jet, Sinatra flew his Palm Springs neighbors back to his desert retreat at the ninth hole of the Tamarisk Country Club. There the festivities continued, with Sinatra himself serving fried chicken. It reminded friends of parties to which Sinatra, a man who exists on little sleep, invited friends: "Black tie and sunglasses."

It was a most memorable evening for a man with a continuing and memorable career, a man whose popularity and renown were so great that Caesars had begun advertising his appearances in a most-novel manner. A limited number of superstars were publicized in Vegas with the use of only their first names: "Sammy" meant Sammy Davis, Jr., as "Engelbert" referred to Engelbert Humperdinck, and "Diana" to Diana Ross. However in 1979 Sinatra's appearances at Caesars were announced in newspaper ads, on billboards, and on the hotel marquee with two indeterminate words, "He's here" or "He's back"—and nobody had to be told who "he" was. It was rare recognition of the man's renown.

On New Year's eve, 1979, Mutual Radio presented a three-hour Sinatra retrospective titled "It Was a Very Good Year." The host was Sid Mark, a Philadelphia disc jockey who is a Sinatra buff and whose special guest was Sinatra himself. Looking back, 1979 was the first year since *The Main Event* LP of 1974 in which Frank spent considerable time in the recording studio, always a haven and a refuge, cutting the album that was issued as *Trilogy.*

As a performer, he became the first singer in history to present a program of pop songs in the awesome shadows of the Pyramids and the Sphinx in Egypt. A series of concerts in Atlantic City at Resorts International produced a gross of over $1 million. At the Universal Amphitheatre in L.A. he outgrossed his record-breaking figure of $800,000.

Pursuing as he had in the past an arduous and munificent schedule of benefits, he distinguished himself in a program at the Metropolitan Opera House in behalf of the Sloan-Kettering Cancer Center that brought in over $2 million. For the Juvenile Diabetes Association in Denver, he helped raise $500,000. He participated in benefits for Nazi hunter Simon Wiesenthal, the World Mercy Fund, the Republicans, the Buckley School in Los Angeles, and the family of the late mayor of San Francisco, George Moscone, who was assassinated in 1978.

Columbus Day 1979 in New York City found Sinatra leading the annual parade as the grand marshal, a position he also occupied at the Tournament of Roses in Pasadena.

His 40th year in show business was a very good year, indeed.

1. "I Sing The Songs": The Singer

"Frank is a singer who comes along once in a lifetime," said Bing Crosby, "but why did he have to come in my lifetime?"

Actress Betty Grable said: "He sings like Clark Gable makes love."

Novelist-columnist Joyce Haber said: "Sinatra does to a song what Hemingway does to prose."

Of 100 jazzmen queried by jazz critic Leonard Feather, 56 named Frank Sinatra as "the greatest ever" male vocalist. In a survey covering the years 1945 to 1972, Sinatra scored as the Number One Album Artist, with Elvis Presley in the Number Three position and the Beatles, Number Six.

The Sinatra singing style trades on at least four elements: (1) a warm, rich, appealing baritone voice with a unique sound; (2) phrasing that is magical in its clarity and smoothness; (3) crystalline diction in which consonants, even hard terminal ones, are distinctly articulated — a rare accomplishment in pop as well as classical circles; and (4) a depth of feeling that involves and overwhelms listeners.

For Sinatra, singing was not merely a form of entertainment, but also of autobiography. Following in the footsteps of blues singer Billie Holiday, he became the first major pop singer to sing his innermost feelings.

Francis Albert Sinatra was performing at Caesars Palace in the spring of 1979 when composer-conductor-arranger Gordon Jenkins and the late record producer Sonny Burke drove in from Hollywood to see him.

Burke had been the producer of a score of Sinatra albums, including the award-winning *September of My Years, A Man and His Music,* and LPs of Sinatra collaborations with Count Basie, Duke Ellington, and Bossa Nova king Antonio Carlos Jobim. Gordon Jenkins was the writer of such standards as "P.S., I Love You" and "Homesick, That's All" and had worked on various projects with Sinatra since 1957, arranging and conducting, among other albums, *London By Night, All Alone,* and *September of My Years.*

When they met with Sinatra, Burke asked: "We want to know why you're not recording?"

Frank had not had a new album release in over five years, the last being *The Main Event,* a live recording of his 1974 concert at Madison Square Garden.

"What the hell are you guys talking about?" Sinatra demanded. "You know damn well why I haven't been recording. Because there's a lot of garbage out there. I can't record garbage. Nobody's writing any songs for me and I don't know what to do about it."

Sonny Burke said: "Well, we brought you something that Gordy has written. It's about time you got back into the record business."

That night, in Sinatra's suite, Gordon Jenkins played a demo tape he had made with a synthesizer and six voices, not of a song but of a large work — call it a cantata or a mini-opera, something in the extended vein of his famous *Manhattan Towers* opus. *Reflections on the Future in Three Tenses,* as he titled it, ran over 38 minutes. While the first half dealt with the future in terms of space exploration, rockets, computers, and the possibility of a world without war ("World War None"), the second half explored the future of a man facing his mortality, "the cat with a scythe." Lefty, as Frank called Jenkins because he conducted and wrote with his left hand, well knew Sinatra's penchant for autobiography in his singing. ("His life is a mirror-image of the songs he's made famous," a perceptive critic wrote.) The cantata was replete with references to Sinatra's world: his home in the desert, his nights at Las Vegas's gaming tables, and his friends — Dino (Dean Martin), Chester (songwriter Jimmy Van Heusen), and even Lefty himself.

"You gotta do this album," said Sonny Burke, who died suddenly, not long after the album's release. "It's a legacy you're gonna leave behind. More than just 32-bar songs. This thing is gonna be great. People are gonna play it for years and years."

Reflections on the Future became the basis of *Trilogy,* released in the spring of 1980. Once Sinatra approved the Jenkins opus on the Future, Burke persuaded him to expand the idea by including a record on the Past ("Collectibles of the Early Years"), arranged and conducted by Billy May, and the Present ("Some Very Good Years"), arranged and conducted by Don Costa. A third longtime collaborator, Nelson Riddle of the Capitol years and many Sinatra film scores, was very involved in other projects but scored ex-Beatle George Harrison's "Something" in the Present album.

The *Trilogy* was not only an ambitious undertaking but also a demanding and mammoth project, especially for a man who had made his first recordings over forty years earlier. Material for *The Past* and *The Present* was screened during a period of almost a year, with Sinatra, Sonny Burke, and Sarge "The Torch" Weiss, Frank's longtime music coordinator, considering as many as 500 different songs. During Frank's long career he had recorded something like 1,200 titles, and the search was for evergreens he had not previously recorded as well as suitable new material. In the final choice of selection, 16 of the 29 songs

NEAL PETERS COLLECTION

were new in Frank's recorded repertoire. They included contemporary material by such pop-rock writers as Billy Joel ("Just the Way You Are"), Neil Diamond ("Song Sung Blue"), Carol Bayer Sager and Peter Allen ("You and Me—We Wanted It All"), and Jimmy Webb (an abbreviated version of the surrealistic "MacArthur Park"). Among the new standards there were "My Shining Hour" by Johnny Mercer and Harold Arlen, "But Not for Me" by the Gershwins, and Vincent Youman's "More Than You Know."

As for the recording sessions, enough musicians were employed to staff several symphony orchestras: 56 on *The Past* LP, 68 on *The Present*, and no fewer than 142 on *The Future*, including four harps. In addition there were mixed choruses of over 90 voices. Despite the numerous recording studios in Hollywood, there was not one that could accommodate the enormous complement of musicians and singers for the Jenkins cantata. The work was finally recorded at the giant Shrine Auditorium, where the curtain and scenery had to be removed to permit the 142 musicians and 50 singers to work on stage. "Let's do it first class all the way," Sinatra had told Sonny Burke once he had approved the project. People inside the business estimate that the recording cost of the 3-record set, done first class, may have run as high as a whopping $200,000.

"With *Trilogy*," John Rockwell wrote in *The New York Times*, "Sinatra proves that his singing remains one of American popular culture's great treasures. He's singing better now than he has in recent years." Ken Tucker of the *Los Angeles Herald-Examiner* "doffed his hat" to two of the three records, expressing reservations about the Jenkins opus just as Rockwell had done.

But jazz critic Leonard Feather of the *Los Angeles Times*, sharing his confreres' enthusiasm for the first two discs, found Gordon's work "as extraordinary a piece of special material as has ever been written for Sinatra." Feather concluded his thumbs-up review: "If Sinatra and Jenkins left us nothing more than *Reflections on the Future in Three Tenses* to show the 21st century what popular music could achieve in the 20th, their accomplishment could hardly have been more ideally designed."

Industry recognition of *Trilogy* came in the form of six Grammy nominations. The "New York, New York" track, released as a single, garnered three: Record of the Year, Best Song, and Best Arrangement. Sinatra was nominated as Best Pop Male Vocalist, while the LP itself was in the running as Album of the Year. Of the multi-nominations, it came as no surprise, considering the tenor of the pop market, that only the literate liner notes by David McClintick walked off with an award.

Crowd control needed in Pasadena, California, 1943.

Band Vocalist (1939-1942)

Sinatra began, as singers did in the 1930s, as a band vocalist. When he stepped forth as a soloist, he was the bedroom baritone par excellence, at first of sensuous romance and then of the pain of hurt love. On his rise from the depths to which he had fallen, emotionally and career-wise, in the early '50s, he emerged as the swinging Sinatra. Through the rock years he managed to produce hits by a judicious selection of songs and sounds: "Strangers in the Night"; "Something Stupid" (a duet with daughter Nancy); "Send in the Clowns"; and "New York, New York." *Trilogy* went Gold in 1981. *She Shot Me Down* (1981) reaffirmed his mastery as the poet of loneliness, lost love, and the wee hours of the morning.

What a journey — 1939 to 1982 — and over so many dips in the road and uphill climbs! The journey to greatness actually began on Route 9W, near Alpine, New Jersey, at a roadhouse called the Rustic Cabin, where Frank sang, emceed, and occasionally waited on tables for $15 a week in 1938 and 1939. In retrospect the beginning might be moved back to five years earlier, for it was then that an appearance by the celebrated and venerable Bing Crosby at a Jersey City vaudeville house triggered young Frank's determination to make it as a singer. Sweet-talking his doting mom into buying him a $65 portable P.A. system and counterboys (like Hank Sanicola) at New York publishing companies into supplying him with free orchestrations, he spent five years gigging around Hoboken and Jersey City, making free appearances on Newark and New York City radio, and touring for a time with the Hoboken Four as part of a Major Bowes vaudeville unit.

Like all budding singers of the day he had his eyes fixed on a berth with name band. Eighteen months at the Rustic Cabin led to the fledgling Harry James Band, and after six months (July 1939 to January 1940) to the prestigious Tommy Dorsey Band. "Singing with a band," he later said on many an occasion, "was like lifting weights." Unquestionably, Sinatra's technique and style were honed on the bandstand of the two dance bands.

The first time that he stepped in front of a recording microphone was on July 13, 1939. The initial label that bore the legend "Vocal Chorus Frank Sinatra" was the Brunswick recording by Harry James and His Orchestra of "From the Bottom of My Heart" backed with "Melancholy Mood." Frank cut only six discs with the James band. They were not well received by the reviewers nor were they good sellers. However when the August 3,

1939, recording of "All or Nothing at All" was reissued in 1943 after Frank had taken the solo route, the disc, which sold a paltry 8,000 originally, became a runaway best-seller and Sinatra's first record hit. By then, the large type on the record label read FRANK SINATRA, not HARRY JAMES.

Despite the financial problems that Dorsey created when Frank left him and the confrontations between the two hot-tempered hombres during the 32 months of Sinatra's tenure, Frank always acknowledged the tremendous musical debt he owed the gifted trombonist. "The man was a real education for me," he has said, "in music, in business, in every way possible. From the way he played his horn I learned about dynamics, style, and phrasing; and because he always saw to it that his singers were given a perfect setting, working with him was a delight." Sinatra's early velvet-smooth, bel canto sound and legato style were modeled on the Dorsey trombone. Studying his performances night after night, Frank mastered the art of breath control and was able to free the phrasing of a lyric from dependence on one's breathing.

In musicologist Henry Pleasants's words: "He achieved the instrumentalist's control of 'the seamless line,' never forgetting the priority of the lyric. . . . Given the electronic assist of the microphone, he could resort to such age-old devices as slur, portamento, appoggiatura, mordent, and tempo rubato — in the original sense of stolen time — to set the words in a conversational prosody independent of the time values of the printed notes."

The Dorsey experience also contributed such perennials to the Sinatra repertoire as "I'll Never Smile Again," I'm Getting Sentimental Over You," "There Are Such Things," "I'll Be Seeing You," "Polka Dots and Moonbeams," and "The One I Love Belongs to Somebody Else," among other songs. Sinatra may be heard on 90 Dorsey recordings, covering the period from February 1, 1940 through July 2, 1942. By the end of 1941 he had replaced Bing Crosby as the top male vocalist in the annual *Down Beat* poll, a position that Der Bingle had held since the inception of the poll in 1937.

The Paramount Panics (1943-44)

The Sinatra charisma and sex appeal, manifest on the bandstand in the latter days of his Dorsey association, began to exercise their magic on the female sector as early as his first appearance at the New York Paramount. When he stepped out on the stage on December 30, 1942, he was billed just as an Extra Added Attraction to the then reign-

ing King of Swing, Benny Goodman. But the reaction of the bobby-soxers was so explosive that Goodman apparently exclaimed, "What the hell was that!" After the Goodman band departed, Sinatra stayed on, extending his booking to eight weeks, a record in which he equaled the Vagabond Lover, Rudy Vallee, and was exceeded only by Crosby. The hysteria built. From the Paramount Frank walked into the top vocal spot in radio — lead singer on the Saturday night Lucky Strike "Your Hit Parade" show, with his first broadcast on February 6, 1943. Shortly afterward he was booked into a chichi East Side nightclub, the Riobamba, where owner Arthur Jarwood was jittery that the Voice's appeal was solely to adolescents. But females of the mink-and-martini crowd reacted so strongly that Sinatra's stay was extended to a riotous ten weeks, during which his pay doubled and the Riobamba was saved from bankruptcy. The swooning syndrome, which had begun to take shape at the Paramount, was now so widely publi-

cized that the media began referring to Frank as Mr. Swoonatra.

Looking back on those days, Jack Keller, who worked with publicist George Evans, has said: "We outfitted Frank with break-away suits and hired girls to scream when he sexily rolled a note. But we needn't have. The dozen girls we hired to scream and swoon did exactly as we told them. But hundreds more we didn't hire screamed even louder. Others squealed, howled, kissed his pictures with their lipsticked lips and kept him a prisoner in his dressing room between shows at New York's Paramount Theatre. It was wild, crazy, completely out-of-control."

The description applied particularly to Sinatra's third appearance at the theater, which occurred in October 1944. The booking included Columbus Day, a school holiday. By 3:00 and 4:00 A.M. that morning, subway employees, late-night truckers, and police sensed that something explosive was developing in the city: high

Live at the Hollywood Bowl, August, 1943.

school girls from all the boroughs and from New Jersey were flocking into the Times Square area of Manhattan. Eventually the throng grew to a crush of over 30,000 tremulous youngsters, all scrambling to get into the Paramount. To control the massive assemblage, a mighty army of police was called out: 421 police reserves, 200 detectives, 70 patrolmen, 50 traffic cops, 20 policewomen, 12 mounted police, 2 assistant chief inspectors, 2 inspectors, 2 captains, 4 lieutenants, 6 sergeants, 2 emergency trucks, and 20 radio cars. Nevertheless, the ticket booth was destroyed, windows of Broadway shops were smashed, passersby were trampled, and traffic was at a standstill.

Inside the theater, 50 extra ushers were added to the normal complement in an effort to cope with the hysterical crowd. When the first show finished only 250 seats were vacated of the 3,600 in the house. Kids remained glued to their seats for three and four shows, chattering and paying no attention to the film on the bill. What with the excitement and the unwillingness to leave one's seat for any reason, there was, according to theater employees, more urine on the seats and carpet than in the toilets. Girls did faint, some from sheer hunger, and a few because they were paid to do so by press agent George Evans.

But there is no question that New York's adolescent females were in a "Sinatrance," as *Variety* typed it. *Newsweek* observed: "He is undersized and looks underfed—but the slightest suggestion of a smile brings squeals of agonized rapture from his adolescent admirers." *Time* said: "Not since the days of Rudy Vallee has American womanhood made such unabashed love to an entertainer."

The phenomenon was hardly limited to New York. Martha Weinman Lear, a contributor to *The New York Times Magazine* who went to see Sinatra at Madison Square Garden in 1974 and became, in her words, "a 13-year-old again, packing my peanut-butter sandwich off to the RKO-Boston to shriek and swoon through four shows live, along with several thousand other demented teen-agers. . . . 'Frankie!' we screamed from the balcony, because you couldn't get an orchestra seat unless you were standing in line at dawn, and how could you explain to Mom leaving for school before? 'Frankie, I *love* you.' "

The love affair did not end in the 1940s. It went on and on. At a performance at Caesars Palace in 1981, as he approached the edge of the stage, a middle-aged woman sitting with her family just below gently handed him one long-stemmed rose.

At the height of the hysteria in 1944–1945, buckets of ink were spilled by reporters, columnists, lay psychologists, and psychiatrists in an attempt to explain Sinatra's necromancy. Jack Keller, the publicist, voiced an oft-repeated hypothesis: "The explanation for the hysteria," he said, "was the *time*—early in the war years

when girls were without men and romance." But if that were the case, why didn't they swoon over all the other crooners of the time, singers like Jack Leonard, who was Dorsey's vocalist before Frank, Bob Eberly, Bing Crosby, Dick Haymes, and so on. Surely the time was a factor, the environment in which the hysteria erupted. But the explanation had to lie in something Sinatra *had* and *did*, something that made him different from all the other singers.

"The microphone is the singer's basic instrument," he has said, "not the voice. You have to learn to play it like it was a saxophone." And play it he did, with sensitivity, understanding, and artistry. Thus it was the way he sang as well as the way he looked that made the difference.

Recalling those days at RKO-Boston, Ms. Lear wrote: "That glorious shouldered spaghetti strand in the spotlight would croon on serenely, giving us a quick little flick of a smile or, as a special bonus, a sidelong tremor of the lower lip. I used to bring binoculars just to watch that lower lip. And then, the other thing: The Voice had that *trick*, you know, that funny little sliding, skimming slur that it would do coming off the end of a note. It drove us bonkers. . . . It was an invitation to hysteria. He'd give us that little slur—'All . . . or nothing at a-alllll . . .' and we'd start swooning all over the place, in the aisles, on each other's shoulders, in the arms of cops, poor bewildered men in blue. It was like pressing a button. It *was* pressing a button."

In short it was his singing style—sensuous, romantic, tender, intense, full of yearning and feeling—that did it to the girls. He was making love to them via a song. It was also his look—thin, hollow-cheeked, jug-eared, gawky. He was the boy next door, and he looked so vulnerable. And then there was the look that he gave each girl. He had those blue, blue, cerulean eyes—eyes that Roz Russell raved about even at his "retirement" concert in 1971—eyes that were almost hypnotic in their effect and that made each girl they speared feel that he was singing just to her, making love to her alone.

Turning back to Ms. Lear once again: "The sociologists were out there in force, speculating over the dynamics of mass hysteria, blathering about how his yearning vulnerability appealed to our mother instincts. What yo-yo's. Whatever he stirred beneath our barely budding breasts, it wasn't motherly. . . . The thing we had going with Frankie was sexy. It was exciting. It was terrific."

It was the intensity, the extravagance, and the unbuttoned character of the female reaction that made the wartime balladeer a phenomenon—"an American phenomenon," as *The New Yorker* termed him in a three-part profile in 1946.

Beginning with the reissue of "All or Nothing at All" in 1943, Sinatra scored a succession of record hits for three years as "the bedroom baritone" of Columbia Records. Among the songs that are remembered from these booming years, there are "You'll Never Know," "Sunday, Monday or Always," "I Couldn't Sleep a Wink Last Night," "Saturday Night (Is the Loneliest Night in the Week)," "Nancy (With the Laughing Face)," and "I've Got the World on a String."

The swooning and the hysteria were wartime phenomena of such an explosive magnitude that the postwar dip in Frank's popularity, which became evident in 1947, was not too surprising, even if its suddenness was something of a shock. Suddenly there was a new Frankie on the scene— Frankie Laine—and a new style, belting instead of crooning, was grabbing record buyers. A shout style derived from rhythm and blues, belting brought fame to Eddie Fisher, Johnnie Ray, Don Cornell, Rosemary Clooney, Kay Starr, Georgia Gibbs, the Four Aces, and the McGuire Sisters. Their delivery was more muscular, more rhythmically propulsive, and louder than that of the baritone balladeers.

The downward spiral for Frank was accelerated by crises in his domestic and romantic life. The separation from his children, the divorce from Nancy Barbato, his first wife, the ups and downs of his relationship with Ava Gardner, his own manic reactions, and the intemperate outbursts and clashes with the media—all played havoc with his following. By 1952 Frank had hit bottom: Columbia Records had not renewed his contract; a deal with ABC-TV was down the tubes; there were no offerings from film companies with whom he had worked; and his agent, MCA, in the unkindest cut of all, dropped him.

An appearance at the New York Paramount, the scene of his canonization as the great male sex idol, elicited a newspaper article headed "Gone on Frankie in '42; Gone in '52," with a subhead that read "What a Difference a Decade Makes—Empty Balcony." Lamenting his fall, but not without a smirk, reporter Muriel Fischer told of how she heard three girls at the stage door murmuring "Frankie." When she asked, "How do you like Frankie?" they replied, "Frankie Laine, he's wonderful!" When she heard another girl sighing, "I'm mad about him," *him* turned out to be Johnnie Ray.

In the years of the downdraft created by Hurricane Ava and the rise of new singing idols, perhaps the most poignant and dramatic moment came on May 2, 1950. Frank was performing at the Copacabana in Manhattan. Here is how conductor Skitch Henderson described what

happened during the third show of the evening: "He opened his mouth to sing after the band introduction and nothing came out! Not a sound! I thought for a fleeting moment that the unexpected pantomime was a joke. But then he caught my eye. I guess the color drained out of my face as I saw the panic in his. It became so quiet in the club—they were like watching a man walk off a cliff. His face chalk white, Frank gasped something that sounded like 'Good Night' and raced off the floor, leaving the audience stunned. It was tragic and terrifying."

Always the autobiographical singer, Sinatra now turned to songs that reflected the trauma of his depressed feelings. The songbird of yearning and tender romance became the bittersweet balladeer of heartbreak. Instead of euphoric songs like "People Will Say We're in Love" and "Oh, What a Beautiful Morning," he recorded "No One Cares," "It's a Blue World," and the melancholy "In the Wee Small Hours." The lush, romantic string-and-flute backgrounds of arranger Axel Stordahl were superseded by the brooding cello-and-trombone scores of Gordon Jenkins. The depth of his emotional travail over Ava was sounded in a disc of "I'm a Fool to Want You," recorded in March 1951 on an evening when he was so overcome by his feelings that he was compelled to leave the studio.

"At 38 years old," he later wrote, "I was a has-been, sitting by a phone that wouldn't ring, wondering what happened to all the friends who grew invisible when the music stopped, finding out fast how tough it is to borrow money when you're all washed up. Yes, when 1953 slid down the pole in Times Square, my only collateral was a dream, a dream to end my nightmare."

That dream was, of course, to play the role of Private Angelo Maggio in the film *From Here to Eternity.*

The Swinging Sinatra (1953—1960)

"The most admirable thing about Frank," Bing Crosby wrote in a letter to George Simon, "is his great determination. After a meteoric beginning, he had every conceivable reversal and disappointment, socially, professionally, and privately. Very few people in our business can rally from something like this. But he did—and big! And all by himself."

The buoyant Sinatra who emerged from the memorable role of Maggio and the Oscar award ceremony of March 25, 1954, came roaring back on records with a Top Ten hit in "Young at Heart." Having moved from Columbia Records to the smaller, Hollywood-based Capitol label, he moved away from the beatless, string-and-flute romanticism of Axel Stordahl's arrangements to a style marked by swinging rhythm and walloping brass. Scores were provided by two new men: Nelson Riddle, a former Dorsey trombonist-arranger and Billy May, a jazz-oriented, former trumpeter-arranger with Charlie Barnet and Glenn Miller. Riddle was the major architect of a kick-ballad style, compounded of finger-snapping rhythms and a bouncy insouciance, embodying the toughness as well as the tenderness of Sinatra. At year-end 1954, "Young at Heart" scored as the Number One song in *Billboard*'s annual poll while Sinatra was named Singer of the Year by *Metronome* and Most Popular Male Vocalist by *Down Beat*, a title which he was again awarded in 1957.

Now Frank recorded upbeat albums with titles like *Come Fly with Me, Come Swing with Me!, Swing Easy, Come Dance with Me* (with a come-hither wink-and-smile photo on the cover), and *Songs for Swingin' Lovers*. His world and his career were epitomized in songs like "I've Got the World on a String" and "Don't Worry 'Bout Me," the two sides that he cut on April 30, 1953, and that cemented his relationship with Nelson Riddle.

"Young at Heart" was followed by two other Gold records. "Learnin' the Blues" harked back thematically to songs he had been singing in anguish over Ava. "Love and Marriage," featured in the TV version of *Our Town* which became the second song hit (after "Let Me Go Lover") to develop from a television show.

"Love and Marriage" was the work of Sammy Cahn and James Van Heusen, a writing team that emerged from the breakup of Johnny Burke and James Van Heusen, and Sammy Cahn and Jule Styne. Burke and Van Heusen, who had originally been Bing Crosby favorites, won an Oscar for "Swinging on a Star" in 1944 and Cahn and Styne had carried off an Oscar for "Three Coins in a Fountain" from the film of the same name in 1954. The two teams had been favorites of Sinatra's during his Columbia years, with Cahn and Styne accounting for eight of nine hits produced by them, "Five Minutes More," "Let It Snow, Let It Snow," "Saturday Night," and "Time After Time," among others. Now, Cahn and Van Heusen became a major source of Sinatra songs, writing the title tunes of some of his films as well as other songs. "The Tender Trap" (1956) and "All the Way" (1957) were both Top Ten hits, with the latter being the first of three songs that Sinatra helped power into Academy Awards. "High Hopes," from his 1959 film *A Hole in the Head* and "Call Me Irresponsible" (1963) were the other two Oscar winners for Cahn and Van Heusen. Through the years gifted Sammy Cahn has written witty lyric parodies of songs used by Sintara on special occasions.

The Capitol years were some of the most-concentrated recording years for Frank. Not only did he regain his position among the top vocalists of the day in trade-paper polls, but two of his albums brought him Grammys. In 1959 he walked off with two NARAS

awards for *Come Dance with Me,* one for Best Vocal Performance (Male) and the other for Best Album of the Year. In the preceding year *Only the Lonely* was awarded a Grammy for the Best Album Cover of the year.

Voyle Gilmore, who was his Capitol producer from Frank's first date in 1953 until March 1958, has said: "As a singer, there was no one like him. As a guy, there's no one more difficult to handle." The late Dave Cavanaugh, who succeeded Gilmore and worked with him until Sinatra left to form his own label, said: "It was always challenging to work with him because his musical intuitions were always so right. . . . For him, a record session was like a night-club appearance. He has his crowd and he's putting on a show. . . . You're not just an A & R [Artists & Repertoire] producer. You're straight man for his jokes."

The Ring-A-Ding Ding Years (1961–1971)

In December 1960 Frank was strolling past the Capitol Records circular tower building on Vine Street, just north of Hollywood Boulevard. Looking up, he reportedly said to Mo Ostin, who soon became head of Reprise Records: "I helped build that. Now let's build one of my own." Roughly three years later, when he sold Reprise Records to Warner Bros. in a deal that also encompassed future film productions, he was paid $10 million and retained a one-third interest in the company.

Ring-a-Ding Ding, his initial Reprise release in June 1961, suggested Sinatra's upbeat frame of mind. If the album title also had a cash-register ring, it may have been because Frank involved himself in every phase of the company's administration. He was not one to forget the snubs he had suffered from an agency, a record company, and others in the early '50s. He had begun building an empire that would make him independent immediately after the *Eternity* Oscar had put his career in a new, ascendant orbit. To accelerate Reprise's growth, he produced three albums in rapid succession before the end of 1961 in addition to *Ring-a-Ding Ding, Sinatra Swings,* and *I Remember Tommy.* These and other albums continued to exploit the swinging concept initiated on his Capitol albums, so much so that Capitol went to the law courts to try to stop him but merely succeeded in forcing a change of title on the album finally released as *Sinatra Swings.*

The Reprise years, certainly through the '60s, were musically challenging to Sinatra, who had no sympathy with the sound of the mainstream. Like Mitch Miller, whom he blamed for his decline at Columbia, he was one of the outspoken critics of rock. He referred to it at one point as "a rancid-smelling aphrodisiac" and at another as "the martial music of every sideburned delinquent." The antagonism inevitably moved him in the direction of jazz.

In fact, the *Ring-a-Ding Ding* album was arranged and conducted by Johnny Mandel, whose score for the film *I Want to Live* (1958) is considered the first successful use of jazz in a movie score. In succeeding albums he used other jazz-oriented arrangers like Neal Hefti, Quincy Jones, Billy May, and Sy Oliver. He did several albums with Count Basie: *Sinatra–Basie* (1962), *It Might As Well Be Swing* (1964), and *Sinatra at the Sands* (1966). In 1967 he collaborated with Duke Ellington, whose orchestra he named his favorite, on an album titled *Francis A. and Edward K.*

But he was listening and studying songs by the younger writers and the work of arrangers of the new music. Finally, in 1964, he recorded what is frequently referred to as his first rock song, "Softly, As I Leave You." It is a curious misnomer since the ballad has a lovely modulating melody and was an import from Italy with a delicate English lyric by a British songwriter. The confusion doubtless arose from the fact that the song was arranged and conducted by Ernie Freeman, a man with a substantial rhythm and blues background.

It was Freeman who helped Sinatra break into the Beatles–Rolling Stones-dominated charts of 1966 with "Strangers in the Night," a record that went to Number One over a 15-week period on the charts, won a Grammy as Record of the Year, and gave him a Grammy for the Best Male Vocal. Later that year Freeman arranged and conducted "That's Life" (an earlier version of the song remains unissued) and helped Sinatra climb to Number Four on the charts. The following year Sinatra went for broke on "Somethin' Stupid," a duet with daughter Nancy, arranged and conducted by Billy Strange, a young rock arranger. It went to Number One and became the biggest single of his post-*Eternity* years.

Sinatra was now ready for a full-scale invasion of the teenage market. He found little to his taste in the more raucous forms of rock like acid or electronic rock. But in folk rock, country rock, and pop rock he was able to select songs that did not violate his interest in words and expressive melody. The album titled *Cycles* after a song by Gayle Caldwell contained Joni Mitchell's "From Both Sides Now," John Hartford's "Gentle on My Mind," Bobby Russell's "Little Green Apples," and Jimmy Webb's "By the Time I Get to Phoenix," among other recent hits.

Nineteen sixty-nine was the year that Paul Anka took a French song and produced the superlative lyric that became "My Way"—his "national anthem," as Sinatra took to calling it—a song that he was compelled to sing so frequently that he eventually dropped it, though the music is used at times as entrance or exit music for his personal appearances. In 1969 he also continued his exploration of teenage music, recording Lennon and McCartney's "Yes-

terday," Jimmy Webb's "Didn't We," Paul Simon's satirical "Mrs. Robinson" (in a sardonic big-band treatment), and even Ray Charles's "Hallelujah, I Love Her So."

Sinatra's adventuring mind took him in other directions as well. The soft Bossa Nova sound had samba'd into this country in the early '60s with Stan Getz, Charlie Byrd, "Desafinado," and "The Girl form Ipanema." In 1967 Frank undertook a collaboration with the Brazilian guitarist-composer of these works and produced the album *Francis Albert Sinatra & Antonio Carlos Jobim.* The following year his search for new material led him to singer-songwriter Rod McKuen, who was attracting tremendous press as America's best-selling poet. Sensitive to Sinatra's power in dealing with the theme of loneliness, McKuen created a series of songs under the title *A Man Alone.* It proved less than an ideal collaboration. Whatever the merits of the low-keyed lyrics, McKuen's lackluster melodies and lack of passion failed to elicit the expressiveness and feeling of which Frank is the master.

Unquestionably, the peak of Sinatra's recordings of the '60s came with *September of My Years,* one of the most perfect albums Sinatra ever made. Keyed to his 50th birthday in 1965 and unified in theme, it had a series of eloquent songs concerned with a man facing the problems of aging. Cahn and Van Heusen contributed the thematic title song and the moving "It Gets Lonely Early." Gordon Jenkins raised the question "How Old Am I?" and tried to find some answers in "This Is All I Ask." There were nostalgically romantic songs: Rodgers and Hammerstein's "Hello Young Lovers," "Last Night When We Were Young" by Yip Harburg and Harold Arlen, "When the Wind Was Green," and the bittersweet remembrance of things past in Ervin Drake's "It Was a Very Good Year." Bart Howard of "Fly Me to the Moon" fame dealt with "The Man in the Looking Glass" and Alec Wilder and Bill Engvick waxed philosophical in "I See It Now." Dramatically and neatly structured, *September of My Years* closed appropriately with the haunting Kurt Weill–Maxwell Anderson ballad "September Song." It came as no surprise when the members of the National Academy of Recording Arts and Sciences named the LP Album of the Year, a Grammy award that also went the following year to the retrospective 2-volume collection *A Man and His Music.*

During the 1970s, a dull period in rock and pop music but an era in which country music came sweeping into the mainstream, Sinatra was not only out-of-sync with the time musically but in a troubled state about his records. He did no recording between 1970 and 1973, the years of his "retirement" from show business. But he also stayed out of the studios in 1978. And in 1977, when he participated in a dozen sessions, he rejected most of the sides, which remain unissued to the present.

Nevertheless, during the '70s he made standards out of two songs. With his unending search for superbly written songs, he dug a gem out of the score of the Broadway show *A Little Night Music,* which opened in February 1973 and ran for over a year. Like the rest of Stephen Sondheim's ingenious score, "Send in the Clowns" was in waltz time, melodically intriguing but offbeat, and lyrically quite subtle. Sinatra recorded it in a Gordon Jenkins arrangement late in June 1973, opening the door to its belated recognition as Song of the Year at the Grammy awards ceremony of 1976.

In the final year of the '70s, he did for the Big Apple what he had previously done for the Cahn-Van Heusen swinger "My Kind of Town" for Chicago. "New York, New York" was the theme of the 1977 film of the same name, written by John Kander and Fred Ebb of *Cabaret* fame especially for Liza Minelli, who starred and sang it in the movie. It remained for Sinatra to capture its effervescent flavor and to transform it into an exciting evergreen, a song that he included in his *Trilogy* album and that now closes virtually every one of his live performances, during which he converts his audience into an exuberant hand-clapping crowd.

The Jazz Singer

One evening in the summer of 1980 Sinatra was having dinner in New York City when he encountered Ahmet Ertegun of Atlantic Records and Warner Bros. Communications. Ahmet suggested a new recording direction for Frank: "Get myself six or eight guys, the best jazzmen in the world and go into a studio without arrangements," as Frank later described it, " have each of the men submit ten or fifteen songs *they* like to play. Pick the standards I've never done and just keep recording. If one song runs six minutes, let it run six minutes. In other words— into a vocal, out of the vocal, half a chorus, jump to a trombone player. I liked the idea and I think we're gonna do it after New Year's."

Sinatra told Mitchell Fink of the *Los Angeles Herald-Examiner* about another LP he was planning—"a complete saloon album—tear-jerkers and cry-in-your-beer kinds of things. We may prepare the saloon album, do the arrangements and put it in a drawer but get everything set. We'll do the jazz album first, then the saloon album."

But 1981 saw the release not of the jazz album but of the saloon album, a collection of songs of lost love, which he called *She Shot Me Down.* In Sinatra's conversation with the *Herald-Examiner* staff writer, he had said: "Essentially I'm not a jazz singer." It's an opinion that many jazz critics share, without rejecting the idea that his singing is jazz-oriented, but which one of the most probing of critics

slowly came to question.

When Whitney Balliett, the longtime jazz analyst of *The New Yorker,* heard Sinatra at the Newport Jazz Festival in 1965, he wrote a rather snide review, characterizing the evening as "a circus." "After a dozen desultory Count Basie numbers," he observed, "Sinatra paraded onstage with his own drummer, his own trumpet player — and his own arrangements. Basie put on a pair of businessman's glasses and started reading his part." Balliett wrapped up his acerbic review: "Sinatra was airborne (he had also arrived by helicopter) before the Basie band, struggling to regain its soul, had finished a concluding *One O'Clock Jump.*"

That was 1965. Just about nine years later Balliett's evaluation of Sinatra as a singer took an entirely different turn. Reviewing a concert at the Nassau Coliseum in April 1974, he wrote: "He is singing better now than he ever has, for he has gradually become, in a startling reversal of the usual jazz-singer-to-popular-singer trek, a first-rate jazz singer."

Of his debt to Billie Holiday, the first lady of jazz singing, Sinatra has never made a secret, dating her influence—"the greatest single musical influence on me," in his words—back to the days when he first heard her in 52nd Street clubs like the Famous Door in the early '30s. But it was not until 1970 and *Sinatra and Company,* the last album released before his short-lived retirement, that he paid heartfelt homage to her on a record. Written by Bob Gaudio and Jake Holmes, "Lady Day" went through three sessions and two arrangers before the date arranged and produced by Don Costa in November 1969 yielded the emotive version released in the album.

In documenting Sinatra's growth as a jazz singer, Balliett observed: "He has become fascinated by the rhythmic possibilities Billie Holiday endlessly explored. He will, without blurring his crystal articulation, jam words and syllables together, as she did, or he will stretch the words out behind the beat, achieving the priceless legato quality that is at the heart of swinging. He will bend notes and coat others with light growls, and he will gentle his words, shaping them into hymns and lullabies."

Serving his apprenticeship with the dance bands of Harry James and Tommy Dorsey, Sinatra learned to sing with a beat from the start. The quality was somewhat clouded during the Columbia years, when Axel Stordahl's arrangements catered to a generation of boy-starved, love-hungry bobby-soxers who responded to slow, lush, dreamy ballads. But even in this period Sinatra displayed an improvisatory feeling for textural variaton, altering the timbre of his voice to suit the sense and tonality of the lyrics. The switch to Capitol in the '50s and to the arrangements of Nelson Riddle and Billy May added drive, bounce, and rhythmic adventure to his singing.

By 1955 *Metronome*'s comment on his album *In the Wee Small Hours* was: "Sinatra has always had a taste and an intuition for jazz nuances, for improvisational ornaments, for swinging beats, far beyond the call of popular singing duty." His succeeding album, *Songs for Swingin' Lovers,* was named by the jazz publication "one of the best jazz albums of the year."

Nevertheless there is an area in which Frank and jazz singers tend to part company. He has never been interested in improvisation merely for the sake of alteration, technical display, or momentary feelings. His abiding concern is almost classical in character, an effort to find the most expressive way of wedding words and music. When he has made three and four different recordings of a song, when he varies the treatment of a given tune on successive nights of a club engagement, he is impelled by a desire to achieve the most compelling rendition of a song. Musicologist Henry Pleasants puts it this way: "Sinatra has not been a notably improvisatory singer, but few have used subtle melodic deviation and fastidious ornamentation as effectively as he has."

Another aspect of Sinatra's singing style poses a problem for a purely improvisatory approach. In explaining how he worked out an arrangement for Sinatra, Nelson Riddle has said: "First—find the peak of the song and build the whole arrangement to that peak, pacing it as he paces himself vocally. . . . One other thing, I usually try to avoid scoring a song with a climax at the end. Better to build it about two-thirds of the way through and then fade to a surprise ending." The reference to the "peak" and the "climax" makes clear that Sinatra and Riddle were both concerned with forcefully structuring a record, with building it dramatically so that it had a beginning, a middle, a peak, and an end. Structure and improvisation frequently do not go together.

It has been said that Lester Young, tenor sax Father of the Cool School of Jazz, became concerned with the lyrics of songs as a result of Sinatra, and that he studied the words of new songs carefully before improvising. Young's respect for Sinatra was widely shared by other jazzmen. In a poll that jazz critic Leonard Feather ran in 1956, Sinatra was chosen "the greatest ever" male vocalist by an incredibly large number of jazzmen. He captured 56 votes to Nat Cole's 13, Billy Eckstine's 11, Louis Armstrong's 9, and Bing Crosby's 7.

On most of his Capitol record sessions, the band included musicians like saxist Ben Webster, trombonist Juan Tizol, and other jazzmen who generally eschewed studio dates with pop singers. Harry "Sweets" Edison, the celebrated Count Basie trumpeter, worked steadily with Sinatra's backup bands during the Capitol years, performing also on his TV shows. At Sinatra's direction Edison recorded on a mike separate from the rest of the trumpet section so that he could interpolate his own improvisational obbligatos behind Frank's vocals.

In the 1970s Sinatra's interest in working with jazz people escalated. As he had done in the 1962-1966 period, he made many appearances with Count Basie in 1974 and 1975. He also did "hot" dates with the Woody Herman Band, with Ella Fitzgerald and Sarah Vaughan. But a completely improvised album poses serious problems for the architect and the perfectionist in him. It is a musical challenge as great as he has ever faced.

Singing In The Dark

Sinatra's penchant for making his singing a form of autobiography—whence the immediacy, involvement, and poignance he achieves—has led him since he turned 50 to confront his mortality in song. *September of My Years,* the album that marked his fiftieth birthday, dealt with the loss of innocence, of youth, of young love. He was a man in his prime looking backward and wondering: "Where is the star that shone so bright? . . . Why must the moments go by with such haste? . . . The world I knew is lost to me. . . . Where did it go? . . . And now the days grow short. . . ." Was that why he then wooed and married a woman (Mia Farrow) who was younger than two of his children?

Since the *September* album the shadows in his work have grown deeper and heavier. Perhaps it was the loss of both of his parents that turned his thoughts from autumn to winter, from the passage of time to dying. On the stage at Harrah's in Lake Tahoe he did say one night: "Dying is a pain in the ass."

Not long after his 50th birthday he recorded "That's Life," a world-weary look at living. There was resignation in its existentialism. Several years later, just before his father died, he cut "My Way." It made its impact not only because of the assertion of his self-willed, indomitable course in life, but also because it was framed by the line—"And now the end is near."

In *Trilogy,* "time's winged chariot" became "the cat with the scythe." "I'll be singing as I leave," he chanted. But he was facing the moment when the music would end and he was indeed leaving. Critics of Gordon Jenkins's cantata about the Future seemed to miss the point. The trip through space, with which the work began, was just the flight of a man's imagination—his thoughts about the future world of spaceships, rockets, and computers, and the world his children would inhabit. But what was the dreamer doing? He was sitting "outside his desert home on a summer night with a drink in his hand and a little moonlight music." The man is "no longer young," and he's thinking about things he must and would like to do before the music ends. That's what *Reflections on the Future*

in *Three Tenses* is about—a man facing his terminal moment of truth.

The album that followed *Trilogy* at the end of 1981, Sinatra's saloon album, was a *weltschmerz* set, made up entirely of songs of love. *She Shot Me Down* was, in Leonard ·Feather's view, "a show of strength," with the Voice delivering "a message as firmly convincing as it has been in years." But it was shadowed by reflections on his mortality in Alec Wilder and Loonis McGlohon's ballad "South to a Warmer Place."

"Heading for 67," Feather wrote, "Sinatra has strengths at this age that he lacked in his salad days." As for tomorrow, Frank said it existentially in "How Old Am I?" on *September of My Years*—"Turn the page."

His Achievement

During the 1970s, rock and pop (trade papers call it "Easy Listening") had been involved in a flirtation, which at the beginning of the '80s finds Willie Nelson, Linda Ronstadt, and Carly Simon, among others, recording standards of the 1930s and 1940s. Efforts at a merger of the two forms have been assayed by balladeers like Barry Manilow, Neil Diamond, Billy Joel, and Paul Simon, among other young artists. In *She Shot Me Down*, at least one critic, Stephen Holden, found Sinatra moving "closer to rock than he's ever been" and contended that Sinatra "looks less like the last of a dying breed than the Father of a new one." [Curiously, Holden rated Sinatra's album *superior* both vocally and in the quality of songs" to the latest Neil Diamond *(On the Way to the Sky)* and Billy Joel *(Songs in the Attic)* releases.]

The average life of a popular singer tends to be a decade. Only a few superstars like Elvis, Bing Crosby, Perry Como, and the Rolling Stones have been able to extend their hold on the public into a second decade. Sinatra, however, is sui generis. There is no other singer in the history of American entertainment who has been able to sustain his career for as long as Sinatra—now in his fifth decade—and to produce hits in each of those decades, despite the inevitable changes in public taste. Among the bestsellers he has created decade by decade:

1940s
"All or Nothing at All"
"You'll Never Know"
"I'll Never Smile Again"
"Sunday, Monday or Always"
"Don't Cry Joe, Let Her Go"
"I Couldn't Sleep a Wink Last Night"

1950s
"Young at Heart"
"Learnin' the Blues"
"All the Way"
"Love and Marriage"
"Hey! Jealous Lover"
"Witchcraft"
"(Love Is) the Tender Trap"
"High Hopes"

1960s
"Strangers in the Night"
"Something Stupid"
"That's Life"
"Call Me Irresponsible"
"It Was a Very Good Year"
"My Way"

1970s
"Send In the Clowns"
"New York, New York"

In a survey conducted by Sinatra's P.R. people in 1980, none of the above was named the favorite single recording (Cole Porter's "I've Got You Under My Skin" was chosen). Of the more than 1,600 titles recorded by Frank, a total of 587 figured in the poll, to which responses were received from Sinatra appreciation societies throughout the world. Two other Porter ballads, "Night and Day" and "I Get a Kick Out of You," were among the Top 25 discs named in the survey. Nevertheless Porter came second to Sinatra's close friend and Palm Springs neighbor Jimmy Van Heusen, five of whose titles made the top group: "Nancy," "Here's That Rainy Day," "All the Way," "Come Fly with Me," and "September of My Years." Sammy Cahn was the lyricist on the last three titles.

Discs made by Sinatra during the '50s dominated the survey, with the buoyant years from 1956 through 1958 accounting for almost half of the Top 25. Among the seven different arranger-conductors responsible for the favored platters, the imperturbable Nelson Riddle outdistanced all his competitors by a wide margin. Twelve of the 25 bore his imprint, including the Number One "Skin," Number Two, "The Lady is a Tramp," and Number Three, "Chicago." Then came Axel Stordahl with 4 titles, Gordon Jenkins with 3 and Don Costa with 2.

In studying the lengthy list of Sinatra recordings and trying to determine his favorites, I found three songs that he had recorded four times: "All or Nothing at All," cut in 1939, 1961, 1966, and 1977; "Night and Day," in 1942, 1956, 1961, and 1977; and "I've Got You Under My Skin," in 1956, 1963, 1966, and 1974. All three were in the upper half of the 25 most popular discs.

Considering Sinatra's reputation for unpredictability, moodiness, and irritability, it is noteworthy that he has maintained a creative relationship with a small group of arranger-conductors over long periods of time. Balding Axel Stordahl dominated the discs of the Columbia years (1943–1952) as Nelson Riddle was the engineer of the Capitol sound (1953–1962). Billy May, in a sweatshirt, and Gordon Jenkins, in a neat business suit, both entered the world of Sinatra in 1957 during the Capitol years, and have worked with him through the Reprise years (1961 to the present). Don Costa, who did his first date with Sinatra in 1961, producing one of the most magnificent of albums *(Sinatra and Strings),* is the prime figure of the Reprise years, on stage as well as on disc, sharing chores at times with Gordon Jenkins but playing a larger role than Billy May or Nelson Riddle, who have also been part of the arranging-conducting scene into the present.

Although his voice has deepened with time and the texture has changed from velvet to corduroy, his singing style still trades on at least four factors that made him the preeminent male vocalist of our time: (1) a rich, appealing baritone voice with a sound so unique no one can mistake it; (2) phrasing that is magical in its smoothness, nuance, and expressiveness; (3) crystalline diction in which consonants, even hard terminal "d's" and "t's" are effortlessly articulated, an accomplishment as rare in pop music as classical; and (4) a depth of feeling so profound that listeners are involved, overwhelmed, and mesmerized.

Sinatra's achievement as a singer embodies the painter's feeling for texture, the dramatist's command of tension, the architect's dedication to structure, and the poet's sensitivity to words.

2. "It's Only a Paper Moon": The Actor

The great Humphrey Bogart said of Sinatra: "This guy has the most natural acting talent I've ever seen." But that talent has been spent on a not inconsequential number of films—"squandered" would be more accurate than "spent."

During the filming of *Guys and Dolls,* in which he was miscast as Nathan Detroit and the main songs of the musical were sung by Marlon Brando, Sinatra himself said, "I don't buy this take and retake jazz. The key to good acting on the screen is spontaneity—and that's something you lose a little with each take." To writer-director Joseph Manckiewicz, he said: "Don't put me in the game, coach, until Mumbles is through rehearsing." "Mumbles" was Frank's nickname for Marlon Brando.

Frank Capra, the gifted director, confirmed Sinatra's concept in his own way: "When I directed him in *A Hole in the Head,* I noticed that his best performance came on his first take. As takes continued, he would never reach that first show of brilliance. The other actors were just the opposite, even such an old pro as Edward G. Robinson. They all improved with each take. I devised a simple way of overcoming this. I just had someone else do Sinatra's lines until the other actors had the scene down pat. Then I called Frank. He's a performer first, actor second. That's why his first shot is always the best."

Sinatra the actor started, of course, as Sinatra the performer. He made his first appearance on the silver screen in 1941, singing "I'll Never Smile Again" as the male vocalist of the Tommy Dorsey Orchestra, in an opus quite appropriately titled *Las Vegas Nights.* Between then and 1982 he has starred or made guest appearances in almost sixty films. Even before he carried off an Oscar for his great performance in *From Here to Eternity* in 1954, there had been widespread recognition of his talent as a dramatic actor and comic. But through the years there has been a recurring feeling that he has all too frequently squandered that talent on mediocre vehicles.

Writing in *The New Republic* about *The Naked Runner* (1967), Pauline Kael asked: "It's a Frank Sinatra production, starring Sinatra. Which raises the question: why has Sinatra not developed the professional pride in his movies that he takes in his recordings?"

From 1941 to 1948, the year in which he tackled his first dramatic role as the priest in *The Miracle of the Bells,* Sinatra was basically a screen singer. Whatever the story lines, his films were designed to display his appeal and magic as a vocalist. They were years of growth, during which he learned how to move, dance, and be funny, sad, sentimental, or angry on the screen. By the time he stepped forth as an actor in the Father Paul role in 1948, his

career was in a down-draft, which even *The Miracle of the Bells* could not arrest. For that matter his exuberant and entertaining collaboration with Gene Kelly in the well-received film *On the Town* (1949) failed to brake the down-curve in his popularity.

The turnaround came with *From Here to Eternity* (1953), in which the realism and poignance of his performance as Private Maggio not only revived his sagging career but also established him as an actor of note. From then on he has had his pick of roles and vehicles, and has been able to branch out at will as a director and film producer. He won critical applause as a presidential assassin in *Suddenly* (1954). He was nominated for an Oscar for his powerful performance as the junkie-card dealer-drummer in *The Man with the Golden Arm.* There were bravos for his acting in two contrasting motion pictures, *The Manchurian Candidate* (1962)—a dramatic suspense film—and *Come Blow Your Horn* (1963)—a sentimental comedy in which he played a swinging bachelor. Despite a continuing respect among critics for his talent as an actor and an appreciation among film people of the money-making potential of his projects, they generally failed to arouse the excitement and adulation of his work before a microphone, in a recording studio, or on stage.

The first film in which Sinatra starred, appearing opposite Michele Morgan and Jack Haley, was *Higher and Higher.* The story was inconsequential if not silly. *The New York Times* critic suggested it should be called *Lower and Lower.* But it had songs by Jimmy McHugh and Harold Adamson, two of Hollywood's top songsmiths, and "I Couldı't Sleep a Wink Last Night" made the *Hit Parade.* At this point, 1943, Hollywood was frankly exploiting Sinatra's frenzied fame as a singer, starting with *Reveille with Beverly,* a film in which his leap to the screen was as fast as his ecstatic acceptance by the nation's bobby-soxers. Although he sang just one song, Cole Porter's "Night and Day," he seemingly stirred the same fantastic reactions in movie houses as in his onstage performances at the New York Paramount.

"And this Frank Sinatra!" John T. McManus exclaimed in *PM.* "Well, I am convinced that there has been nothing like him since goldfish-eating. He even out-manias the chain letter rage and the Rudy Vallee crush of 15 years ago. And for the life of me, I can't tell you why.... *Reveille with Beverly* is his first movie, so it is reportable news that at each moan and trick-turn of the Sinatra voice, in fact each time he so much as turns his dead-pan head or flickers an eyelid, the adolescent set goes nuts! They squeal in delight, they rock, moan and make animal cries. When he's finished, they're emotionally spent."

In 'TILL THE CLOUDS ROLL BY, 1946.

Step Lively (1944) also found Archer Winsten of the *New York Post* reviewing the audience as well as the film: "With the Sinatra Swoon & Squeal Society in force, it is not always possible to pay attention to the picture. Whenever Mr. Sinatra does anything the slightest bit endearing, his followers let forth such an ear-piercing shriek that further calm judgment is out of the question. This is usually followed by loud and opposition cries from sailors and others pretending to excess masculinity. . . . But he looks better, acts better, and sings in the manner that has made him famous. Apparently the Voice is here to stay. . . ."

He was not only here to stay. Louis B. Mayer, head of the powerful MGM organization, arranged for him to leave RKO Pictures. In 1945 he starred in *Anchors Aweigh,* the first of three fun films in which he was teamed with dancer Gene Kelly. The other two, both 1949 releases were *On the Town* and *Take Me Out to the Ball Game.* Although *Anchors Aweigh* fared best in the reviews and at the box office, all three were well received, largely because of the infectious interplay betwen Kelly and Sinatra, not to mention the dancing of the duo. But working with Kelly meant much more to young Sinatra than just box-office and good reviews.

Years later—thirty years later—at a Friars Roast of Kelly, Frank said: "We became a team only because he had the patience of Job, and he had the fortitude not to punch me in the mouth because I was impatient. I was in a different world. It took a lot of time to do these things, and I couldn't understand why I took so much time.

"He just managed to calm me when it was important to calm me. We were doing something that we wanted to do. We loved doing it, and I loved it. And we made some fun movies together. He taught me everything I know. I couldn't walk, let alone dance. I was a guy who got up and hung onto a microphone—with both arms together, and a bad tuxedo, and brown shoes.

"And all of a sudden I was a star. And one of the reasons why I became a star was Gene Kelly."

Between the three films with Kelly Sinatra starred in a picture about which he recently said; "All I ask is that my daughter Nancy never let my granddaughter see *The Kissing Bandit.*" In 1948, the year of the *Bandit,* "Sinatra's name on the marquee," according to *Time* magazine, "is sufficient to guarantee lipsticky posters on the outside, moaning galleryites within." Accordingly, Hollywood's search was for properties that would project his sexual charisma, emphasized then by some of his offscreen exploits, as well as his singing magic. A high point, or low, depending on one's view, was reached with *The Kissing Bandit* (1948). Playing the son of an innkeeper who was really a bandit in disguise and who devastated the ladies with his kisses,

Sinatra found himself in a "lavish but limp MGM technicolor musical. . .handicapped by a weak script, silly dialogue, and uncertain direction." Years later, when comic Joe E. Lewis happened to see a late-night rerun of the film in a Las Vegas hotel room, he had a salami delivered to Sinatra onstage at a hotel down the Strip.

But Sinatra was pleased with the last film he made before *From Here to Eternity. Meet Danny Wilson* was released in 1952 at the lowest point of his relationship with the public. Although it garnered good reviews, especially with regard to his acting, it was a box-office bust. The premiere at the New York Paramount, the scene of his greatest triumphs, drew small audiences even though he starred onstage. Nevertheless when he wanted to acquaint the unit publicist on *From Here to Eternity* with his work on the screen, he arranged a special screening of the film for Walter Shenson, later producer of The Beatles films. Sportswriter Jimmy Cannon was also part of the small group that included Shenson and his wife at dinner before the private screening of *Meet Danny Wilson.*

There is no point in repeating here the very well-known tale of the extreme lengths to which Sinatra, then in the pits professionally and emotionally, went to secure the role of Private Angelo Maggio in *From Here to Eternity.* Nor will any purpose be served by repeating the hyperbolic accolades that his superlative acting elicited and that led to his receiving the Oscar for Best Supporting Actor at the Academy Awards ceremony of 1954. No one has more poignantly stated what that award meant to him than Sinatra himself.

"God chose to smile on me," he said of that night, March 25, 1954, at the RKO Pantages Theatre. "It's quite a dream. I still have it three nights a week. I'd have it seven nights a week but I don't go to bed four nights. Talk about being born again, it was one time in my life when I had such happiness I couldn't share it with another human being. I ducked the party, lost the crowds, and took a walk. Just me and Oscar! I think I relived my entire lifetime that night as I walked up and down the streets of Beverly Hills. Even when a cop stopped me, he couldn't bring me down to earth. It was very nice of him although I did have to wait until his partner came cruising to assure him that I was who I said I was and that I had not stolen the statue I was carrying. . . ."

Sinatra was "born again," and the Oscar opened the door to his emergence as the impressive actor he became. When he had asked for the role of Maggio, producer Buddy Adler had said: "But it's an acting part, Frankie." And the late Harry Cohn, who was the head of Columbia Pictures, had said: "Look, Frank, Maggio's an actor's part. You're a singer." Suddenly, the singer was in demand as an actor, in such demand that 1955 saw him starring in five major films and 1956 brought him four films. In several other years (1957, 1960, 1962, 1965, and 1966), he has appeared in three motion pictures. But 1955 and 1956 were the busiest movie years.

The first picture he made after *Eternity* was *Suddenly*. It was a startling role he attempted—playing the part of an ex-GI being paid half-a-million dollars to assassinate the President of the United States. John Baron had no redeeming feature, except, perhaps, his desire to be *somebody*, something he could achieve only by killing. A wholly unsympathetic role, it brought raves from the critics: "The one-time crooner brings spine-chilling reality to the role of the crack-brained hired gunman...." *Newsweek* wrote: "Sneeringly arrogant in the beginning, brokenly whimpering at the finish, Sinatra will astonish viewers who flatly resent bobby-soxers' idols." *Cue*'s verdict: "The dramatic talent Sinatra suggested in *Meet Danny Wilson*, and which came to richer fruition in *From Here to Eternity*, is a solid and richer talent than many suspected. In *Suddenly* Sinatra bears a full load as its star and dominating character. He holds the screen and commands it with ease, authority and skill."

In 1955 Frank starred in more films than in any other year of his crowded career. In rapid succession he appeared in *Young at Heart*, whose title was taken from his hit disc of the same name but which was an adaptation of *Four Daughters*, with Sinatra playing the moody John Garfield role. *Not As A Stranger* followed, with Frank appearing as an amiable doctor opposite Robert Mitchum, a humorless, hard-driving medico. In *The Tender Trap* Frank as the freewheeling bachelor found himself ensnared by the wiles of Debbie Reynolds. Then there were *Guys and Dolls* and *The Man with the Golden Arm*, the last providing as challenging a role as the Frank Loesser musical was a sail-through.

Guys and Dolls, however, posed a problem from the start. Marlon Brando, hardly a singer, was given the romantic lead as Sky Masterson and had the major ballads of the tuneful Loesser score to sing. As the tinhorn gambler Nathan Detroit, running the oldest established floating crap game in New York, Frank was saddled with the production numbers: "Fugue for Tinhorns," "The Oldest Established," "Sue Me," and others. Moreover, Frank had no great love for Brando, who had played the lead in *On the Waterfront*, a role that had been promised to Frank and over which he had sued the film's producers. On the set, he kept referring to Brando as "Mumbles," while Marlon in turn told associates: "When Sinatra dies, he'll complain to God for making him bald."

Although Sinatra frankly felt that he was miscast as Nathan Detroit, he fared well in the reviews: "Sinatra is Sinatra," Hollis Alpert wrote in the *Saturday Review*, "and in this is perfect." But most reviewers felt that Brando, too, was miscast, and the film failed to achieve the acceptance that had made it a hit Broadway musical.

During the filming of *From Here to Eternity*, Sinatra had become close friends with actor Montgomery Clift, who had contributed greatly to Sinatra's masterful acting as Private Maggio. In fact, Frank, Clift, and writer James Jones became inseparable when the shooting was being done in Hollywood and the three were staying at the Hollywood Roosevelt Hotel. Nightly, they ate together at a favorite Italian restaurant. Returning to the hotel, sometimes full of beer or vino, "they would shout obscenities in the lobby," according to Clift biographer Patricia Bosworth, "and throw beer cans from the windows at startled passersby."

In November 1955 when Clift was invited to a preview of *Guys and Dolls*, he went with anticipation to Loew's 86th Street in Manhattan. "I'm dying to hear Marlon and Sinatra try and sing together," he told a friend whom he invited. "It oughta be a gas!"

Not long after the film started, according to the friend, "Monty began making loud derogatory remarks: 'Marlon is vomitable—oh, look at poor Frank!' He got so noisy people in the audience were shushing him. Finally, in the middle of it, he said; 'This picture sucks, let's get out of here.'

"When they reached the lobby, he was still fulminating against Hollywood corruption and lousy values. He was really steamed up. Suddenly, for no reason at all, he smashed his fist through the display case where all the glossy photographs of Marlon Brando, Sinatra, and Jean Simmons were pasted up...."

Whatever its limitations, *Guys and Dolls* hardly warranted so dynamic a critical reaction. But if it proved one of the weaker vehicles in which Frank starred, the force of his performance in the film that followed brought him his second nomination for an Academy Award. Playing the role of an artful card dealer in *The Man with the Golden Arm* —wherefore the title of the film—and a would-be drummer who is struggling to conquer drug addiction, he proved amazing "with his acting ability" to *The New Yorker*'s demanding critic, "terrifying in the vividness of his portrayal" to *Cue*, and "an actor of rare ability" to perceptive Arthur Knight of the *Saturday Review*. Unfortunately, 1955 was the year of *Marty*, a film that swept the awards, so that Ernest Borgnine won the race for Best Actor.

But 1959 saw another film that certified Sinatra's growth as an actor. Reacting sensitively to Frank Capra's discerning direction, Sinatra played a major part in making

A Hole in the Head, one of *The New York Times*'s "Best Ten " motion pictures of the year. Bosley Crowther, *The Times*'s critic, hailed Capra's return to filmmaking after an eight-year hiatus. He praised the Arnold Schulman script for its pithy social observation of a middle-class American family. He lauded the acting of Edward G. Robinson as the older, narrow-minded brother; Thelma Ritter as the compassionate wife; Eddie Hodges as the 11-year-old son; and Eleanor Parker as a widow lined up to wed "the dreamer, promoter, rolling stone."

"But the prize," Crowther concluded, "goes to Mr. Sinatra, who makes the rolling stone...a soft-hearted, hard-boiled, white-souled black sheep whom we will cherish, along with the Mr. Deeds and Mr. Smith, as one of the great guys Mr. Capra has escorted to the American screen."

Through the 1950s and 1960s, Sinatra remained a gleaming box-office name in over thirty films, all of which invariably earned him critical approval even when the films in which he appeared were faulted. In *The Joker Is Wild,* the Joe E. Lewis bio pic, he was "believable and funny— alternately sympathetic and pathetic, funny and sad" *(Variety).* In *Pal Joey* he was "perfectly type-cast as Joey" *(Los Angeles Times)* and "potent" *(Variety).* In *Some Came Running* "Frank Sinatra and Dean Martin punch over two of their best performances" *(Los Angeles Mirror-News)* and "Sinatra, as usual, gives a polished performance" *(Cosmopolitan).* In *Can-Can* "his naturalness makes him all the more effective, and his charm and self-assuredness ably complement a vocal style which fits hand in glove with the Porter tunes" *(Variety).* But there were only two films in which he approached the soaring level of *From Here to Eternity* and *The Man with the Golden Arm.*

Performing as an ex-soldier who had become a major in army intelligence in *The Manchurian Candidate* (1962), he was "in his usual uncanny fashion simply terrific" according to *The New Yorker,* and an actor who offered "one of his strongest portrayals" according to the *Los Angeles Times.* In the view of the *Hollywood Reporter* he gave "a seasoned and in many ways more mature performance than he has ever done before."

"I'm more excited about this part," he told Robin Douglas-Home, "than any other part I've played. I'm saying things in this script that I've never had to speak on the screen before. Never had to speak at all, for that matter. Long wild speeches. For instance, my first words in the film are a long speech about the different note value systems on the Boehm clarinet. Sometimes I've even ad-libbed for three whole pages of script, just been myself talking as I would do normally. But this is different. Very, very different."

Douglas-Home, who stayed at Sinatra's home when he was working on his book about Sinatra, noted that Frank would appear at breakfast with the script and delightedly read long passages out loud and would keep the script close to himself all through the day. Sinatra's trenchant handling of his role as Captain Ben Marco was a confirmation of what director Stanley Kramer had once said: "If Sinatra really prepared for a role, researched it, he'd be the greatest actor in the world."

During the '60s when the fear of a nuclear war, the conflict in Vietnam, and the struggle for civil rights engaged the energies and commitment of young people, polarizing the country into an arena of real tension and turmoil, Sinatra moved in two different and unrelated directions as an actor and moviemaker. Once, at the beginning of his career, he had dared the wrath of the Establishment by his outspoken espousal of racial and religious equality and had won himself a Special Oscar for a short film in which he pleaded for tolerance, *The House I Live In.* Now, in the turbulent '60s, he became involved at first in a series of flippant films, made mostly with members of an in-group known as the Clan, and toward the end of the decade, in a succession of detective pictures.

That these directions were his choice is indicated by his association with the vehicles not only as star but as producer and/or owner. Sinatra made his initial foray into film production as early as 1956. *Johnny Concho,* a western in which he also starred, playing the unsympathetic role of a coward who eventually musters the courage to face the killers of his brother, was hardly a resounding success. Nevertheless he was fascinated by the whole business of making movies, and through the '60s, he became involved in the production of more than a dozen films. Although he himself served as producer of only three, all of these were mounted through the initiative of Sinatra-owned companies like Essex, Dorchester, Arcola, Sinatra Enterprises, and Artanis (Sinatra spelled backward).

Working with Dean Martin, Sammy Davis, Jr., Peter Lawford, and Joey Bishop—who were part of the so-called Clan, though not all of them appeared in all of the films—Sinatra starred in (and sometimes produced) *Ocean's Eleven* (1960), *Sergeants 3* (1962), *4 for Texas* (1964), and *Robin and the 7 Hoods* (1964). The public seemingly liked them well enough to make them pay off at the box office. But the critics were critical, unfriendly, and even antagonistic, depending on their attitude toward the high jinks and shenanigans of the Clan.

Newsweek wrote of the first of the series: "*Ocean's Eleven* is a genial group effort by a bunch of real-life pals. First Peter Lawford found the property. Frank then formed a producing company, and sold shares in it to Peter and Dean. Then they all went out to Las Vegas and filmed it while entertaining the club customers at night. Unfortunately, it is all so genial that the major suspense lies in whether Frank, Dean, et al., will get their hands out of their pockets long enough to pull the robbery [of five casinos], which the movie is all about."

Of *Sergeants 3*, produced by Sinatra, *Playboy* wrote: "It's the Rat Pack reprise of *Gunga Din*, transposed from the Queen's Own in Inja to the American West, with the U.S. Cavalry riding to a great many rescues. And away we go with Feisty Frank Sinatra, Dashing Dean Martin, Pistol Peter Lawford [the three reenacting parts played in the 1939 George Stevens's epic with Cary Grant, Victor McLaglen, and Douglas Fairbanks, Jr.] and Sammy Davis, Jr., trailing along via white mule (the real thing, not the firewater)." While *Playboy's* review might have been tongue-in-cheek, the *Hollywood Citizen-News* rejected the film as "a movie mish-mash" and "downright amateurish."

In the eyes of James Powers of the *Hollywood Reporter*, reviewing *Robin and the 7 Hoods*, "One fault of these star-studded enterprises has been that the stars frequently gave the impression that they could give only a small part of their attention and talent to the work at hand." *Time* had previously observed regarding *4 for Texas*: "The Clan constitutes an in-group, and they seem bored with the outside world. . . . They seem less concerned to entertain the public than to indulge their private fantasies."

Sinatra himself told Douglas-Home: "Of course they're not *great* movies. No one could claim that. But every movie I've made through my own company has made money, and it's not so easy to say that. *Ocean's Eleven* has grossed millions of dollars, and *Sergeants 3* is already on the way doing the same."

Two films released in 1965 tackled more serious subjects. *None But the Brave*, in which he made his directorial bow, dealt with the relations between Japanese and American troops on a deserted Pacific Island during World War II. In *Von Ryan's Express*, which followed, he played a cool but unpopular American officer engineering a flight of British war prisoners from an Italian Nazi camp. It won plaudits for his acting—"expertly done" (*Life*); "Sinatra at his best as an actor" (Hollywood *Citizen-News*); "at last he has made a good picture" (*Playboy*).

Von Ryan's Express was filmed in Spain. Cinematographer Ted Allan—whom Frank endearingly called Farley Focus—recalls an incident, which did not make the American papers. Sinatra had finished his stint and was in a bar of the hotel where they were staying when he was approached by a young woman. Holding a cocktail glass in her hand, she asked if Sinatra would take a picture with her. He declined. As he turned back to his drink her glass went flying in the air—either accidentally spilled by another customer or thrown by her. And suddenly there was a photographer snapping the scene.

"The next we knew," Allan recalls, "police, armed with machine guns, arrived at the hotel to arrest Frank. The woman claimed that she had been injured when Frank threw a glass at her. Considering the stories about his temper and his belligerence toward people who invade his privacy, one might easily have believed her version. But I was there at the bar. I saw the whole thing, and I know Frank did not throw the glass.

"We managed to sneak him out of the hotel before the armored police could get to him, drove him to an airport, and got him out of the country on a private plane. He had to borrow money from several of us since in the hurried flight from the hotel, he left empty-handed.

"When he returned to the States, he never said a word about the incident. A crew had remained behind for some location shooting. Frank was concerned that anything he said might create problems for them. In fact, several were put under arrest but released soon after.

"Many of us believed the whole thing was a setup. Frank had made adverse comments about the Franco regime at various times—and we thought this might have entered into the situation. The fact that this woman had a photographer with her made it look like a plot.

"Incidentally, it was Frank who suggested the downbeat ending used in the film. In the original script he was supposed to make the train carrying the escaping British at the last moment. Instead, he gets killed by the Nazis as he is running after the departing train. That flop he took on the tracks was downright dangerous. The tracks were set on real sharp rocks, not pebbles. When I worked with him on *Sergeants 3*, he also insisted on doing all the stunts himself, including one bit where he had to climb out from under the wheels of a wagon racing at over 30 miles an hour. That was even more dangerous than the last-minute fall in *Von Ryan's Express*."

As for other films in which he appeared during the '60s, Sinatra himself was criticized for "sleep-walking," "gold-bricking," and a "walk-through." The adverse comments reached a peak in Pauline Kael's review of *The Naked Runner*, a 1967 film. "It might be a good movie," she wrote, "to read by if there was light in the theatre. . . . An implausible, unconvincing spy story without a single witty idea, and the star's role, that of an anxious, lifeless mouse. Sinatra wouldn't come on that way to the television audience; why does he have so little regard for the movie audience?"

The Naked Runner prompted Bosley Crowther of *The New York Times* to make a different kind of observation: "It is curious," he wrote, "how Frank Sinatra repeatedly gets himself involved in films about fellows who do violent things with guns—gangsters, soldiers or assassins. He seems immensely attracted to stories in which he as the leading character is called upon to kill." A provocative statement, it proved statistically sound. A survey revealed that Frank has played a man with a gun and/or killed—as a gangster, crook, soldier, or detective—in no fewer than 22 films. And a number of films that Sinatra made later, *The Detectives* (1968), *Contract on Cherry Street* (1977), and *The First Deadly Sin* (1980), seemed to confirm Crowther's thesis.

Sinatra, however, rejects Crowther's contention. "There have been a number of those," he told Neil Hickey. "But I didn't go looking for them, in most cases. I'm always dying to do comedy. But you can't find them. So when other things come up, you do those instead. I'd also like to do musicals, but who's making musicals any more? I'm always reading, always looking, always talking to people."

Although the number of comedies is smaller than the films with guns, Sinatra has appeared in such farcical, lightweight, or ring-a-ding-ding vehicles as *A Hole in the Head* (1959), *Can-Can* (1960), *Come Blow Your Horn* (1963), and *Marriage on the Rocks* (1965).

During the '60s, Sinatra moved for the first time—and so far, the last—to a chair behind the camera. Making his directorial bow in *None But the Brave* (1965), which he also produced and in which he starred, he was characterized as "impressive" and "straightforward and understated" as a director. *Time* felt that "Director Sinatra and his scriptwriters goof away tension at every turn." A melodrama of World War II, involving Japanese troops who spoke in their native tongue, the film posed problems that led to generally mixed reviews. While Sinatra continued to involve himself in film production, he did not again assay the directorial chore as of 1982.

By the year of *The Naked Runner* (1967), many felt, as

Hollis Alpert wrote in the *Saturday Review*, that "ever since *The Manchurian Candidate*, Sinatra has been a talent in search of a role." The film that provoked this comment by Alpert was actually the first of three in which Sinatra apparently attempted to establish a role for himself. It was a curious choice, considering his early, well-publicized aversion to "cops and reporters." In *Tony Rome* (1967) and in *Lady in Cement* (1968) he played a Miami private eye. In between he starred in *The Detective*, wearing a badge as detective Joe Leland.

He fared best in *The Detective*, which was based on a best-selling novel, well in *Tony Rome*, and better in *Lady in Cement*. In *The Detective Motion Picture Herald* saw "his most effective performance in a long time," and the *Hollywood Reporter* commented: "Sinatra has honed his laconic, hep veneer to the point of maximum credibility, and his detective Joe Leland is his best performance and role since *The Manchurian Candidate*."

In the Tony Rome character many critics saw an attempt by Sinatra to emulate Humphrey Bogart or, at least, to update Bogey's "Shamus" formula. Both Charles Champlin in the *Los Angeles Times* and Hollis Alpert felt that Sinatra had found himself, playing the tough, wisecracking, worldly but idealistic dick of Bogey's *Maltese Falcon*. With *Lady in Cement*, Champlin felt that Sinatra had gotten the Tony Rome character down perfectly. "He projects the ex-cop-turned-private-shamus," he wrote, "with a time-tested fictional blend of insouciance, cynicism, battered but surviving idealism, wisecrackery, courage, libido, thirst and all the more interesting hungers. He clearly enjoys the role and it is this evident pleasure which carbonates the thin material with lively amusement."

Both *Time* and *The New York Times* turned in minority reports, echoing a view previously expressed by Pauline Kael. Of *Tony Rome*, *Time* observed: "It remains one of Hollywood's major mysteries why a performer who puts so much style into his records so often sabotages his genuine talents in shoddy and ill-chosen movie vehicles." In the *Times*, Bosley Crowther's epithet was "strangely tricky and trashy motion pictures."

Whatever shortcomings the Tony Rome films had may have been in part the result of the pace at which they were shot. Never noted for his patience on a movie set, Sinatra arranged for the interiors of *Lady in Cement* to be filmed while he was at the Fontainebleau in Miami. Ted Allan, who was Sinatra's personal photographer for a number of years, recalls that all the interior sets were built in the basement of the hotel. All that Frank had to do to appear in a given scene was to take the elevator from his room down to the basement.

In his comments on *Tony Rome* Bosley Crowther began his analysis with a full recognition of Sinatra's sta-

ture: "It has not escaped the attentions of a few million persons in the land that a gentleman named Frank Sinatra is one of the phenomena of our age. Certainly his range and vitality as an entertainer are phenomenal, and his extracurricular reputation is awesome, to say the least. That's why it is provoking—nay, disturbing and depressing beyond belief—to see this acute and awesome figure turning up time and again in strangely tricky and trashy motion pictures." Crowther found little to recommend in *Von Ryan's Express, Marriage on the Rocks, Assault on a Queen*, or *Tony Rome*, which he felt fell short of Bogey's "me-first, loner" style. The clue to the shortcomings of *Tony Rome*, Crowther contended, was in Sinatra's willingness or carelessness in "pandering to those who are easily and crudely amused." Crowther concluded his evaluation in a spirit of nostalgic regret: "What grieves a longtime moviegoer is to remember how bright and promising Sinatra used to be, beginning with his charming performance in *Anchors Aweigh* and moving on into his poignant performance in *From Here to Eternity."*

Perhaps the most adverse critical reaction came in 1970 when Sinatra starred in the MGM film *Dirty Dingus Magee*, which seemed to bear out Crowther's reference to "sheer bad taste." Even from critics who had generally been friendly to his work, Frank took a lambasting. Kevin Thomas's review in the *Los Angeles Times* was peppered with phrases like "description-defying silliness," "enough to make you cringe with embarrassment for Frank Sinatra and George Kennedy," and "the burlesquing of Indians and their ways that we're supposed to find so funny is merely disgusting." In the *Hollywood Reporter* Craig Fisher characterized the film as "the most tasteless, witless and fatuous spoof on Western conventions yet to be filmed." Of Sinatra, Arthur Knight wrote in the *Saturday Review*: "He seems ineffably bored and totally uncommitted as well he might be."

Under his flip exterior Sinatra is a sensitive and extremely intelligent man. That he might have taken the criticism to heart is not beyond the realm of possibility. That he might have been involved in other enterprises or been unable to find suitable scripts are likewise possibilities. In any event, it was seven years before he made a new film. But *Contract on Cherry Street* was made for and shown on television in 1977.

Three years later Sinatra starred in *The First Deadly Sin*. Faye Dunaway was his costar as the bedridden wife dying of a mysterious disease. A film with a "deft *Naked City* beat and a solid cast," according to Jack Kroll's *Newsweek* review, it displayed Sinatra acting with "the same God-given rhythm he has as a singer."

Charles Champlin of the *Los Angeles Times* also found him "in top form" and playing "a charged roll with a fresh charge of passion and commitment" that reminded one that *From Here to Eternity* was not an accidental performance." Nevertheless, Champlin thought the tale was "pretty ordinary stuff, a police story not radically different from the stories TV and the movies have ground out by the tens of miles of footage." On the other hand, Arthur Knight, writing in *Variety*, thought it was "a dandy mystery story" and "a taut, skillfully paced melodrama." Agreeing with his confreres, he felt that Sinatra's performance "transformed the picture into the kind of class act that has always been associated with the Sinatra name in recordings and concerts."

Sinatra has at various times expressed regret that he never studied acting. His intuitions about being a good actor are, nevertheless, as sound as if he had taken a doctorate in acting. Explaining his philosophy as a film actor, he told Robin Douglas-Home: "I always try to remember three things as a movie actor. First, you must know *why* you are in the movie, understand all the reactions of the man you are playing, figure out *why* he's doing what he is doing. Secondly, you must know the script. . . . I keep a script in my office, my car, my bedroom, by the telephone, even in the john. And I read the whole script maybe fifty or sixty times before shooting even starts. Then, when it comes to shooting a particular scene, you just have to glance at the script to remember the lines and, more important, you know how the scene fits into the picture as a whole. Thirdly, you must learn and listen to the lines of others; it's no good just learning your own."

Of his performance in *From Here to Eternity*, director Fred Zinnemann said: "He played Maggio so spontaneously, we almost never had to reshoot a scene."

And Buddy Adler, who produced the film, said: "He dreamt, slept, and ate his part. . . . He never made a fluff. And this from a fellow who never really had any training. Once the test was made, it was a case of the natural performer up against some great actors. The natural performer was better."

The natural performer was better not only in *From Here to Eternity*, but in *Suddenly, The Man with the Golden Arm, A Hole in the Head, The Manchurian Candidate,* and *The Detective*, among other films. These pictures certify Sinatra's achievement as an actor in the history of the American film. But considering how many other films he made, it seems not inappropriate to say, as Pete Hamill has said, "A Sinatra film never reached down into the darkness the way the songs did. . . . He never cheated on songs." There's only one thing wrong with Hamill's statement. The first "never" should be replaced with "seldom."

In VON RYAN'S EXPRESS, 1965.

II

The Retirement Concert

JUNE 13, 1971

THE RUMOR THAT FRANCIS ALBERT SINATRA WAS RETIR-
ing from show business first surfaced in Joyce Haber's column in the *Los Angeles Times* of March 9, 1971. Two
weeks later Ms. Haber confirmed it: "Passing from happy
events to sad," she wrote, "it's happened. Frank Sinatra,
the King of Them All, has announced he's retiring. No
more Sinatra-starring movies. No more Sinatra TV
specials. No more Sinatra smash engagements in night
clubs. No more Sinatra-stunning songs on LP's. . . ."

The formal announcement of the retirement came
through another columnist in the last week of March.
Suzy (Aileen Mehle), syndicated society columnist of the
New York *Daily News* and an occasional Sinatra date, in-
formed the public of his exit, "effective immediately," on
the basis of a six-paragraph statement she received from
Frank.

"It has been a fruitful, busy, uptight, loose, sometimes
boisterous, occasionally sad, but always exciting three
decades," Sinatra wrote. "There has been at the same time
little room or opportunity for reflection, reading, self-
examination and that need which every thinking man has
for a fallow period, a long pause in which to seek a better
understanding of the vast transforming changes now
taking place everywhere in the world. . . . This seems a
proper time to take a breather.

"I look forward to enjoying more time with my family and dear friends, to writing a bit—perhaps even to
teaching."

In the vast media coverage that followed the
announcement, there was considerable speculation as to
what really prompted the retirement. Many papers referred to problems he had had with Dupuytren's Contrac-
ture, a shortening of muscular tissue in the palm of the
hand that forces fingers into a clawlike position. Frank had
undergone surgery for the ailment in July 1970. The following month he appeared at his daughter's opening at
Caesars Palace with his right arm in a sling. Although the
operation had been successful there was continuing pain in
the hand, so much so that he withdrew from a Warner
Brothers's film he was to make in November 1970.

The suspicion that ill health was the cause of the
retirement continued to grow. Soon, some of the more
lurid publications began circulating rumors that he was
suffering from muscular dystrophy or cancer of the throat.

Frank Jr. felt impelled to speak up. "There is no truth
to the cancer rumor. Everyone agrees he looks better than
he ever has in his life. I know for a fact that he is just taking
it easy. Just eating good food and exercising, and drinking

a little good whiskey now and again, and just sitting in the sun, but hopefully not letting his mind wander. He still reads a great deal and is still practicing his golf swing.....He's doing what I think is very nice for a man in his mid-50s....He's worked hard for 35 years and I think he deserves a little time to himself."

Sister Nancy added her words to the denial. "No, he isn't sick or dying from an incurable ailment. He's very much alive and well and kicking, thank you. But he says it's the end of an era, and he's right. His kind of show business has ended. So he's going to take it easy and enjoy himself."

Eventually, toward the end of the year, Sinatra brought a $5-million lawsuit against one of the gossip tabloids that had printed stories about his suffering from throat cancer. The suit was settled out of court in May 1972, with the publication printing an apology and contributing a near six-figure sum of money to the Martin Anthony Sinatra Medical Education Foundation in Palm Springs.

In all the speculation no one apparently mentioned the establishment of the $805,000 facility, which had occurred just about two months before he announced his retirement and which he had established in memory of his father. But columnist Jim Bishop, who did not feel happy about Frank's exit, suggested: "I suspect that when an artist of Sinatra's stature steps down, it may be because he reads too many obituary columns." Apart from his father's death, Frank had suffered or would suffer the loss of a number of close friends, all within a few years: Joe E. Lewis, restaurateur Mike Romanoff, publisher Bennett Cerf, producer Leland Hayward, and boniface Jack Entratter of the Sands Hotel. He had said at one point: "Life's too short in this rat race. I want to do some other things before they put me away."

But when Sinatra was pressed for an explanation, his answer tended to be on the flip side: "Hell, I just quit, that's all. I don't want to put on anymore makeup. I want to relax and do absolutely zero." And he would add: "I want to read Plato and grow petunias." Looking back after he came out of retirement, he said: "Being a public figure got to me. People were always spiritually peeking in my window."

An altercation in which he was involved at Caesars Palace late in 1970 may also have figured in his retirement. It could have triggered a decision, which was subconsciously in the making. In the wee hours of September 7 Sinatra got into a heated argument with one of the Palace's casino bosses. Apparently it had something to do with extending his credit, though this is not certain. San-ford Waterman drew a gun on him. In the splurge of news accounts that followed, there was no agreement on what, how, or why it happened. But both the district attorney and sheriff of Las Vegas came down on Sinatra in public statements that caused him to say: "I'll never go back to Nevada." (Both of the incumbents were out of office by the time Sinatra returned to perform at Caesars in 1974, and Sinatra was not entirely benign in the campaign to unseat the D.A. who had been antagonistic.)

My reference to a "decision subconsciously in the making" stems largely from the tenor of the songs he chose for the album *Sinatra and Company,* which he recorded just before he announced his retirement. The songs had a world-weary quality, and at least two, "Lady Day" and "Leaving on a Jet Plane" dealt with departures and good-byes.

In trying to analyze the motives for his retirement, two perceptive columnists reached contrasting conclusions, although each felt that it had something to do with the temper of the times. In the view of Charles Champlin of the *Los Angeles Times ,* Sinatra had always done much more than just sing "all the good songs there are, better than any other popular male singer of our time." He had somehow reflected changes in the world: at first, "the youthful romantic idealism"; later, "the world-bruised wisdom and lightly cynical defiance of the inconstant fates"; and more recently, "gratitude for the good ladies and the good years, [seeking to assess] where we've been and where with luck we'll yet get to go."

Pete Hamill of the *New York Post* felt that Sinatra was out of joint with the times. "In the past five years," he wrote, "Sinatra and his America began to drift apart." Sinatra's support of Ronald Reagan for governor of California was the firecracker that lit up the change. The Ronald Reagan thing, as Hamill called it, expressed "his disgust with the glib contempt of so many young . . . , the resentment of a self-educated man" against attacks on the universities; and "a drift into a kind of natural conservatism that comes with age."

Like Jim Bishop, both Charles Champlin and Pete Hamill regretted his decision, a decision, whatever the underlying or immediate motivation, from which he was not going to retreat in 1971. "It will not be the same America," wrote Pete Hamill.

A grandmother in England, unconcerned with motives but feeling very much as Hamill did, wrote the London *Evening Standard:* "Sad, sad, sad to learn that the prodigious, phenomenal Frank Sinatra has called a halt. I was one of those adoring teenagers many years ago, and now, a grandmother, I feel he is still the greatest.

Never can there be another Frank Sinatra. . . ."

The farewell concert would be on June 13. The choice of date was, perhaps, accidental. About a year before he made the announcement of retirement, actor Gregory Peck, a trustee of the Motion Picture and Television Relief Fund, had begun working on a benefit to amortize a large deficit in the fund. He had lined up a stellar cast of performers, including Bob Hope, Jack Benny, Cary Grant, Sammy Davis, Jr., Pearl Bailey, Barbra Streisand, as well as Sinatra. With the two most celebrated singers of the day, Streisand and Sinatra, on the program, tickets went fast at $250 a seat.

When Sinatra indicated that the June 13 benefit was to be his last public appearance, the event assumed an historical significance and the demand for tickets escalated unbelievably. People were now willing to contribute as much as $5,000 for a seat. When the receipts were finally tallied, the take was over $800,000. Not only was the deficit wiped out, but the fund for needy film and TV actors wound up with $125,000 in the till.

Regardless of the original purpose of the concert, the evening's doings became a tribute to Sinatra, with fans flying in from all parts of the United States as well as England and Australia. Among those who came to hear his swan song, there were, according to reporters, "more big names and more Beautiful People than all the Hollywood social and political chroniclers boasted in their heyday." The luminaries included Princess Grace of Monaco, Cary Grant, Steve Allen, Polly Bergen, Carol Burnett, Diahann Carroll, David Frost, Clint Eastwood, Susan Hayward, Charlton Heston, David Janssen, Ali MacGraw, Ryan O'Neal, Robert Wagner, Natalie Wood, among others.

At the private house party in Beverly Hills that Rosalind Russell gave after the gala let out at 1:05 A.M., attendees included such political bigwigs, weighted on the Republican side, as Vice-President Spiro Agnew (who had been staying at Sinatra's home in Palm Springs), Henry Kissinger, and Governor and Mrs. Reagan.

Sinatra spent the afternoon of Sunday, June 13, playing twelve holes of golf. As he sat in a dressing room of the Los Angeles Music Center, sipping vodka and lemon juice, and kidding with Don Rickles and Cary Grant, his retirement was foremost in the mind of every person attending the gala. Her Royal Highness Princess Grace (Kelly) Rainier had flown in from Monaco to serve as the evening's patroness. The benefit, with an attendance of over 5,000 patrons, was to be staged in all three theaters of the music center—the same show being performed live,

first in the Chandler Pavilion and then in the Ahmanson while a special, historical film short, *The Movies,* was being shown in the Mark Taper Forum.

David Rose conducted the orchestra in an overture. Opening the proceedings, Jimmy Stewart hop-scotched onstage to introduce Bobby Sherman, a young rock entertainer. Approaching from opposite ends of the stage, Ryan O'Neal and Ali MacGraw introduced Jimmy Durante, who was followed by the master of the oneliner, Bob Hope, who was followed by Mitzi Gaynor and her entourage. Singing the title song from *Hello Dolly,* Pearl Bailey, assisted by a curious chorus line, scored "a showstopper of such mammoth proportions" that the audience demanded and received a reprise. The chorus line consisted of Rock Hudson, Greg Morris, Joe Namath, Jack Lemmon, Sammy Davis, Jr., David Niven, and Don Rickles. It did a mock Rockette kicking routine, which ended in a free-for-all pileup after Lemmon accidentally took a pratfall.

The second half of the concert proceeded rapidly, after starting with a Cary Grant introduction of Princess Grace, who introduced The Fifth Dimension. To boogaloo with them in their final number, the group attracted onstage Ryan O'Neal, Ali MacGraw, Natalie Wood, David Janssen, and Barbi Benton. The Fifth Dimension was followed by a Jack Benny original violin concerto and routine, with Jimmy Stewart acting as straight man. A monologue by David Frost brought Barbra Streisand onstage in a program of five songs. As Barbra was completing a swinging version of "Oh Happy Day," Sinatra slipped into his tuxedo jacket and started for the wings. Don Rickles yelled to the backstage crowd of stars: "Somebody help the old man on with his coat. Make way for the old timer. Help him go out in a blaze of glory. Remember, Frank, pity!"

The appearance of chairperson Rosalind Russell onstage, four hours after the show began, signalled the approach of the evening's climactic moment. Struggling to keep her voice under control, Miss Russell, in shining rhinestones on white crepe, announced: "This assignment is not a happy one for me." Her voice cracked. "Our friend has made a decision"—she fumbled for words—"a decision we don't particularly like but one which we must honor. He's worked long and hard for us for 30 years with his head and his voice," she sighed, "and especially his heart. But it's time to put back the Kleenex and stifle the sob, for we still have the man, we still have the blue eyes," she paused, "those wonderful blue eyes, that smile. And for the last time, we have the man, the greatest entertainer of the 20th century. . . . "

As Sinatra, wearing black patent leather boots, came onstage, waving a finger and cautioning her softly, "Don't you cry," the audience leaped to its feet—the first of three standing ovations and the start of an emotion-racked interplay between performer and audience.

"Here's the way it started," Sinatra announced, as he launched into "All or Nothing at All," followed by "I've Got You Under My Skin," a tender "I'll Never Smile Again," a flip "The Lady Is a Tramp," and a stirring, rich-toned "Ol' Man River."

("He sang with power," Thomas Thompson observed in *Life*, "with breath strong enough to hold the notes, keep the notes—strong, full, lush Sinatra notes. There was the old phrasing, the attention to the lyric, the delicate shading, the long melodic line. He sang almost as if throwing out a challenge!")

During the singing of "Nancy (With the Laughing Face)," his eyes filled with tears. The words of "My Way"—"I face the final curtain"—brought a ripple of sighs from the audience. Barbra Streisand, by then in a seat in the orchestra, dabbed her eyes with a handkerchief. As the song ended, Sinatra was given a second standing ovation. Having delivered the existential "That's Life," Frank now chose for his final number "Angel Eyes" because, as he explained, "It's a saloon song and I've been a saloon singer." As he began the song, the stage was darkened, and he was picked up in a dramatic silhouette by a pin spot. He staged the finale with style and feeling. Mid-song, he lit a cigarette. He exhaled and the smoke billowed around him. He was building toward the last line of the song. "'Scuse me while I disappear," he sang. The pin spot of light blinked out—and he was gone.

The suddenness of the departure stunned the teary-eyed audience. There was a shocked moment of silence, and then thunderous applause crashed through the theater as the audience leaped to its feet. Thompson later called the exit "the single most stunning moment (he had) ever witnessed on a stage." Sinatra returned for one, two, three curtain calls. The audience wanted more song. But he would not do an encore. Sammy Davis, Jr., bounded on the stage, dashed into the wings, and led Sinatra out, feigning anger. The applause rose to a new crescendo. He embraced Frank, who turned to the audience, and said "Love you all," blew a kiss of thanks—with many ladies instinctively reaching for their compacts—and was gone.

"Gone but not forgotten," observed Joyce Haber, "the Italo-American kid from Hoboken who fought his way to the very top—top singer, top movie star, top entertainer, top womanizer and, at times, top anonymous

philanthropist, top legend and top champion of the under-privileged. Sinatra is, perhaps, the only really great idol of our day whom the public accepts, nay, loves, despite the fact that it cannot identify with him. He's talented, he's rich, he lives on a super-scale. . . ."

Of the concert, *Daily Variety* editor Thomas M. Pryor wrote: "Sinatra sang in top form. He sounded like a man at the peak of his talent rather than one who had decided to close the cover on his professional life."

In confronting the retirement announcement, Pete Hamill had written: "It doesn't seem right that he should depart this way—a statement issued from Palm Springs isn't the way to go out. This isn't Vic Damone: this is Sinatra. I wish he'd give us one for the road. In the Spring, in New York where it started, at Madison Square Garden now that the Paramount is gone. Just one more time. Let him come out on a bare stage, elegant and proud, to sing the Jimmy Van Heusen songs or about Nancy with the laughing face, and give us one final chance to thank him before he leaves us forever with his style and his sorrow."

Perhaps Frank had heard him. Regardless, he had done it exactly as every Sinatra admirer would have wanted him to do it if he insisted on going off. And so the career of 58 films, 100 albums, and nearly 2,000 singles seemed to end for the Hoboken kid with the caved-in cheeks and an oversize Adam's apple who first appeared before frenzied crowds on the Paramount stage in a floppy, polka-dotted bow tie and a double-breasted suit with wide lapels.

"It was a night of charity," Thomas M. Pryor noted, "a night of sentiment, a night of tribute, a night of wondrous entertainment, a night when Hollywood glistened amidst its travail. A night to be remembered."

Departing the theater, Frank entered a waiting limousine, which took off for Beverly Hills and the home of Rosalind Russell. Thomas Thompson of *Life*, who was in the Cadillac with Sinatra and Russell, reported that Frank leaned back against the cushioned headrest and said: "I'm tired. It's been a helluva 35 years. I always sang a tough book. Not a lot of phoney talk. It used to wring me out. I used to do five full shows a night at the Jersey shore. From 8:15 P.M. to 4:00 A.M. I'd see the sun come out as I walked home. And then at the Paramount in New York, we did 10 shows a day. . . . 11 on Saturday. . . ."

Over a Spanish language station, as they were driving, a south-of-the-border ballad came on. Frank improvised a lyric and sang a few bars. "And that, ladies and gentlemen," he said, "is the last time Frank Sinatra will open his mouth."

Everyone in the speeding Cadillac laughed. "But in our laughter," Thompson wrote, "was the unmistakable edge of sadness."

Before the concert Thompson had asked whether Sinatra was *really* quitting. To which Frank replied: "I'm absolutely serious about retirement. You can't make an idle statement like the one I made. At least, *I* can't. I'm not built that way." He added: "I've had enough. Maybe the public's had enough, too."

To another reporter, he said in a lighter vein: "I'm quite serious about quitting. I've got things in my life I haven't had a chance to do. Like meet some girls and things like that."

On another occasion, he said: "I want to get out while I'm ahead, not when I'm a has-been."

The retirement process reached its, perhaps, unexpected climax on June 30, 1971, when Sinatra journeyed down to Washington, D.C., with a group of friends —the Bennett Cerfs, the Gregory Pecks with their teenage daughter, and others. Sitting in the Senate gallery, Sinatra heard nine senators—the papers reported only seven, omitting Muskie and Pell—rise in Congress to heap words of praise upon him. The 45-minute tribute was initiated by Senator John V. Tunney (D-Calif.), who was joined by two Republican Senators (Jacob Javits of New York and Charles Percy of Illinois) and by four Democratic Senators (Birch Bayh of Indiana, Hubert H. Humphrey of Minnesota, Alan Cranston of California and Howard W. Cannon of Nevada). All expressed regret over Frank's desire to remove himself from the entertainment scene and voiced the hope that it would be temporary.

Referring to him as "the greatest entertainer the United States has ever known," Senator Tunney praised him as "a master of the performing arts." But the name "Sinatra," he said, "symbolizes more than just a star or a legend. It symbolizes a man of genuine warmth and deep feeling, who in a thousand silent acts has worked to better the lives of those around him." The two themes were taken up in succeeding tributes.

Senator Hubert Humphrey, whose statement was more extended than the others', took the time to elaborate on Sinatra's humanitarian activities, noting that "the moneys he has raised for a wide variety of charities spiral to astronomical proportions." Harking back to the period of World War II, Humphrey observed that "no man in the entertainment field has done more in the field of human rights" in speaking for and fighting for the little people.

Humphrey was echoing a note first sounded by Senator Cranston, who said: "Some may say that Frank Sinatra is all voice. Those who know him well know that he is really all heart. They also know that he is all guts." Thinking back to a Democratic rally in 1955, Cranston recalled that there were two dramatic moments: the first was when Henry Wallace and Harry Truman walked in arm in arm to signal the healing of a division in the party; and the second, when Sinatra appeared onstage. Sinatra had said he was well aware that many thought entertainers should stay out of politics and that he had been warned that he would ruin his career. But Sinatra had added he believed "so deeply in the cause that brought him there, that if it meant the end of the entertaining phase of his life, then so be it."

In his tribute Senator Javits said: "One thing he has taught us, and that is that American life, notwithstanding its materialism, can also be romantic." In a supplementary statement in which Sinatra's "great persistence and perseverance" were praised, Senator Tunney read a poem, "On a Tree Fallen Across the Road," by Robert Frost, celebrating man's indomitable spirit.

During the tribute Frank sat in the second row of the Senate's family gallery between Mrs. Gregory Peck and Mrs. Bennett Cerf, his chin resting on his right hand. As the speeches ended he turned to Gregory Peck, who was sitting in the row behind him, and said: "What a marvelous thing to do!" Then, overcome by the tributes, he added: "Never in my life—with Oscars, Gold records, or anything—have I been so rocked as I was today."

Afterward, Frank and his friends attended a private luncheon hosted by Senator Tunney. "I know my wife and children envy my chance," Senator Muskie had said in his remarks on the Senate floor, "to have lunch with him." Included in the Sinatra party, in addition to the Gregory Pecks and the Bennett Cerfs, were Peck's 13-year-old daughter and Mr. and Mrs. Daniel Schwartz, a longtime business associate and executive vice-president of National General Corporation, a company in which Sinatra held a considerable batch of stock.

As he walked out of the luncheon into the steamy heat of a late June day in Washington, Frank was thinking about Senator Javits' words: "I feel that he has retired from show business to take a more active part in life. I feel that his impulses and motivations will lead him to a higher role in our times."

Frank had told Thomas Thompson of *Life:* "I've got things to do. Like the first thing is not do anything at all for eight months, maybe a year. . . . Roam around the desert taking pictures of cactus. . . . Paint a little, maybe try once again with watercolors. . . . I've never been able to control them. . . ."

In its retrospective following Sinatra's announcement of retirement, *Time* had observed: "It is questionable how long a mercurial and sleepless man like Sinatra can be happy as a professional dropout, ruminating and writing." An executive of Frank's recording company was quoted as saying: "I have yet to recall an entertainer who stayed in retirement. A great artist is a great artist. How many times did Judy Garland retire? And each time she came back. Singers retire, actors retire, bullfighters retire, but they all come back. Who knows?" The words turned out to be prophetic.

3. "Witchcraft": The Showman

"A Sinatra opening," wrote Charles Champlin, the analytical entertainment editor of the *Los Angeles Times,* "is like nothing else in show business."

Las Vegans say other performers fill a showroom, a casino, a hotel. Sinatra fills the city.

"No one else around," exulted the rock critic of the *Los Angeles Herald-Examiner* in 1980, "demands just as

much attention from his audience as he gives to his work."

When Sammy Davis performs in Las Vegas or Engelbert Humperdinck appears at the MGM Grand, the hotel marquee, newspaper ads, and billboards around town herald the appearance with the use of only their first name—"Sammy," "Engelbert," and so on. It is a token of status and acceptance granted to a small coterie of headliners. But when Sinatra appears at Caesars Palace, his performances are advertised with the simple phrase "He's here" or "He's back." No identification is made of "he" and none is needed. Vegas hotel executives say: "Other performers fill a showroom or a hotel. Sinatra fills the city."

Sinatra's charisma as a showman is a worldwide phenomenon. An announcement of his forthcoming appearance brings out long lines of ticketbuyers in Australia, South America, and even South Africa. When he appeared in Sun City in 1981, 20,000 people drove from Johannesburg to Pretoria to see him. In Buenos Aires, also in 1981, 1,000 seats were sold at $1,000 a seat for his performances at the Sheraton, and it was reported that $25 seats were scalped for as high as $2,500 a seat.

What is, perhaps, more remarkable is the reaction of the critics. "The voice was more secure and wider in range both for dynamics and pitch," wrote a *New York Times* reviewer of his Carnegie Hall concert in 1981. "If he is the best in the business, he is also an artist. . . . He is the master of his field, and his field is the American song." Filling Radio City Hall's 6,000 seats for 10 consecutive performances in 1978, he was characterized in the *Village Voice* as "brilliant.*"That,"* wrote the critic,"is the only word that will describe the effect with which he took over the stage at the Radio City Music Hall."

Sinatra has been doing that to audiences for over 40 years—captivating, titillating, mesmerizing, overwhelming, seducing them. No need to go back to the World War II years when his appearances at the New York Paramount brought swooning back into vogue.

"We loved to swoon," Martha Weinman Lear recalled, almost 30 years later. "Back from the RKO-Boston, we would gather behind locked bedroom doors, in rooms where rosebud wallpaper was plastered over with pictures of The Voice, to practice swooning. We would take off our saddle shoes, put on his records and stand around groaning for a while. When the song would

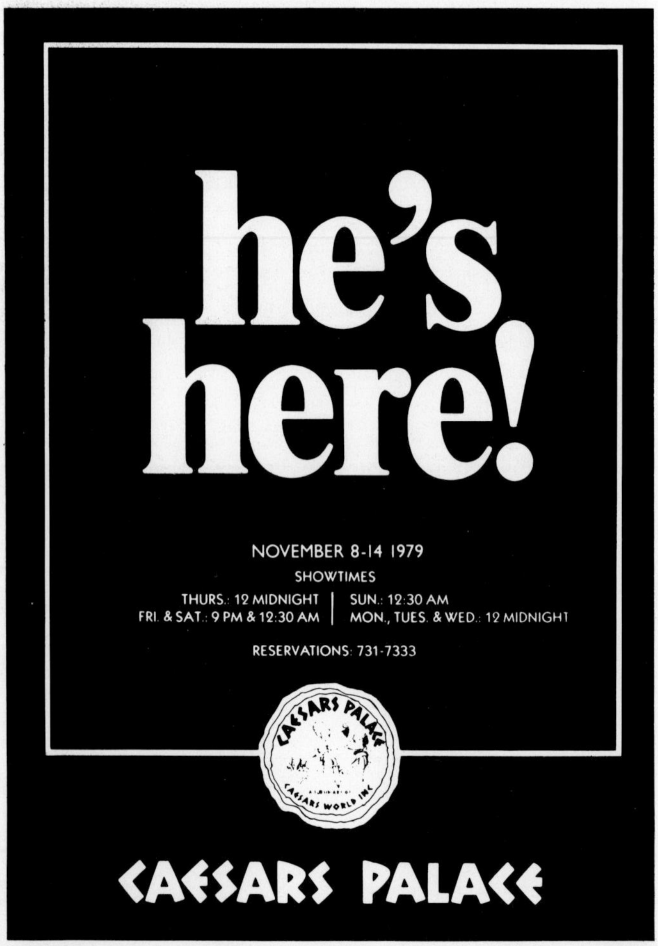

he's here!

NOVEMBER 8-14 1979
SHOWTIMES
THURS.: 12 MIDNIGHT | SUN.: 12:30 AM
FRI. & SAT.: 9 PM & 12:30 AM | MON., TUES. & WED.: 12 MIDNIGHT

RESERVATIONS: 731-7333

CAESARS PALACE

end we would fall down on the floor. We would do that for an hour or so. . . . "

It was thought at first that his appeal was only to the bobby-sox crowd, to the teenagers who sat hungry and spent through a day of panty-wetting ecstasies. But he quickly demonstrated that he could overpower the wives of the expense account crowd and the jet setters who frequented the Waldorf-Astoria's Wedgwood Room and East Side chichi night spots such as the Riobamba. Today his audience stretches from Las Vegas to South Africa, and from the bigwigs of government and industry to the rock crowd, whose music he cannot stand.

Potent as he is on wax, Sinatra is an in-person warlock. The record has the voice but it does not have the eyes—those cerulean blue eyes that have transfixed audiences for 40 years. No one who has ever seen Sinatra in person ever forgets those eyes. No matter where they sat—at remote tables at the top of the Circus Maximus or at a distant spot on the carpet-covered sands near Cairo—those eyes speared them with an electrical charge

that eliminated the space in between. That was what always made each female feel that Sinatra was singing just to her.

But Sinatra's impact was not just a matter of sound and contact. Almost from the beginning, he was never just a voice. He was always an image, a romantic image that embodied toughness as well as tenderness, challenge as well as comfort, vulnerability as well as violence. It was a complex image, full of contradictions. He was a high-liver and a giver, enigmatic as well as outspoken, intemperate and the acme of courtesy, a swinger and a sad-sack, hurt as well as hurting. The contradictions freighted the onstage figure with a fascinating charisma and added to the witchcraft of his singing and showmanship.

"What Sinatra has," director Billy Wilder said at one point, "is beyond talent. It's some sort of magnetism that goes in higher revolutions than that of anybody else, anybody in the whole of show business. Wherever Frank is, there is a certain electricity permeating the air. It's like Mack the Knife is in town and the action is starting."

The move from the Copa in New York City to the Sands in Las Vegas was as natural as it was inevitable when Copa boniface Jack Entratter took over at the Sands in 1952. If Las Vegas had not existed, Sinatra could have invented it. "He is the swinging image on which the town is built," his reporter-friend James Bacon has said. In truth, no other entertainer embodies as fully the glamour, the excitement, the vitality, the rhythms, and the sleeplessness of the 24-hour capital of gaming and entertainment.

But that was not how his roaring relationship with the gaming city began. One of his earliest Vegas appearances occurred in September 1951 at Wilbur Clark's Desert Inn, at the time when the tide of public opinion was running against him. Critic Bill Willard of the *Las Vegas Sun,* noting that there was "a tendency to scalp the Voice before it had a chance to be heard," praised Sinatra's performance of several songs and hailed the seven-minute version of "Soliloquy" from *Carousel* as "a Sunday punch"—"he KO's the whole room, but good." Willard also indicated that, regardless of the knocks he had been taking, Frank remained "one of the most colorful guys in showbiz."

The following day the publisher of the *Sun*—later one of Frank's strongest supporters and a business associate—took issue with his own critic. Addressing himself to Sinatra, whom he described as an anemic Clark Gable fallen under the spell of Hollywood," Hank Greenspun wrote: "You leave me *sooo* cold. You do nothing to me. You had it at the Waldorf. You were hungry." When Willard took issue with his publisher, suggesting that "styles change with time," Greenspun struck back in his column, *Where I Stand:* "I am no critic, just a fan who paid $33.00 [sic!] for a group of friends," he wrote, and protested that "the $15,000 a week being paid Frank was a lot of money [sic!]," considering that he "offered little to resemble performances of the past."

Incidentally, it was at this time, possibly during this very engagement, that Sinatra initiated a relationship with pianist Bill Miller that lasted over 25 years. Miller,was then playing an all-day, all-night grind in the Lady Luck Bar of the Desert Inn with a group called The Majors, became Frank's accompanist, and eventually, his conductor.

A high point in the life of the city and in Sinatra's career as a showman came in 1960 with the so-called Summit meetings of the Clan. Sinatra's Dorchester Production company was then shooting *Ocean's Eleven,* the story of a group of war veterans who execute a miraculous $10-million dollar heist of five Vegas casinos. In return for opening their establishments to on-location shooting, Sinatra and his cohorts nightly mounted the stage of the Sands and put on an ad-lib show that was the talk of the town and, with media coverage, became the talk of the nation. Although only Sinatra's name appeared on the marquee, he was joined onstage nightly by Dean Martin, who played the lush, Sammy Davis, Jr., the minstrel man, Peter Lawford, the British buffoon, and Joey Bishop, the cool comic—all of whom were in the cast of *Ocean's Eleven.* Their improvised shenanigans and offbeat humor, sometimes off-color, drew brickbats from some customers. But *Playboy* ran an almost verbatim account of some of their routines, reflecting the feelings of most people that the Clan was "the inmost in-group in the world." The Summits were a testimonial not only to Sinatra's showmanship but to his business savvy. Premiering in downtown Las Vegas, *Ocean's Eleven* toppled box-office records on its opening at New York's Capitol Theatre and went on to become one of Warner Brothers's five biggest box-office attractions as of that time.

When George Wein, the indefatigable impresario of the Newport Jazz Festival, announced in 1965 that Sinatra would appear on the final evening of the four-day fete, there was an outcry of criticism from jazz purists. Sinatra, they argued, was not in the same groove as Ella Fitzgerald, Sarah Vaughan, or Carmen McRae. And they were right, as Frank himself would be the first to admit: he was not a jazz singer. But much of his singing was melodically and rhythmically jazz-inflected, and from the beginning of his recordings on Reprise, the label he had founded, he had used jazz arrangers such as Johnny Mandel, Neal Hefti, and Quincy Jones. With Count Basie, he had done two albums, *Sinatra-Basie* in 1962 and *It Might As Well Be Swing* in 1964, and he was to be accompanied at the festival by the Count Basie Band.

Regardless of the purists, Frank's name worked its magic. I attended the festival, as I had over the years since its inception in 1955, and the chatter from the time I arrived at Newport's Viking Hotel until the final concert on Sunday evening, July 4, was about Sinatra—some of it pro, some of it con, but all of it "Sinatra." As *Variety* observed in its review, it was "Sinatra's festival." At previous fetes the last evening was always the most poorly attended. But in 1965 it was the first to sell out and the best-attended, filling the cash register with $38,952 over and above the $40,000 fee paid to Sinatra. Moreover the festival's attendance, which had been slipping for several years, climbed to a figure 6,000 over the previous year.

Newport is an island of stately millionaire mansions (some converted to other uses) to which most people travel from the Rhode Island mainland by slow ferry. But during the day of Sinatra's concert, word spread that he was flying into the area. Somehow this caught the imagination of young jazz fans, accustomed to the more mundane arrival of other artists. All through the day, fans chattered about Frank's arrival time. *Would he fly in for an afternoon rehearsal?* At concerts and workshops, heads were constantly turned upward and the skies were watched. But the afternoon passed without Sinatra. He'd been on tour and the program was worked out in advance.

At dusk, the concert field began to crowd with anxious members of the audience. Any strange noise in the air brought a tilt of heads toward the sky. The Basie band was assembling onstage when the distant whirring of helicopter blades suddenly became audible. Concertgoers arose en masse from their chairs to watch the appearance of the chopper. Eyes were rivetted on its descent in a field near the concert area. Sinatra's emergence from the helicopter could not be seen. But his appearance onstage after the Basie band had completed the playing, had the mythic quality of the arrival of a being from outer space.

He did a full program of eighteen songs, opening with "Get Me to the Church on Time," from *My Fair Lady* and closing with a rousing version of "My Kind of Town," his exit number of that period (succeeded later by "My Way" and most recently, by "New York, New York"). After a standing ovation, he left by helicopter, the sound of the chopper in its initial ascent contributing a dissonant counterpoint to the Basie band's concluding number, "One O'Clock Jump."

In *Variety*'s view he contributed "glamour, showmanship and his own kind of casual hipness" to the event. Although festivals of previous years had had their great moments, it was undeniable that no artist had possessed the four-day round of concerts as had Sinatra in 1965.

From Newport Frank went to the West Side Tennis Club in Forest Hills, New York, where he gave a well-received concert, again with the Basie band. Through the 1970s when he was battling the rip current of the pop mainstream, he found kindred spirits in the world of jazz and, for a brief time, even in the country-folk cosmos of John Denver. With Basie, Sinatra concertized in London in 1970. Basie was with him again in 1974 and 1975; at Caesars Palace where they were joined by Ella Fitzgerald in 1974; and both in London and New York, being joined by Sarah Vaughan in London in 1975 and by Ella again in New York. Woody Herman provided the backing for a

September 1974 date at Harrah's in Lake Tahoe and for a concert stand at Madison Square Garden thereafter. These collaborations produced two high points in Sinatra's concertizing in the '70s.

One was the concert Sinatra gave at Madison Square Garden in October 1974 in the course of a nine-city tour with the Woody Herman Band. It was billed as "The Main Event," and Frank performed on a raised platform, disguised as a boxing ring, with the audience of 21,000 spread around on all sides as at a boxing match. He entered the "ring," wearing the kind of robe that prizefighters do, with sports announcer Howard Cosell acting as the emcee, and displayed no difficulty in meeting the challenge of working on the unconventional stage.

The New York Times heralded the concert in its Sunday Arts and Leisure section with a front-page, 8-column banner headline, "That Old Sinatra Magic Is a Mix of Musicianship and Sex Appeal," and with two long articles that added up to at least a full page of copy. Under the heading "Appoggiatura, Tempo Rubato, Portamento —He Uses 'Em All," London-based musicologist Henry Pleasants assessed Sinatra's historical role in the development of microphone-singing technique, dubbed him the Master of Pop Bel Canto, and suggested that he used all the devices of ornamentation and embellishment employed by classical singers, regardless of whether he or his audience knew what "appoggiatura" was. Middle-aged Martha Weinman Lear, reviewing his career from the swooning era of which she was a part, admitted that, despite reservations about his "seamy, tawdry" personal development, he made her feel 13 again and "what's left of the voice still gets to me like no other voice."

Reviewers of "The Main Event" found him in top form, still "the consummate showman," and a singer who enraptured the preponderantly middle-aged crowd. To John Rockwell of *The New York Times*, the show was "superb," the audience "rapturous," and Sinatra emerged still "the master of his generation" as the avatar of the pop-jazz sensibility. Harking back to the days of bobby sox hysteria, somebody at ringside threw a handkerchief, a towel, or a piece of female underclothing onstage. Never at a loss for words, Sinatra reacted quickly: "I don't do laundry anymore."

The Saturday evening performance was a rehearsal for the live ABC-TV presentation that followed on Sunday night and that was sent by satellite through the Western Hemisphere (from Canada to South America) to an expected audience of 490-million people.

"I have never felt so much love in one room in my

whole life," he told his live audience. But the in-person impact, despite expert pacing and skillful camera technique, somehow was not reflected on the tube. "Frank flops in ratings," was the statistical assessment: he failed by three points to make the 30 percent share of an audience, regarded as a mark of a show's success, and "The Main Event" did not register as one of the week's most popular programs. It was not the first time, or the last, that a televised appearance failed to project the magic of his in-person charisma.

The other high point was "The Concert," as it was billed, at the Uris Theatre, starting on September 8 and lasting two weeks in 1975. It occurred during the musicians' strike, which closed every Broadway musical. Apparently, Sinatra's attorney, Mickey Rudin, and producer Jerry Weintraub were so persuasive that the head of local 802 granted a dispensation, and the show went on. Jazz critic John S. Wilson of *The New York Times* found Sinatra "in strong voice and good spirits" and reported: "He was easiest and at his best when he joined Ella Fitzgerald for a finale in which they bounced lines off each other, she singing a gentle obbligato to his 'They Can't Take That Away from Me,' he belting out a lusty 'At Long Last Love,' and both of them swinging through 'The Lady is a Tramp.'"

Observing that Sinatra was 58, Ella 57, and Count Basie 71, Wilson was impressed by Frank's command of the audience. "If they had once been wide-eyed, skinny kids," he wrote, "hanging around the stage door of the Paramount Theatre hoping to catch a glimpse of Mr. Sinatra, they were now well-fed and well-groomed but scarcely less titillated by his presence. They cheered his songs, laughed at his jokes, and seemed thoroughly to enjoy themselves being in the palm of his hand."

A certain zest was added to the proceedings by the presence, on at least one evening, of Jacqueline Onassis, with whom Frank first dined at the 21 Club and later attended a Pat Henry show at the Rainbow Grill. The electricity generated by the two was fodder for many column items and food for thought back in Palm Springs where Barbara Marx awaited his return. In actuality Jackie's interest in Frank was of a purely business character: She was working for a New York publisher and was apparently interested in Frank's autobiography. Be that as it may, the show at the Uris was a howling success. In fact, it was pegged as "Broadway's first million-dollar gate," by producer Jerry Weintraub, who expressed the opinion that it would never happen again. With top seats selling at $40, the gross was eventually tallied at $1,088,000. Sinatra's crack during one of his mid-show monologues was: Back

when, the price of seats at the Paramount was not $40 but 40¢, and people were saying "40¢ for what?"

Nineteen seventy-four was a most significant year in Sinatra's career as a showman or, to use the term that he prefers, "saloon singer." It marked his return to Las Vegas and a busy schedule of live performances after a hiatus of more than three years.

He had come to Caesars Palace in September 1968 after performing at the Sands for more than a dozen years. He had terminated his association with the Sands quite suddenly one explosive night in 1967 when he had been refused the gambling credit he demanded and a high-decibel argument with beefy casino boss Carl Cohen had led to an altercation in which Sinatra lost two front teeth. Caesars Palace was delighted to add the disgruntled entertainer to its distinguished roster of stars. But in the late hours of September 7, 1970, only two years later, Frank had once again become involved in a heated argument with a casino boss, who had inexplicably pulled a gun on him. Sinatra had stormed out of Caesars, canceling the rest of the engagement and vowing never to return to Nevada. The announcement of his "retirement" came about six months later in March of 1971, followed by the emotional farewell concert in June at the Los Angeles Music Center. Despite his retirement Sinatra managed sagaciously to keep himself on the performing scene—not in professional engagements but by singing at political, private, and charity happenings.

Shortly after his angry departure from Caesars Palace, he performed at San Francisco's Hilton at a high-level "Californians for Ronald Reagan" fund-raiser. He sang again for Reagan at his Inaugural Gala as governor in Sacramento in January 1971. In the latter part of January, he participated in a Beverly Hills fund-raiser for Democratic Senator John Tunney, who later in the year initiated the Senate tribute to Frank on his retirement. In 1972 he sang at a celebrity night salute to Spiro Agnew, held at the Americana in New York City. Along with Jerry Vale, Vic Damone, Trini Lopez, and others, he performed at an Italian-American Civil Rights League benefit, held at the Felt Forum in New York City and emceed by Ed McMahon of "The Tonight Show."

Between times, he sang at a "Night of Nights" charity at the Royal Festival Hall in London, at a "Shower of Stars" benefit in Memphis for St. Jude's Research Hospital, and, of course, at the celebrated 1973 White House reception for the Italian prime minister.

"The town that Sinatra built," in James Bacon's words, "was hardly happy over his retirement, for no one grabbed an audience the way he does." How much he was missed is suggested by the ardent expressions of "Welcome Back" that emanated in 1974 not only from Strip bonifaces but from the Vegas newspapers and the offices of the sheriff and district attorney, both of whom had been quite antagonistic at the time of Sinatra's fracas at the Palace. "Celebs Jam Vegas for Sinatra Opening," the *Los Angeles Times* headlined his comeback in January 1974.

Having demonstrated, after his three-year layoff, that he was still "a magical performer with undiminished powers," he soon embarked on a series of ambitious appearances and tours that brought his in-person showmanship before audiences not only in this country, but around the world. Taking a leaf from the bookings of superstar rock groups, he performed in huge arenas, eventually establishing a world record for playing before the largest audience in January 1980 in Brazil.

Embarking on a 13-day tour in April 1974 that took him through nine cities, he played giant arenas like the 16,715-seat Nassau Coliseum in New York, the 17,165-seat Omni in Atlanta, the 20,000-plus-seat Capitol Center in Washington, D.C., and the 20,000-seat Chicago Stadium. Between April 8 and April 27 almost 200,000 people paid over $3 million to hear him. So great was the demand for tickets not only among middle-aged Americans but among young people that *Rolling Stone* devoted an article to charges made by other publications that politicos and Sinatra friends received preferential treatment at the box office.

"I never swooned," said a woman who brought her 11-year-old daughter by bus and train to hear him. "But I used to bring my lunch to the Paramount and stay all day. It cost only 28¢." And now she was unable to resist the tug of those memories and was full of hope that Sinatra would stir up once again the ashes of the fires that burned in the '40s.

Then there were those like a *Rolling Stone* reviewer who had grown up with the songs and lyrics of Bob Dylan but who found himself at one with the excited middle-aged folk filling the Chicago Stadium. "It is almost as if the haunting, beautiful voice," wrote Paul Hendrickson, "has a life of its own. As if it doesn't depend on earthly concerns like time or change.... He never sings a song quite the same way. And for that, he truly can be called the Chairman of the Board...." Henrickson was surprised, nay, startled that the voice he had set out to write about "with almost no emotional involvement has suddenly got inside my soul."

What was, perhaps, even more revelatory in indicating Sinatra's amazingly long-lived vogue was Hendrickson's reaction to the final song, "The House I Live In." He called it "an old jingoistic ballad, corn higher than an elephant's eye." Obviously Hendrickson and other reviewers of his generation were too young to know that when Sinatra used the song as the title and subject of an award-winning short in 1945, it was regarded by many as a liberal or left-wing plea for brotherhood and tolerance.

In September 1974, the main showroom of Caesars Palace presented not one but three Sinatras. Frank had his daughter Nancy Jr. and his son, Frank Jr., with him in a rare onstage family reunion. Midway in his stint, as was his wont, he joked with the audience: "A funny thing happened to me on the way to Australia," he said. "I got off the plane. I used to blow whole countries. Now, I blow continents."

The first time the family had worked together was actually at Harrah's in Lake Tahoe during the preceding week. Then, mid-way in his monologue, Frank had referred to the Australian incident in somewhat different terms: "I want to make a public apology," he said. "I would like to apologize to the Madonnas of the evening for comparing some women reporters to them."

It was a renewal of his July feud with the press in Australia when he blasted women reporters as *hookers* and men reporters as *parasites and bums* who had never done an honest day's work in their lives. As in other confrontations there were major disagreements as to what occasioned Frank's outburst. Scheduled to give two concerts in Melbourne and three in Sydney, he canceled after the first night in Melbourne and took off in his private jet for Sydney. Here he faced a tense and troubling situation. The demand for an apology made by the Professional Musicians Union and the Theatrical and Amusement Employee Associates—a demand that had ended in a stalemate and caused the cancellation in Melbourne—was now supported by the Hotel Employees' Union and the Transport Workers' Union. The Hotel Employees' Union refused to service Sinatra's party in any Aussie hotel, while the Transport Workers' Union refused to refuel his plane, thereby making it impossible for him to leave the continent.

The unions were enraged not only by Sinatra's onstage reflections on the country's working press but by the alleged manhandling of newsmen before, and a TV crew after, the sellout show to which 8,000 paid as much as $26 a seat. According to *Life* editor Thomas Thompson the trouble had started almost immediately after Frank's arrival in Melbourne when a press representative of the organization sponsoring the Australian concerts informed

him that the media were waiting for him and that he *had* to hold a press conference.

"The one thing I know about Frank," Thompson later wrote, "is that nobody tells *him* what he is going to do, and I suspect Frank told this woman what *she* could do." Thereafter, while he was trying to relax and hoping to see a bit of the country, his $220-a-day suite was besieged by the press. In the evening when he was leaving the hotel for the concert hall, he had to "walk through" a wall of reporters. Thompson explained that what the press referred to as bodyguards were actually musicians who were traveling with him.

The impasse and confrontation in Sydney were not resolved until Sinatra's attorney met with Australia's top labor official. A three-hour meeting produced a joint com-

promise statement. Without making a general apology, Sinatra stated that he did not intend "any general reflection upon the moral character" of the Australian media while they in turn expressed "regrets for any physical inconvenience" they might have caused him. And so the front-page headlines in Australia and around the world disappeared, and Sinatra was able to depart, having given but one concert at Festival Hall in Melbourne and one at the Harden Pavilion in Sydney.

That the incident rankled and was not quickly forgotten by Sinatra became apparent at a November 1975 Friars Roast when he said to Aussie singer Helen Reddy, after leading the crowd in singing "Happy Birthday" to her: "You showed great class when you left Australia. Schmucks! At least they let you out of there."

At Heathrow Airport, July 18, 1974.

Despite constant references to the inevitable aging of his vocal instrument, Sinatra pursued a heavy and enthusiastically received series of Caesars Palace appearances and concert tours through Europe and the United States all through the '70s and into the '80s. In 1975 he repeated his previous year's spring tour of American cities, but added Montreal and Toronto to the schedule. Toronto was again the scene of a confrontation with the press. Interrupting his May 10 appearance at the Maple Leaf Gardens, he held up a copy of the *Toronto Star* and told the audience that he had two uses for newspapers: "to cover the bottom of my parrot's cage and train my dog on." With the paper claiming that a Sinatra bodyguard had punched a freelance photographer, Sinatra offered $1 million if the photographer could prove that he was responsible.

Returning from his final concert of the American tour on May 14, 1975, Sinatra embarked on his first European tour since 1962 just five days later. The first stop was at the Sporting Club in Monte Carlo, which brought a renewal of his friendship with Princess Grace (Kelly) Rainier, with whom he had appeared in *High Society* almost 20 years earlier. The tour included programs in Paris, Vienna, Munich, Frankfurt, London, and Brussels, terminating on June 2 in Amsterdam. It was marked by travail, as in Germany, and triumphant moments, as in Great Britain. In Munich (Olympia Halle) and in Frankfurt (Festhalle), Frank performed to half-empty houses. But what was even more aggravating was the violent antagonism of the German press, which reached its peak about the time that he headed for a concert in Berlin. About one-fifth of the seats (2,000 out of 10,000) had been sold at the Deutschland Halle, partly, perhaps, because the stories in the

German papers were not only hostile but so provocative that Frank's associates felt he might be physically assaulted if not kidnapped. The Berlin concert was canceled, and Sinatra, troubled by the fiasco of his German dates, returned $85,835 to the promoters to help offset their losses.

From Berlin Sinatra went to London, where the demand for tickets at his Royal Albert Hall concert was so great that scalpers were reportedly getting as much as $575 for good seats. "I don't understand the German press," Sinatra told British interviewers. "They call me a super-gangster! Germans are the gangsters. I could have mentioned Dachau."

The Albert Hall triumph of May was duplicated, actually surpassed, in November when Sinatra, abetted by Sarah Vaughan and the Count Basie Band, gave ten concerts at the Palladium. The advance sale was so great that the British correspondent to *Daily Variety* described Frank as "the biggest draw this town has seen in a hardtop situation."

Not too long after Sinatra returned home from the Albert Hall concert, newspapers carried headlines about the gangland slaying of Chicago crimelord Sam Giancana, the man whose stay at Sinatra's Cal-Neva Lodge had led to the cancellation of his Nevada gaming license and whose friendship with Judith Exner was the subject of a congressional investigation when it became known that she had been JFK's mistress during the same period.

Sinatra was rumored to have introduced her to both JFK and Giancana. Ms. Exner later wrote a book about her experiences and Sinatra reportedly said: "Hell hath no fury like a hooker with a literary agent."

With Grace Kelly in HIGH SOCIETY just before she became Her Serene Highness of Monaco, 1956.

One of the most curious collaborations in Sinatra's concertizing came in 1975 when he did a back-to-back show at Harrah's in Lake Tahoe with John Denver. It would be difficult to conceive of two men so different in style, point of view, and age. The only thing that Sinatra and young Denver had in common was Jerry Weintraub, the brilliant agent-producer who was able to entice them into working together. It turned out to be a spectacularly successful booking, with Denver performing at the 8:00 P.M. dinner show and Sinatra appearing at midnight. If Harrah's is to be believed, its switchboard was swamped with an absolutely fantastic number of phone calls, running into the thousands, the moment the pairing was announced. One year later the two did not work in tandem but together. After doing 30-minute segments each, they joined forces in a 30-minute segment, sitting next to each other on stools.

If you can visualize it—the youngish country boy in metal-rimmed glasses, with the wide, smiling mouth, and the world-weary 60-year-old swinger—together in a kind of warm father-and-son relationship, generated a magical chemistry. The medley they performed consisted mostly of Sinatra evergreens—"Learnin' the Blues," "Witchcraft," "Nancy," "All the Way"—but included Denver favorites like "My Sweet Lady," "Leaving on a Jet Plane," and "A Sad Song." It was a sufficiently startling collaboration to bring the popular music critic of the *Los Angeles Times* to Lake Tahoe. Robert Hilburn termed the show a "natural" and applauded their being "linked by their respect/love of music and their obvious desire to entertain/touch others."

By 1977, disco music with the heavy, thumping, four-to-the-bar, bass-drum beat, was beginning to assume the proportions of a craze, peaking the following year with the popularity of the *Saturday Night Fever* film. It had first begun making the ears of listeners stand up with Gloria Gaynor's record of "I Will Survive" and the feet of dancers move with Van McCoy's Number One hit of 1975, "The Hustle," which became the biggest dance disc of the '70s and the basis of disco dancing. Always ready for adventure Sinatra had a brief flirtation with the sound in 1977 when he experimented briefly with a disco arrangement of the Cole Porter perennial "Night and Day," performing it in April in California and at the Forest Hills Tennis Stadium in July 1977.

The Forest Hills concert apparently marked the last appearance of pianist-conductor Bill Miller with Sinatra, for in October 1977 Vincent Falcone, Jr., performed those twin chores for Frank at Harrah's in Lake Tahoe. When Bill Miller joined the Sinatra musical family in November 1951, he came out of a big band background that included

playing and recording with the Charlie Barnet, Jimmy Dorsey, and the lesser-known Joe Haymes bands, but also went back to the emergence of Benny Goodman as the King of Swing in 1936, a year in which he composed and arranged "Riffin' at the Ritz" for the Goodman orchestra. Miller also worked with Red Norvo's small combo in the 1930s and 1940s, a combo that traveled with Sinatra to Australia in 1959.

Miller's tenure with Sinatra began about a year before Frank started recording for Capitol. His first stint as Frank's accompanist was on the weekly "Frank Sinatra Show" on CBS-TV. A radio show that premiered in November 1953 and remained on the air into 1955, "To Be Perfectly Frank" found Miller not only serving as Frank's accompanist but also occasionally soloing.

Miller did not take up the baton for Sinatra until the late sixties, his first stint as conductor occurring in May 1969 when he led the Nat Brandwynne Orchestra at Caesars Palace. Thereafter he functioned as Frank's pianist-conductor, touring with him, rehearsing with him, and wielding the baton, except on occasions when Sinatra turned to Don Costa or Gordon Jenkins. In the 1974-1975 period he conducted the orchestras of Count Basie, Woody Herman and Brian Farnon at various bookings. He led the band for Sinatra's "Main Event" concert at Madison Square Garden and his two-week stand at the Uris Theatre, among other notable engagements. In 1975 when Frank was on tour in Europe and Don Costa became ill, Miller took on the conducting assignment after the concert at Frankfurt, Germany.

Despite Sinatra's reputation for being moody, demanding, capricious, and intemperate, there is not another entertainer in pop music who has maintained continuing relationships for as long as he has with arranger-conductors Don Costa, Gordon Jenkins, Nelson Riddle, Billy May, and Quincy Jones; songwriters Jimmy Van Heusen and Sammy Cahn; inspired the late producer Sonny Burke; and sidemen such as drummer Irv Cottler, guitarist Al Viola, among other musicians.

Over a period of years he has worked with a small group whom he calls the Fearsome Fivesome. "I never leave home without them," he has said. In addition to Cottler and Viola, the Fivesome has in recent years included Charlie Turner (trumpet), Gene Cherico (bass), and Vinne Falcone (pianist-conductor).

When Vincent Falcone, Jr., assumed the post of pianist-conductor upon Miller's retirement in 1977, "Sun Tan Charlie," as Frank loved to call him because of his pallor, had completed just about a quarter-of-a-century of work with Sinatra.

Nineteen seventy-nine was the year of an experience as unique as any singer could envision or enjoy. On the night of September 27 Sinatra sang in the shadow of one of the Seven Wonders of the World—the Sphinx and the Pyramids just outside Cairo. A much less prestigious booking was his appearance in the spring of 1979 in Atlantic City. But his still undiminished power to draw a crowd was indicated when he was chosen to initiate the entertainment program of Resorts International, the first casinotel to open its doors on the refurbished Atlantic City scene. No less than a full-page advertisement in the Sunday *New York Times* heralded his reappearance at the gaming hotel in the spring of 1980.

On the West Coast the Universal Amphitheatre in Universal City was the scene of blockbuster concerts in 1978, 1979, and 1980. These invariably drew not only adulatory audiences but also equally admiring critics. The climax came in 1980 when the rock publication *Rolling Stone* headed a probing review, "The Majestic Artistry of Frank Sinatra." Considering how little regard Frank has for the music to which the publication is dedicated, it was a rare testimonial, suggesting the remarkable span of his appeal. Not even the younger, so-called rock generation was immune to Sinatra's charisma, vocal artistry, and showmanship.

About his first two songs, Harold Arlen's "I've Got the World on a String" and Cy Coleman's "The Best Is Yet to Come," Mikal Gilmore wrote, "Sinatra not only made good on his reputation as America's preeminent romantic vocalist, but also served notice that he was making one final high-reaching bid for artistic apotheosis." The critic saw it as an extension of the objective of his latest album, *Trilogy*: "to make a monument of one man's renaissance."

Approving *Trilogy* as an album of better singing than Sinatra had done on record in fifteen years, Gilmore felt Sinatra came closer to his goal onstage than on record because he sang better. "It was as if the presence of an audience," he concluded, "impelled him to renewed levels of ingenuity and intensity." Gilmore ended his words of applause: "When Sinatra left the stage, we realized we might never witness artistry that big and that provocative again."

Earlier in 1980 Sinatra traveled to Brazil, where he sang in the world's largest soccer stadium, located in Rio de Janeiro. The concert was cancelable if it rained, mainly because of possible damage to the musical instruments. But after raining a good part of the evening, the downpour stopped promptly at 9:00 P.M., when the concert was slated to begin at Marcãna Stadium. If the *Guinness Book of World Records* is to be believed, Sinatra sang that

evening (January 26, 1980) to an estimated 175,000 people, establishing a record as the solo performer who warbled for the largest live audience in history.

James Bacon, who accompanied Sinatra on his visit to Brazil, later wrote in the *Herald-Examiner* of the incredible interaction between Frank and the audience: "It was incredible. Here were 200,000 people whose language is Portuguese and who sang *Come Fly With Me* with Sinatra. He just turned the concert into an intimate experience." Including four nights at the Rio Palace Hotel, the promoters grossed $1,800,000 and Sinatra came away with $850,000.

During the summer of 1980 when he performed at the Universal Amphitheatre near Los Angeles with Sergio Mendez, reviewers noted that he had made his debut as a conductor. The composition for which he waved his arms, instead of vibrating his tonsils, was pianist-conductor Vincent Falcone's "Bossa Nova in C." In actuality Sinatra's debut as a conductor—unknown, perhaps, to the current generation of reviewers—occurred about 35 years earlier. In 1945, at the height of the Sinatra frenzy, he persuaded an uneasy Manie Sachs, then head of Columbia Records's A & R department, to let him conduct an album of Alec Wilder concert (not pop) compositions. Sinatra was not aware when he arrived for the first session on December 5, 1945, that a professional conductor was standing by in case Frank could not make good on his desire to conduct. The pro never got an opportunity to wave his baton. By the time the session was over, all the symphony cats with their goatees and Stradivarius violins were applauding Sinatra.

The album *Frank Sinatra Conducts Alec Wilder* is out-of-print. But through the years various arranger-conductors have said that despite his lack of formal training, Sinatra had an amazing, intuitive grasp of the art of conducting and could have been a very successful conductor. In 1982, when he urged a singer whom he greatly admires, Sylvia Syms, to make a new album and she asked who would conduct it, his reply was, "Me."

Frank Sinatra Conducts Alec Wilder was not his only foray into the conducting sphere. At the peak of his Capitol years, the West Coast company released *Frank Sinatra Conducts Tone Poems of Color*. This was also an album of concert pieces, impressionist pieces commissioned by Frank and composed mostly by arrangers with whom he had worked to poems on color by Norman Sickel. Again, not too long after he launched his own record label, Reprise issued *Frank Sinatra Conducts Music from Pictures and Plays,* an album with no vocals.

The conducting gambit at the Universal Theatre emphasizes a development that has occurred recently in Sinatra's public appearances. As the normal aging of his vocal cords has begun to create problems for him as a singer, he had become more theatrical at concerts, relying on his craft as a showman to make up for inevitable shortcomings as a singer. Robert Palmer of *The New York Times* and other critics have noted that he has begun thinking of himself as "more of an entertainer than a musician." In fact, Palmer was overwhelmed by Sinatra's performance at Carnegie Hall in 1980 because "everything he sang sparkled" and "he gave a show that was one extended high point."

But age is slowly taking its toll. Frank has begun using a music stand with the lyrics of songs to serve as a prompter, and he is pacing his shows with solos by instrumentalists in his backup band, during which he sits among the musicians.

Nineteen eighty-one brought a significant change in Sinatra's performing style. For years the band that backed him in live appearances consisted of a large complement of strings, violins, violas, and cellos in addition to brass, rhythm, and woodwind-sax sections. Now, in 1981, just before an appearance at Caesars Palace in Lake Tahoe, his P.R. firm released a statement informing the press and his audiences that he was adopting "an Up-beat Band Sound" in future showroom and concert bookings. What that meant was that he was dropping the string section and reducing the instrumentation to a dance band, the type of band he had worked with in his early days with Harry James and Tommy Dorsey — a band made up of a sax section, brass section of trumpets and trombones, and a rhythm section (piano, bass, guitar, and drums) — except that the brass was augmented with two French horns and there was a harpist for special effects. Such a band would have more drive, bounce, and kick that a string-filled orchestra.

Sinatra's musical director, pianist, and conductor, Vincent Falcone, Jr., felt that the new orchestrations they would use "really expose the vocals even more without a giant string section." They would also give added punch and verve to the vocals.

In 1981 Sinatra continued his concertizing around the world, certifying the sway of his artistry and showmanship over people as distant from Hollywood as South Africa. From August 5 he sang for four nights at the Sheraton in Buenos Aires where one thousand seats sold at $1,000 a seat. The fee fixed for the four concerts, negotiated when the Argentine promoter flew up to Lake Tahoe where Sinatra was then appearing, was $1.65

million, plus $500,000 in taxes payable to Argentina. The promoter expected to gross $2.5 million. If the story is to be accepted, one avid female fan reportedly bought $200,000 worth of tickets. Although an unfriendly press story in a São Paulo daily branded Frank "obsolete," it did report that $25 ringside seats were being scalped for $2,500 a seat. Pretty good for an "obsolete" singer who was able to command $400,000 for an evening's performance!

When it was announced that he would perform at the Sun City Hotel in the South African Republic of Bophuthatswana from July 24 to August 2 (preceding the South American engagement), 20,000 tickets were reportedly sold on the first day, $42,000 crossed booking-office counters in the first eight minutes, and the entrepreneur had $1,150,000 in the till at the end of the first week. People came to hear him by private jet, buses, helicopters, and automobiles. At the conclusion of standing-ovation concerts, the President of the Republic conferred the high Order of the Leopard on him and gave him a chair made just for a chief or, as it was suggested, for the Chairman of the Board.

Although the date was an outstanding success financially and in terms of audience reaction, it was not without its tensions. The problem was that Bophuthatswana was one of three homelands for blacks that white minority-ruled South Africa had set up as part of its apartheid or segregationist policy. Black entertainer Ben Vereen canceled a scheduled date at Sun City because of pressure from black nationalists. The Reverend Jesse Jackson, Chicago black activist, blasted Sinatra for agreeing to appear. Sinatra indicated that he had had two of his representatives investigate the seating policy, that they had found that Afrikaners sat side by side with blacks, and that he had stipulated there would be no segregated seating.

"I play to all people," he told reporters after a rehearsal for the first of nine performances, "any color, any creed, drunk or sober."

Commenting on the concerts, James Bacon observed: "He's putting this country on the map just like he did Las Vegas thirty years ago." Bacon noted that over 20,000 people drove from Johannesburg to Pretoria's Sun City in order to hear Frank and that the slot machine alleys of the casino looked like busy supermarkets, with long lines waiting for their turn at the slots.

A number of girls came to the Sun City concerts, wearing T-shirts with "My Way" emblazoned on them. They set up a cry for the song, forcing Sinatra to include it on his program. Having sung it steadily in concerts from

1970 to 1980, generally as his final song, he confessed that he had tired of it. There may be no connection, but in 1978 he added two new numbers to his live performances. One was the lovely patriotic song "America the Beautiful," which closed some of his programs during 1978–1979. The other was "New York, New York," which remained an audience-rouser and closing song into 1982.

Sinatra's concern with new, suitable repertoire involved him in the 1980s, as in previous years, in an unabating search. Standards of the 1930s and 1940s — songs by Cole Porter, Harold Arlen, Johnny Mercer, the Gershwins and others — constituted the bulk of his programs, with Porter's "I've Got You Under My Skin," Matt Dennis's "Angel Eyes," Rube Bloom's "Don't Worry 'Bout Me," and Rodgers and Hart's swinging "The Lady Is a Tramp" scoring as his most oft-repeated songs. Through the '60s and '70s, despite the adverse tenor of pop music, Sinatra found songs by new and young writers that fitted in with his concept of tasteful lyrics and appealing melodies, a partial list of which would include the following:

"Bad, Bad Leroy Brown" *(Jim Croce)*
"By the Time I Get to Phoenix" *(Jim Webb)*
"Close to You" *(Burt Bacharach and Hal David)*
"Cycles" *(Gayle Caldwell)*
"Didn't We" *(Jim Webb)*
"Going Out of My Head" *(Teddy Randazzo and Bobby Weinstein)*
"The Hungry Years" *(Neil Sedaka)*
"If" *(David Gates)*
"I Sing the Songs" *(Bruce Johnston)*
"Like a Sad Song" *(John Denver)*
"Mrs. Robinson" *(Paul Simon)*
"See the Show Again" *(Barry Manilow)*
"Star Gazer" *(Neil Diamond)*
"Send in the Clowns" *(Stephen Sondheim)*
"Something" *(George Harrison)*
"Yesterday" *(John Lennon and Paul McCartney)*
"You Are the Sunshine of My Life" *(Stevie Wonder)*

Jimmy Webb's "Didn't We" competed with the most-performed standards in the number of times Frank performed it through the '70s.

Late in 1981 two new songs made their appearance in Sinatra's concert programs. One was Stephen Sondheim's "Good Thing Going," which he plucked from the score of a show that folded overnight, the musical version of Kaufman and Hart's *Merrily We Roll Along*. The other was a song that started as a Pan Am commercial jingle. "Say Hello," as it was titled, caught Frank's ear. He got in touch with the writers and persuaded them to enlarge the jingle, which they did with the assistance of lyricist Sammy Cahn, transforming it into the song "Just Say Hello."

Sinatra's appearance at Carnegie Hall in September 1981 brought a panegyric from *The New York Times's* reviewer, starting with a headline that read "Sinatra Brings Classy Act to Carnegie." John Rockwell found Frank's voice, despite other critical reactions, "more secure and wider in range both for dynamics and pitch" than in recent years. He added: "He can phrase a conversational song or standard pop ballad like nobody in the business. Those tasty hesitations, those dramatic asides that lapse into melodrama, those gruffly percussive attacks — they add up to a consummate stylist. . . ." And he concluded: "If he is the best in the business, he is also an artist. . . . Mr. Sinatra's feisty personality may not be to all tastes. But he is the master of his field, and his field is the American song."

Rockwell's panegyric echoed an earlier encomium that appeared in New York City's *Village Voice* when Sinatra filled the 6,000 seats of Radio City Music Hall for ten consecutive nights in 1978. Jazz critic Gary Giddins commented: "Sinatra was brilliant. That is the only word that will describe the effect with which he took over the stage at the Music Hall. . . . In Sinatra's art, the singer and the actor are inseparable. . . . His authority comes from a personal elegance and gracefulness kept at a pitch so fine that there is something terrible in his charm — the possibility of unwarranted explosion. . . . This sense of theater has never been so sharply honed as now. . . ."

It may have been just a coincidence. But it was in 1978 that the Songwriters Hall of Fame conferred the title of Entertainer of the Century upon him, a title also proffered to him in 1981 by the *Lampoon* of Harvard University. In a backward glance at the level of showmanship and artistry he has maintained for so long a period — not to mention the breadth of his appeal and the scope of his impact on popular song — is there any entertainer that more richly deserves this accolade?

In February 1982 Sinatra appeared at Caesars Palace together with his daughter Nancy. He was using a music stand to refer to printed lyrics, something he has been doing recently. (He used a stand in his 1980 appearance at

Carnegie Hall, rather than forget a lyric—he told the audience—and louse up a song. Opening night at Caesars, during a duet with Nancy on "Something Stupid," he did louse up the lyric, despite the stand. The audience was sympathetic to the way he shrugged it off. The following day Pete Mikla of the *Las Vegas Review-Journal*, an avid Sinatra buff, secured a copy of the lyrics and typed them on a machine with large oversize letters used for newspaper headlines. He managed to get them to Sinatra before that evening's performance. But that night, despite the very legible lyrics on the music stand before him, Sinatra again loused up the words of the song. The showman had stumbled on an audience-grabber and he was not about to give it up.

4. "Now Is The Hour": Sinatra On TV

Of all the media in which Sinatra has performed, television has presented the greatest challenge, and despite his many forays and the savvy of his producers, the time on the tube has not always been a shining hour. Considering how potent a performer he is in personal appearances, it is a "puzzlement" why the charisma and appeal of the man do not carry over.

Nevertheless, it was a TV special that became the vehicle in 1973 to bring Frank out of a brief hiatus of self-exile and retirement. With Gene Kelly as his sole guest, it was both a sentimental and nostalgic occasion. Taped on a Paramount soundstage that had been reconstructed at a cost of $125,000, witnessed by a well-dressed, high-level crowd of Hollywood celebrities, and festooned with enormous advance media hoopla, *Magnavox Presents Frank Sinatra* or *Ol' Blue Eyes Is Back* prompted columnist Joyce Haber to exclaim: "It was as though a B-52 hit the long-deserted soundstage, as though the Golden Age of Hollywood was reborn!"

The show had imaginative production angles. It opened in pitch blackness, with a pin spot picking Sinatra's face out of the darkness, harking back to his retirement concert in 1971 when he dramatically disappeared from the stage with a pin-spot blackout. To vivify his return to show business, he delivered his first song walking on a treadmill and greeting people seated on two revolving turntables. When he sang "Send in the Clowns," he approached a section of the bleachers filled with such comics as Lucille Ball, Milton Berle, Dick Van Dyke, and Jack Benny, and thus gave an added dimension to the lines "Where are the clowns, send in the clowns . . . don't bother, they're here."

An adroit use of cameras was made by director Marty Pasetta so that Sinatra and his audience were seen from many different angles, from overhead cranes and in hand-held close-ups, from a camera sailing birdlike down from the eaves, and through a lens on a cameraman's shoulder. And then there were the vibrant vocals by Sinatra on saloon songs like "Here's That Rainy Day" and "Violets for Your Furs," and new songs like "Let Me Try Again" and the opening and closing "You Will Be My Music." A standing ovation followed the song and dance by Frank and Gene Kelly on "We Can't Do That Anymore" in which they proceeded to repeat the dances they had done together in musicals of the 1940s.

"The show was so great," Joyce Haber wrote, "that observers [watching it at home] broke out in spontaneous applause. It was Emmy Time!"

But no Emmy was forthcoming. An excellent show, well conceived, well produced, and well performed, it somehow lacked the magic that made the difference between an entertainment and a spellbinder. In fact, only one show of the many in which Sinatra starred yielded an Emmy for his crowded trophy room.

That was *Frank Sinatra—A Man and His Music*, televised November 24, 1965, on CBS-TV and the first of an annual series of specials sponsored by Budweiser beer. The telecast came just eight days after CBS presented a news special titled *Sinatra: An American Original*, a retrospective pegged on the celebration of his 50th birthday (December 12, 1965). Veteran newscaster Walter Cronkite interviewed Frank in between film clips of his life and times, and a segment showing him recording a selection on his *September of My Years* album. Although he cooperated initially with the network, it was rumored that he later demanded the deletion of the interview footage. Whether cuts were made or not by CBS, TV reviewers were puzzled by his truculence. To a man, they felt that the documentary was neither tough nor probing, and that it was "an unmitigated rave for Frankie Goodfellow." Doubtless, the controversy stirred by Sinatra's threats, and the publicity generated by it, helped build a viewing audience. The program registered a higher audience rating than the competing NBC and ABC shows, which had until then consistently outdistanced the CBS hour.

Unlike the documentary, the Budweiser special consisted of songs strung like gems on a thin strand of spoken words—seventeen evergreens, with a brooding, retrospective ballad, "It Was a Very Good Year," serving as a theme. The critics were ecstatic, saluting *A Man and His Music* with epithets like "gasser," "the TV musical of the season," and "the best musical TV hour of the year." And so it was when the top shows were honored. The program garnered not only an Emmy as the best musical show of the year but a George Foster Peabody Award as an outstanding TV show.

The two CBS shows came just about fifteen years after Sinatra's first appearance on the tube. His debut was in the form of a guest shot on a Bob Hope special, *Star-Spangled Revue*. It occurred at one of the low points of Sinatra's career and life, the period when he was torn by his love for Ava Gardner, the struggle to get a divorce from Nancy, and the feeling of guilt over leaving his children. He has never forgotten that it was Hope who opened a door at a time when he was professionally in the pits.

"I couldn't get a job," he said later, "until Bob came along with his first TV spec. In 1950 there weren't many people around like him. People were frightened of me. But Hope! He and his writers wrote his entire spec around me. . . . The show was of tremendous psychological help to me."

The Hope guest shot may also have proved professionally helpful. Just over four months later Sinatra had his own half-hour series on TV. Considering that he himself felt "snake-bitten," it was little short of a shock that CBS came up with a five-year contract at $250,000 a year. The *Frank Sinatra Show* made its debut on October 7, 1950, sponsored by the Bulova watch people. A weekly variety program, it was expanded to a full hour in October 1951 and remained on the tube until April 1, 1952, in a deal originally set for five years.

Frank's guests included a wide variety of vocalists—jazz, pop, country, some on the charts, some past their prime—Sarah Vaughan, Perry Como, Georgia Gibbs, Frankie Laine, Dick Haymes, Peggy Lee, Rudy Vallee, the Andrews Sisters, the Pied Pipers; comics like Phil Silvers, Jackie Gleason, Jackie Leonard, Frank Fontaine, Gary Moore, and Jack Benny; and movie stars like Basil Rathbone, Conrad Nagel, James Mason, and Joan Blondell. Frank sang, dueted with guest vocalists, played in the sketches, and served as the emcee.

From the start the TV critics were unimpressed or negative. Dubbing the program "a drab mixture of radio, routine vaudeville and pallid pantomime," Jack Gould of *The New York Times* quipped: "Sinatra walked off the TV high dive but unfortunately fell into the shallow end of the pool." *Variety* found little to favor in the scripting or pacing of the show, but praised Frank as a performer with "considerable charm, ease and the ability to sell a song." It was precisely a seeming lack of ease that prompted other reviewers to fault him as the program's emcee.

The expanded full-hour version of the show, which debuted on October 9, 1951—just a month before his two-years-in-the-making marriage to Ava Gardner—also got off to a weak start. Apparently the network had great confidence in Frank for they pitted his debut show against *The Milton Berle Show*, then the highest-rated program on the tube. Frank's reaction was, "It's like backing into the pennant. Berle's a big man to knock down." To meet the challenge CBS selected the well-known theatrical impresario Max Gordon as his producer and provided a budget of over $40,000, a high figure for the time. Feeling that his forte was in the vocal department, Frank lined up a stellar array of singers—Perry Como, Frankie Laine, and the Andrews Sisters—all hit makers of the day. Not to be outclassed the Berle show signed Tony Bennett, Rosemary Clooney, and the Mills Brothers in an opposing lineup that ostensibly cost $50,000.

In the battle of the ratings Sinatra could not do more than reduce Berle's by nine points. Although *Variety* praised him as a "hep showman on all counts" and the program as "fast-paced and bright," the critics of the two most important papers, *The New York Times* and the *Herald-Tribune*, down-thumbed both him and his voice. Both felt that time had played havoc with his distinctive styling and the quality of his singing, and that he lacked "the dominant personality needed to sustain a sixty-minute show."

In a sense, the show never recovered from the mixed critical reaction, even though it was to be seen week after week until the end of March 1952. It was a most trying period in Sinatra's life, both domestically and professionally.

Sinatra's next major appearance on the television screen came in September 1955. Although he sang a number of songs in *Our Town*, including "Love and Marriage," which yielded a hit record for him, it was basically a dramatic role he assayed. In fact, his was the key role as the stage manager–narrator in Thornton Wilder's 1938 Pulitzer Prize–winning play. During the rehearsals controversy erupted between Sinatra and NBC-TV, then involved in a negotiation. Column items and headlines appeared when Frank skipped several dress rehearsals and apparently threatened to take a walk.

But on the evening of the telecast—the play was done live on September 8, 1955—Eva Marie Saint, Paul Newman, and Frank all did a superb job. *The New York Times* termed it "magnificent" and reflected the opinion of other reviewers who thought that the five songs written for the production by Cahn and Van Heusen, and sung by Sinatra, enhanced the production. *Our Town* became one of the few television productions that served as the springboard for a hit song, "Love and Marriage," being antedated only by "Let Me Go Lover," the title song of a CBS-TV dramatic show of the same year.

By the time he appeared in *Our Town*, Frank had an Oscar for his role in *From Here To Eternity*, a new recording contract, a best-selling record hit in "Young at Heart," and more offers than he could handle for films, TV shows, and live appearances.

"Man, I feel eight feet tall," he was telling everybody. "Everything is ahead of me. I'm on top of the world. I'm buoyant." And so he was.

Between 1957 and 1960 Sinatra spent much time before the movie camera, starring in as many as ten films. They were equally busy years in terms of the TV tube. By October 1957 he was walking around Hollywood with a $3-million check in his pocket from ABC-TV. He had begun work in the Goldwyn studios on a new TV series, scheduled to premiere on October 18. The series was to include 13 half-hour musicals, an equal number of half-hour dramatic shows, and a number of hour-long specials. The musical series ran from October 1957 through May 1958, interspersed with dramas, which continued on the tube to the end of June. *The Frank Sinatra Show*, as the series was called, was a workmanlike production, with entertainment values that varied, depending on how singers interacted with Frank on a repertoire made up mostly of his standards and, in the case of the dramas, on the quality of the scripts and acting. Between times Frank also made appearances on *Club Oasis*, *The Chevy Show* and *The Bing Crosby Show*, as well as on *Some of Manie's Friends*—all NBC programs. *Some of Manie's Friends* was a March 3, 1959, tribute to the recently deceased Manie Sachs, the man who had befriended Sinatra at the beginning of his solo career in 1943 and who was both his producer and mentor at Columbia Records before the advent of Mitch Miller.

Beginning in October 1959 Frank appeared in the first of four annual, hour-long specials sponsored by Timex. The first featured Bing Crosby, Dean Martin, and Mitzi Gaynor as his guests. The second, titled "An After-

With Der Bingle at the time when Sinatra and Crosby were friendly competitors for the title of
America's favorite male singer, 1948.

noon with Frank Sinatra" and presented in December 1959, took a jazz direction and featured Ella Fitzgerald, the Hi-Lo's, and Red Norvo & His Jazz Group. The third, telecast on February 15, 1960, was a Valentine Day's bouquet with the theme "Here's to the Ladies!" Included in the cast was Juliet Prowse, who had also appeared in the December show, danced in his film *Can-Can*, and to whom he was briefly engaged at that time. Lena Horne performed a medley with him while Eleanor Roosevelt recited the lyrics of the Oscar song "High Hopes," written by Cahn and Van Heusen, to a special arrangement created by Nelson Riddle.

It was the fourth of the Timex series that proved the blockbuster. By then Frank was determined, as Sammy Cahn, who served as producer, told reporters, "to prove that he can go big on TV." And the show was a biggie both in terms of the press it drew and the audience that watched the telecast on May 12, 1960. "Welcome Back Elvis" was its title, and it marked Elvis's return as a performer after a two-year stint in the army. Sinatra, it was reported, paid $100,000 for the privilege of reintroducing the King of Rock 'n' Roll to civilian life, much of it shelled out of his own pocket. With an almost inborn instinct for grabbing space, Frank sensed the potential in publicity of a show embracing two artists, each of whom had detonated a "pop explosion."

Media coverage was extensive, invited, perhaps, by the two-month gap between the March taping and the May telecast, and enhanced by the circumstance under which the show was taped. The setting was the Fontaine-bleau Hotel in Miami Beach where Sinatra was headlining and to which he summoned his buddies of the Clan for a so-called Summit meeting. Sammy Davis, Jr., Peter Lawford, and Joey Bishop participated not only in evenings of improvised, show-stopping comedy but also in welcoming Elvis back, thereby contributing entertainment values inherent in the interplay between the day's teenage idol and the swingers of an older generation. Nancy Sinatra added youth to the proceedings, which were witnessed by a sizable group of Presley fans. The excitement, verging on hysteria, that attended Elvis's appearances was reminiscent of the Sinatra Paramount panics. It was more than audible in screaming that irritated some of the older reviewers and members of the audience.

Of the confrontation between the idols of two generations, Alan Levy later wrote in *Operation Elvis*: "Ex-bobbysoxers who once risked truancy to venture within swooning distance of The Voice watched their idol nostalgically and viewed with parental alarm their daughters' rapture over the Pelvis."

Apart from the Niagara of publicity that poured over the show, "Welcome Back Elvis" was an audience killer, despite mixed critical reactions. When the Trendex ratings came out the show scored a staggering 41.5 mark against NBC's 21.1 and CBS's 4.2. Trade papers noted that the rating represented a five-year high.

In *SUDDENLY*, 1954.

1955.

1945.

TED ALLAN

Count Basie, 1958.

In SERGEANTS 3, 1962. (left)

In VON RYAN'S EXPRESS, 1965.

With Dino.

(L-R) Jill St. John, Phyllis McGuire, Frank and Barbara Rush.

Receiving the Jean Hersholt Humanitarian Award at the 43rd Oscar ceremony, April 15, 1971.

Sinatra as Director, directs the character "Little Fisherman," in a scene from NONE BUT THE BRAVE and (left) checks stills with Director of Photography, Harold Lipstein. 1965.

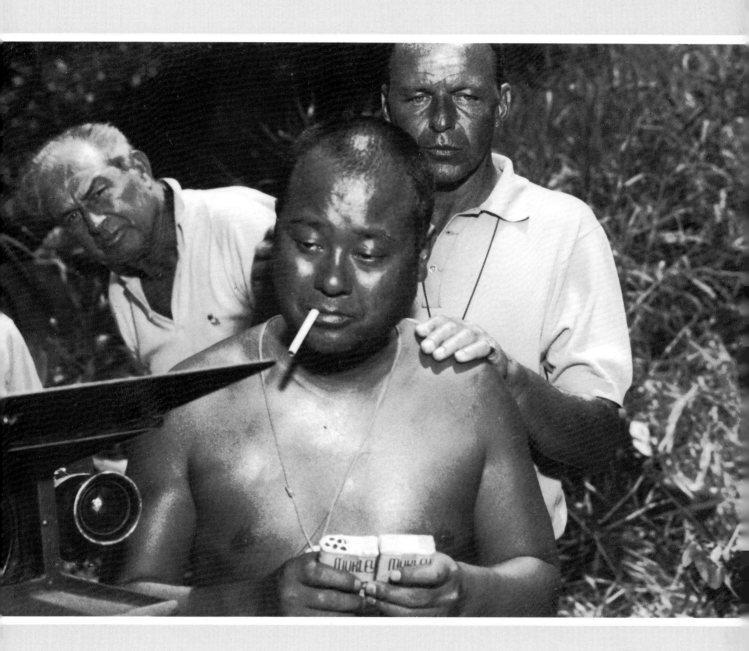

Although he made guest appearances on various specials, it was just about five years before Sinatra became involved again in a series. These were the annual specs he mounted for Budweiser beer, starting in November 1965 with the show that brought him an Emmy and a Peabody and that was repeated in May 1966.

By the time he appeared in the second version of *A Man and His Music* in 1966, daughter Nancy had scored a smash single hit—it went Gold in a record eight weeks—in "These Boots Are Made for Walking." Frank was trying to walk with the young, being involved at 51 years of age in a romance with actress Mia Farrow (who was younger than Nancy) and in a show in which Nancy was his only guest. Sinatra was now attracting attention among teenagers as "Nancy's Pop," as at a later date Pat Boone and Neil Sedaka were each to widen their following as the result of hit records by their daughters. A high point of the special was Nancy's rendition of her "Boots" hit. It was neatly preceded by Sinatra's singing of an old standard, made to order for the occasion, "Yes Sir, That's My Baby." Audience reaction was strong enough so that the program was repeated on April 3, 1967, in part, perhaps, because he had by then scored his first hit single in years with "Strangers in the Night," winner of four Grammys at the NARAS awards of 1967.

That year Sinatra devoted his Budweiser special to a treatise on rhythm, with Ella Fitzgerald and Antonio Carlos Jobim as guests. Two jazzy medleys with the swinging Miss Fitzgerald included such oldies as "Stompin' at the Savoy" (the Benny Goodman standard) as well as the new Jimmy Webb-Fifth Dimension hit, "Up, Up and Away." Jobim was the South American guitarist-composer who had launched the Bossa Nova in Brazil with singer Joao Gilberto, whose compositions "Desafinado" and "The Girl from Ipanema" were American hits in the early '60s and who had recorded an album of Bossa Novas, which was then on the market, with Frank. The contrast between Sinatra's swinging balladry, Ella's jazz styling, and Jobim's Brazilian rhythms made for a delightful musical hour, which enjoyed a repeat telecast on April 21, 1968.

Reacting, perhaps, to the surge of soul music into the pop mainstream—these were the years of the Motown sound—Sinatra's fourth Budweiser special in November 1968 featured the Fifth Dimension and Diahann Carroll. Titled *Francis Albert Sinatra Does His Thing* (in contemporary jargon), the show included a duet with Diahann on "Lonesome Road" and with the pop soul group on "Sweet Blindness." In the final of the series, telecast November 5, 1969, it was *Sinatra* alone singing mostly the standards with which he had been associated for years. The conductors for the series had also all been longtime associates—Nelson Riddle for the first, Riddle and Gordon Jenkins for the second, Riddle for the third, and Don Costa for the last two. None of these shows managed to approach the level of the award-winning special in 1965.

An "arresting" father-daughter situation. Nancy Sinatra, filming a TV special at 20th Century-Fox, takes a lunch break with her father, in uniform for his role in THE DETECTIVE, 1967.

The discrepancy between Sinatra's consistent in-person sorcery and his inconsistent impact on television remains one of the enigmas of his fantastic career. Perhaps the explanation lies in the nature of the tube itself—the contrast between the lifeless, one-dimensional TV image and the animate person. In Frank's work before the television camera, there were a number of cogent instances of the contrast.

Sinatra: The Main Event, telecast live from Madison Square Garden in February 1974, found him overwhelming audiences in-person and then attracting only a limited public on ABC-TV—and even alienating some of the critics. In trying to cope with the problem posed by TV, Sinatra was attempting a live show, hoping thereby to capture the immediacy, intensity, and spontaneity with which he was able to invest his personal appearances. John J. O'Connor of *The New York Times* expressed admiration for Frank's derring-do, aware that he was "putting himself on the vulnerable line, vocal warts and all." Praising the expert pacing and professional polish, and recognizing the enthusiasm of the 20,000 spectators, he nevertheless concluded his review: "Watching the program at home, about midway through the proceedings, I heard a guest announce that she was going home to finish reading a mediocre novel. Given a choice in the matter, I would have gladly settled for a similar alternative."

Frank fared better in his TV outing with John Denver in March 1976. Viewers and critics alike were intrigued by the sharp contrast between the two men in style, personality, and even age. Here was a young man who traveled "Country Roads" and an older man who raced the jet stream. How could nature boy mesh with the swinging sophisticate? What kind of crazy mix would result from a blend of Denver's smiling effervescence and Sinatra's commanding strut? But the interplay between the two was so good-natured and natural that the show turned into simply good-time entertainment. *John Denver and Friend*, as the program was titled, was a triumph of chemistry as well as personality. Country pop and swinging balladry did not clash. In truth, Denver displayed no discomfort in a medley of Sinatra standards and was perfectly at ease in songs like "My Kind of Town," "The Lady Is a Tramp," and "I Get a Kick Out of You."

John Denver was also one of Frank's guests on *Sinatra and Friends*, a show telecast just about a year later in April 1977. Sinatra's other friends included Dean Martin, Natalie Cole, Leslie Uggams, Loretta Lynn, Tony Bennett, and Robert Merrill—a potpourri of artists representing every

major trend in American pop. Who could ask for anything more? Some reviewers felt, however, that the show suffered from a richness of singing talent and a shortage of explosive chemistry. The sponsorship by Sears was deemed quite appropriate. Everybody could find almost anything they wanted to buy, except dynamic thrust and depth of feeling. Other reviewers were quite pleased by the absence of chatter and wisecracks, and felt that the wholehearted dedication to song produced a musical winner.

During the latter part of the '70s and into the '80s Sinatra was visible on the tube mainly in news clips, various telethons, guest appearances on various programs, including *The Tonight Show*, $1-a-year commercials for Chrysler, a Dean Martin celebrity roast, and so on.

His only major appearance in this period occurred with the showing of the film *Contract on Cherry Street* in November 1977. A Columbia Pictures 3-hour television film, it was shot on the streets of New York City. As a result of visits paid to the sets by various political figures then involved in a race for the mayoralty and gubernatorial posts, it received extensive advance coverage in the media. The picture was a continuation of Sinatra's interest in cops-and-robbers stories, although it was reported that he made it because of the partiality of his mother to the novel on which it was based.

Once again as in *Tony Rome*, *Lady in Cement*, and *The Detective*, he was a crime fighter, playing a veteran deputy inspector in the New York Police Department. Frustrated and angered by departmental restraints and distressed by the murder of a fellow officer, he and several members of his unit took the law into their hands and contrived the murder of the chief of one of the underworld mobs. They thereby provoked retaliation by a rival mob, which resulted in a blood bath that decimated both groups. *Los Angeles Times* critic Cecil Smith's verdict on the film was "tawdry, slow and tacky." Of Sinatra, he wrote: "I do not mean to fault his performance—he always is an actor of astonishing power and persuasion." In short, this was an instance, and hardly the first, in which the actor was faulted by story and script.

But the problem posed for Sinatra by the television medium was of a more generic character. The glass tube was seemingly a barrier between the performer and the viewer, preventing Sinatra from projecting qualities that made him an overpowering in-person entertainer. He and his handlers never quite succeeded in sorting out the problems.

Ol' Blue Eyes
Is Back

NOVEMBER 18, 1973

AT A WHITE HOUSE RECEPTION IN APRIL 1973, SINATRA sang for the Premier of Italy and heard himself called "The Washington Monument of Entertainment." President Richard Nixon reportedly said to him sotto voce: "You must get out of retirement."

Later, in September 1973 when he was taping the TV special that brought him out of retirement, Sinatra said: "I don't find retirement all that I expected it to be. I was under constant pressure to return to work."

He was also under constant pressure from the media. The press was still "spiritually peeking" in his window. "In retirement," he told Dwight Whitney of *TV Guide*, "it was worse than ever. Some of the picayune stuff would cease but there was always the press. I call them garbage collectors, the columnists without a conscience, the reporters who take longshots based on the idea that where there's smoke, there's fire. I'm blunt and I'm honest. I could call them pimps and whores."

There was a constant barrage of rumors about his health, so much so that in an April 1972 article in *Coronet*, film star Burt Lancaster, who was a good friend of Sinatra's, felt impelled to state flatly: "Frank is not dying of cancer." Frank had already brought a lawsuit for $5 million against a Fawcett publication for a story claiming he was suffering from cancer of the throat. During the year he also filed a libel suit against the British Broadcasting Company (BBC) for its handling of his problems with a congressional committee investigating the infiltration of organized crime into sports.

The sparring with the House Select Committee on Crime began in June, when Sinatra was scheduled to testify but showed up instead in London, where he was involved in discussions of a role in the film *The Little Prince*, which ultimately fell through. Even before his appearance in mid-July to answer questions, the American Civil Liberties Union issued a statement terming the testimony of one of the witnesses, Joseph Barboza (a New England Mafia gunman), "one example of a congressional committee publicly hearing adverse testimony, unproved, unchecked and unrebutted, which could cause irreparable damage to the reputation of the person discussed." Barboza's assertion that Sinatra had been a front man for Mafia money in the Fontainebleau in Miami Beach and the Sands in Los Vegas was the target of Frank's attack on the committee.

The headlines, big and front-page in Vegas, tell the story: "Sinatra Tells Congressmen Off" *(Las Vegas Review-Journal)*; "Hot Frank Sinatra Storms U.S. House" *(Las*

Vegas Sun). The *Los Angeles Times* head was more specific: "Sinatra Scores Crime Hearing as 'Indecent' and 'Irresponsible'/Charges Congressional Panel Should Have Challenged Mobster's 'Hearsay' Testimony Linking Him to Mafia."

Moments after he had been sworn in, Sinatra held up a news clipping with a headline that read "Witness Links Sinatra to Reputed Mafia Figure" and exclaimed sarcastically, "That's charming. And that's all hearsay testimony, isn't it." Committee counsel agreed. The committee chairman also acknowledged that it had received an affidavit from the owner of the Fontainebleau denying that Sinatra had ever held any interest in it.

"Like most of the committee members," the *Los Angeles Times* reported, "Chairman Claude Pepper seemed taken aback by Sinatra's aggressiveness." And *The New York Times* observed: "The audience was with him all the way, laughing and clapping at his belligerent attacks on the committee."

The attacks did not stop when Sinatra left the House Caucus Room. In a by-lined article on the editorial page of *The New York Times* of July 24, he accused congressmen of seeking publicity "during an election year when they have difficulty getting their names into the newspapers." But the crux of his article was "the rights of a private citizen in this country when faced with the huge machine of the central government." Noting that congressional investigating committees are in theory fact-finding devices, he observed: "In practice, as we learned during the ugly era of Joe McCarthy, they can become star chambers.

"In my case," he continued, "a convicted murderer was allowed to throw my name around with abandon while the TV cameras rolled on.... Sure, I was given a chance to refute it, but as we have all come to know, the accusation often remains longer in the public mind than the defense."

He concluded: "My privacy had been robbed from me. I had lost hours of my life. I was being forced to defend myself in a place that was not even a court of law. It wasn't just a question of them getting off my back; it was a question of them getting off everyone's back."

Sinatra was sufficiently irked and angered so that he ran his article, titled "We Might Call This the Politics of Fantasy," as a paid advertisement in the *Los Angeles Times*. It was only one indication that his first year of retirement (1972) was not as relaxed as he had doubtless hoped it would be. Nineteen seventy-two was the year of *The Godfather* movie, and Frank was reportedly not pleased at being linked by the media as the model for the young singer in the book.

The year was not without its honors and awards: the Cecil B. De Mille Award at a Golden Globe Award ceremony (accepted for Sinatra by Joan Crawford); a plaque from the March of Dimes naming him Man of the Year; a State of Israel dinner honoring him for his efforts in behalf of Israel Bonds; a Medallion of Valor awarded by the State of Israel for his "unprecedented humanitarian efforts in behalf of his fellow man."

Between times Frank did some painting, as he had planned. Columnist Joyce Haber reported in December 1971 that daughter Nancy was displaying a new oil by her dad—a moonlight landscape of trees on the rim of a valley. Frank did some traveling, visiting Monaco and vacationing in Greece. When he was home in Rancho Mirage, he entertained and played golf with an assortment of political bigwigs, including Vice-President Spiro Agnew, a frequent visitor, California Governor Ronald Reagan and Mrs. Reagan, and others.

But even his friendship with the Vice-President led to adverse publicity. In a column headed "Agnew, Sinatra Very Close Friends," Jack Anderson reminded his readers that the late President Kennedy had "quietly dissociated himself from an admiring Frank Sinatra after reading a Justice Department dossier on the singer's racketeer friends" and noted that the Vice-President had "disregarded advice that he, too, should keep Sinatra at arm's length." When Frank received the Israeli Medallion of Valor, Agnew had announced: "I'm proud to know Sinatra as a friend. He is a legend in his time not only in the world of entertainment but in the world of philanthropy." Items in other columns led the Vice-President to issue a statement, which was headlined on the front page of the *Los Angeles Times*: "Agnew Denies He And Sinatra Are 'Raising Hell Together.'" "Every time I see Mr. Sinatra," the Vice-President was quoted as saying, "my wife is with me."

The biggest barrage of adverse publicity came in January 1973. Having contributed $50,000 to the campaign to reelect Richard Nixon, whom he publicly supported, Sinatra was invited to the 1973 inaugural in Washington. At midnight of January 19, as he and Barbara Marx were entering the Fairfax Hotel to attend the pre-Inaugural champagne breakfast sponsored by the Republican National Committee, he was approached by Maxine Cheshire, who had dealt with the Agnew–Sinatra and the Sinatra–Barbara Marx relationships in her columns. In a lobby full of reporters and Inaugural guests, Sinatra exploded with a torrent of abusive epithets, many of which the newspapers regarded as unprintable. There were front-page headlines like "Washington Columnist Seeking Public Apology from 'Frankie,'" and later, the attorney for

The Washington Post, Edward Bennett Williams, asked Frank's attorney, Milton Rudin, for an acceptable apology.

Some columnists claimed that Sinatra's intemperate outburst was the result of Ms. Cheshire's items about Barbara Marx, who was Frank's frequent companion but who was not then yet divorced from Zeppo Marx. But James Bacon of the *Los Angeles Herald-Examiner* was one of the few reporters, possibly the only one, who indicated what had really caused the blistering attack. According to Bacon, Frank was Charlie Charm to Ms. Cheshire until she asked him whether he thought his "Mafia" connections would hurt Agnew's chances for the Presidency.

Bacon later explained: "Of course, the beef made front-page headlines. Ms. Cheshire, who was selling her column in a new syndication deal, knew what politicians had long known. Get in a beef with Sinatra. He'll get you on page one. None of the stories, except mine, ever reported what touched off Frank's tirade. And none even mentioned that nothing sells syndication like page-one controversy."

Some papers reported that Richard Nixon felt the incident had "besmirched" his inauguration. Other stories indicated that an event to honor Sinatra, nurtured by Vice-President Agnew, was still in the making. The honor came in April when Sinatra was invited to sing at a White House reception and state dinner for Italian Prime Minister Giulio Andreotti. April 17 became a dramatic moment for Sinatra, the most significant of several events that led to his return to the entertainment world.

From his retirement in June 1971 until then, Sinatra had done no singing in public, except for private events. He had sung at an intimate party in September 1971, given by Rosalind Russell for Henry Kissinger; at a Friars' testimonial for Jack Benny and George Burns, using a Sammy Cahn parody of "Love and Marriage"; at a Republican fund-raising dinner and salute to Veep Agnew, at which he delivered a Sammy Cahn parody, "The Gentleman Is a Champ." But he made no professional appearances and did not set foot in a recording studio from November 2, 1970, until June 4, 1973.

In introducing Frank to the 200 guests assembled in the East Room of the White House, President Nixon referred to Sinatra, as has been mentioned, as "The Washington Monument of Entertainment. This house is honored," he said, "to have a man whose parents were born in Italy and [who] from humble beginnings rose to the very top of the entertainment world."

Concentrating on the oldies he loved, and backed by the U.S. Marine Band, conducted by longtime friend and arranger-composer Nelson Riddle, Sinatra opened with "You Make Me Feel So Young" and segued into "Moonlight in Vermont," "One for My Baby," "I've Got You Under My Skin," and "I Have Dreamed." He followed with "Fly Me to the Moon," "Try a Little Tenderness," the eloquent "Ol' Man River," and concluded with "I've Got the World on a String."

Before he sang an encore, demanded by the audience, he talked of the days when he was growing up in New Jersey and of what a thing it was to get a glimpse of the mayor in a parade. "Tonight," he said, "here with my President, the Italian Prime Minister and their guests, it's quite a boost to me. . . . Thank you, Mr. President, for inviting me here." The encore was "The House I Live In," which reporters described as a patriotic number, apparently not recalling that he had introduced the song in 1945 as a plea for tolerance in a short film of the same name, which won him a Special Oscar.

President Nixon, who had led the standing ovation before the encore, said in closing: "Once in a while, there is a moment when there's magic in the room—when a great performer, singer and entertainer is able to capture us all. Frank Sinatra did that tonight."

As the Nixons began to escort their guests from the East Room to the North Portico, Sinatra slipped behind the bandstand. He stood there suffused with emotion as tears welled up in his eyes. A moment later White House Press Secretary Ron Ziegler led him to an elevator that took him up to the Nixon family's living quarters. It was during the brief chat here that the President quietly told Sinatra: "You must get out of retirement." Sinatra replied: "Mr. President, after tonight, I'll have to think about it." Within days the *Los Angeles Times* reported that Sinatra was planning to come out of retirement via an NBC/Magnavox special, scheduled for a November 11, 1973, telecast.

"Sure, the President's remarks moved me," Sinatra later told Dwight Whitney of *TV Guide*. "But they weren't what made me come back. I think maybe it was those 15-year-olds who said, 'Gee, we've never seen you work. Did you move like Elvis? Did you gyrate your hips? . . . I had a helluva time explaining I just move."

To another reporter, Frank explained how he made an overseas call and after he spelled his name, the operator asked, "Junior?"

That, as Elvis's fans would say, apparently *shook him up*. But, according to Thomas Thompson, the *Life* editor who had long known him, something else shook Sinatra up. Thompson is perfectly willing to grant that he has no way of substantiating his contention and "it is, perhaps, nothing but coincidence. But it *is* worth noting that at approximately the same time Spiro Agnew felt the fires of scandal swirling about him, Frank Sinatra bolted out of retirement. . . . I do not dispute his stated explanation that he was bored with inactivity and that he had received so many exhortations from his fans that he decided to warm up his tonsils once more. But I heard one remark in Hollywood that seemed worth thinking about. 'Frank bet on the wrong horse,' said a Hollywood director. He went on to suggest that he staked so much on his publicized friendship with Agnew that he could not just sit devastated in Palm Springs. He would reclaim the stage. He would prove that neither age nor the disgrace of a friend had withered him." (Thompson was careful to note that Sinatra had not wavered in his loyalty to Agnew and had gone to considerable lengths to help the ex–Vice-President.)

The only thing wrong with Thompson's hypothesis is that Agnew did not resign until October 10, 1973. Even if one takes the date when the public first became aware of an ongoing investigation of kickbacks to politicians in the Baltimore area—August 1973—it came months after Sinatra had decided to give up retirement.

In considering things that led to Sinatra's comeback, one cannot overlook an approach that was made to him by Paul Anka and Sinatra's longtime lyricist friend, Sammy Cahn. Apparently they came to Sinatra urging him to do a new album and may even have submitted a song, "Let Me Try Again," which was at first supposed to be the title song of the album that came out as *Ol' Blue Eyes is Back*.

Sinatra himself told James Bacon when he was already rehearsing with Gene Kelly for the November TV special that marked his formal return to performing: "I don't know what the hell I'm doing here. First, I'm conned into doing a record album, and now this. I never tire of playing golf. It's the game for all retirees. Golf and sunshine is not a bad way to spend a day. Hell, I enjoyed being retired."

Enjoyed? "Sometimes he is bored," Frank Jr. told friends. "Very bored."

But Frank denied that he was disillusioned with retirement in any way. "I just loved doing nothing," he told
Dwight Whitney. "Yes, I am basically a creative person.
But I got to the stage when I didn't need that. For the first
time, I got to see friends I hadn't seen in a long time. I got
to travel without work — which is so hectic. I got time to
delve into art. I did what came to me when I woke up."

Apparently the volume of mail he received also had its
impact. "When I got out of the business," he said, "I
began to get a lot of mail from disappointed people. Thirty
thousand letters. Some of it said, 'How dare you?' Most of
it was very sweet. 'We know you want your privacy,' it
said, 'but just don't close the door completely and at least
make one album.' Then, one day, some discussion came
up about a TV show. 'I don't know,' I said. But before I
knew it, I was into it." By May 22, 1973, just little more
than a month after his White House appearance, he was
really into it. And by May 28 Joyce Haber's column was
headed "Sinatra Huddles on Comeback Album." The
huddle, in Frank's office on the Goldwyn lot, was with
singer-composer Neil Diamond, the first, apparently, in
a series of meetings with other "select and with-it
songwriters."

The May 22 *Variety* article reported that Sinatra and
producer Howard W. Koch were conferring about team-
ing together for his "many-sided comeback" on TV and in
films. The article continued: "Meanwhile, Sinatra con-
tinues to ready his [commercial] return from temporary
retirement via the banquet circle with Republican pals." In
addition to the White House appearance, he performed at
Spiro Agnew's son's wedding and a May 31 salute to Governor Reagan.

One June 3 he would make the annual presentation of
Sinatra Scholarship Awards at UCLA and on June 9 emcee
the annual Alumni Awards at which basketball coach John
Wooden was to be toasted as Alumnus of the Year. In the
meantime, on the Goldwyn soundstage, he filmed seven
teleblurbs: four for the Prevention of Blindness; one each
for Easter Seals and Foster Parents Plan; and an ad-lib
16-mm greeting to a Magnavox convention in Las Vegas,
anticipating his November 18 NBC-TV special for
Magnavox.

It was not until mid-June that Sinatra made a formal
public announcement of his plan to unretire. He was returning, he said in a front page story in the *Los Angeles
Times*, "only when I can control the situation. I'm not
going to put myself in the position of facing big, uncon-
trolled crowds again. Too many times, I became the victim
in such situations, and I'm not going to let that happen
again. I kept getting mail from people who wanted to hear

me sing. There was something like 30,000 letters, and
many sympathized with my desire for privacy. They suggested that there were ways I could perform again without
sacrificing my privacy. I'll make records, but I can do that
before a small group of friends. I'll have an audience for
the television special; but that can be controlled, too."
Did Sinatra plan to bypass nightclub appearances? It was
not clear.

By the first week in September the Magnavox special
was in rehearsal. At least Sinatra (in a yellow T-shirt with
the legend "Ol' Blue Eyes is Back") was rehearsing with
Gene Kelly, who was to be his only guest. It was a sentimental, heartwarming reunion in more ways than one.

For one thing, Sinatra chose as their rehearsal studio
MGM's venerated Hall B, a large, low, faded-brown
structure on the northern extremity of the old MGM lot,
where most of the celebrated musicals of the 1940s were
developed. "I once spent eight weeks of my life here,"
Sinatra told Dwight Whitney. "And I don't mean just
part-time. We rehearsed *Anchors Aweigh* here for 6 days a
week — for 8 weeks — before our first foot of film was shot
on a soundstage. No way was I a dancer. Boy did we
work — we all did. Gene, Kathryn Grayson — the whole
cast. Later, we did the same for *On the Town* and *Take Me
Out to the Ball Game*. Those were beautiful days.... You
can't imagine what it meant to be a movie performer — a
musical performer at MGM in those days. That was the
end! That was it for a green kid from New Jersey. A performer couldn't have dreamed for more. Metro was arrival
and acceptance. It was a new family and a new life. I never
went to college.... This place is my alma mater." In
1973, the place, a barnlike, sixty-by-sixty-foot room was
heavy with years of grime and dirt. But to Sinatra it was
like a recording studio — home again.

Here Gene and he rehearsed the sequence that was
highlighted by the tongue-in-cheek number "We Can't
Do That Anymore," a song by John Kander and Fred
Ebb, who wrote the script for the Magnavox special.
Composed of film clips from musicals in which he and
Gene Kelly appeared in the 1940s, it displayed them doing
the old, demanding dance routines they claimed they
couldn't do anymore. It was a show-stopping sequence.
Together the two did another number in which Sinatra sat
relaxed in a chair singing "Nice 'N' Easy" while Kelly, in
the background, gracefully danced as only he could.

At a Friars Roast to Kelly two years later, Sinatra paid
homage to Gene for his patience in helping make him part
of a team, and he said: "I love him in many, many ways
because he's a man of great depth. He's a man of intelligence and he's a man who loves me. And I cannot do

more in my lifetime than love a man back the way he loves me — or a woman. And he's the best friend, one of the maybe three or four best friends I have in my entire life."

The actual taping of the Magnavox comeback special, which occurred on September 20, 1973, was greeted by columnist Joyce Haber as follows: "Last Thursday will go down in certain annals as the day that . . . Francis Albert returned to show business, taping a special before the most select '400' since the real Cholly Knickerbocker invented that phrase." The long column that followed contained breathless exclamations like "Has there ever in popular music or among performers been his peer? . . . The show that you'll see on November 18 is called *Magnavox Presents Frank Sinatra*. It might have been called The Reincarnation of the King. . . . A whole new generation will now be able to see the Greatest Legend in Wax since Mme. Tussaud set up her Museum 140 years ago. . . ." Producer Howard Koch had gutted Paramount soundstage Number Nineteen for the taping at a cost of $125,000, clearing the huge arena to the rafters and installing two 38-foot revolving stages. There was room for a 54-piece orchestra, led not by one but two conductors — Gordon Jenkins and Don Costa — and for several sets of odd-sized bleachers of varying shapes and heights, on which sat, in Cecil Smith's words, "a formal assemblage of almost everybody who is anybody in this town [Hollywood]". The 13-minute film clip, previously taped, of the segment with Gene Kelly brought the first of several standing ovations from an awestruck audience.

By October 6 the comeback album, titled *Ol' Blue Eyes Is Back* — his first in three years — was on the market. He had tried at first to record it as most recording was being done in the '70s, section by section. But after cutting one-and-one-half songs in a preliminary session with just a rhythm section, he had given up. "Live is the only way he'll do it," conductor Gordon Jenkins later said — and that was the way the LP was recorded on the Goldwyn soundstage, with a forty-six piece band in July and August.

Jenkins arranged five of the songs while Don Costa did the remaining three. Jenkins conducted the orchestra, while Costa served as producer in the booth. It was a marriage, the first for both, arranged by Sinatra. Of the songs he scored, Jenkins spent the most time on Stephen Sondheim's "Send in the Clowns," which he also thought was the best song on the date. Four of the tunes were by Joe Raposo, best known for his work on the "Sesame Street" TV show ("Being Green," among other hits), who was brought together with Sinatra by Don Costa. *Billboard*'s verdict: "A masterful album of beautiful ballads." Noting

an advance order of 150,000 copies, Leonard Feather of the *Los Angeles Times* wrote: "A mellow ballad set, consistent both in the selection of tunes and level of performance."

On Sunday, September 30, just before the release of the album, Sinatra did a brief stint at a benefit for the Los Angeles Music and Art School at the Dorothy Chandler Pavilion. The pavilion had been the scene of his "farewell" concert of 1971. Introduced by Bob Hope, Sinatra was on his entrance greeted with a riotous standing ovation. Holding his program to four songs and eighteen minutes, he began with "I've Got the World on a String" and concluded with "I Get a Kick Out of You." In the view of Leonard Feather, who loved the saloon song "Here's That Rainy Day," Sinatra "looked and sounded precisely the way his audience had hoped. . . . At no time did he seem to be under any vocal or emotional strain." The trial balloon, as Feather termed the appearance, was "a reassuring demonstration," after the two-year hiatus, that "his chops were in good shape."

And so came the evening of November 18 when the Magnavox special, titled *Ol' Blue Eyes is Back,* was telecast on NBC-TV. It opened almost as a sequential continuation of the moment when Sinatra had left the entertainment scene two years and three months ago. Out of the darkness a pin spot picked up his face, a little rounder and puffier. As the music welled up and the lights came on, he was walking on a treadmill, greeting people in evening dress, sitting on two spinning turntables.

"I didn't know how much I'd miss the business," he said after his opening song, "the records, the movies, the saloons. So here I am for all the young people who wanted to know what I used to work like. . . ."

The opening, as well as the closing song, was Joe Raposo's "You Will Be My Music." Between them were the familiar standards, loved by audiences the world over, and just a few new songs like "Send in the Clowns" and the Paul Anka–Sammy Cahn song "Let Me Try Again." The program closed as it had opened, with the lights fading slowly to a pin spot.

Columnist Joyce Haber, who was watching the show with an in-group, including the Robert Stacks, Fred DeCordova of the *Tonight Show,* and others, reported: "It was so great that observers broke out in spontaneous applause." *Los Angeles Times* colleague Charles Champlin later observed: "Neither the special nor the album were total critical successes."

Just about ten days before the Magnavox telecast, Sinatra's comeback completed its full cycle, or at any rate, announcement was made of its completion. Shortly before his appearance at the White House, the new MGM Grand in Las Vegas had indicated a willingness to pay Sinatra between $250,000 and $500,000 a week if he came out of retirement for its gala opening. But now Sid Gathrid, Entertainment Director of Caesars Palace, advised the public that Sinatra would appear in its main showroom for the first of two dates on January 25 and 31, 1974. "As the most dynamic performer in show business," Gathrid stated, "his engagement will stimulate excitement and electricity not only at the Palace but throughout Las Vegas." To which the Las Vegas *Review-Journal* added: "The controversy surrounding Sinatra undeniably adds to his colorful reputation and consistently makes him the strongest attraction ever to play the Strip."

The following day's *Las Vegas Sun* carried a telegram sent to Sinatra by District Attorney Roy Woofter: "It's so nice to have you back where you belong. Look forward to seeing you and enjoying your songs." It was an entirely different melody than the previous D.A. had sung when Sinatra was involved in a fracas in September 1970 with a Caesars Palace executive who had waved a gun at him. At that time, D.A. George Franklin, who was defeated later that year by Woofter, had announced that Sinatra was wanted for questioning. Sheriff Lamb had then said: "If Sinatra comes back to town, he's coming downtown to get a work card (usually not demanded of superstars like Frank), and if he gives me any trouble, he's going to jail." Now Sheriff Lamb said: "I am pleased that Mr. Sinatra is coming back to show business and especially is making his start in Las Vegas. He is the greatest entertainer of all time and really a superstar. . . . " About the same time it became known that Sinatra had contributed to Woofter's campaign against Franklin—using not money but his influence in getting others to give Woofter financial backing.

When Sinatra finally opened at the Circus Maximus on January 25, the *Los Angeles Times* sent its entertainment editor, in addition to columnist Joyce Haber, to cover the comeback. Charles Champlin found Sinatra "a magical performer with undiminished powers" and his finest moments to be "in the soft, demanding ballads, revealing most astonishingly his gifts of phrasing, control and feeling, and proving beyond doubt the ongoing youthful tenderness of his voice." To Champlin the evening was not an unmitigated triumph because midway, when he paused to sip a glass of wine (plugging his favorite Mouton-Cadet), Sinatra "revived his animosities toward two ladies of the press, Rona Barrett and Maxine Cheshire of The *Washington Post*." Champlin felt that regardless of the distant provocation, "the savagery of the attacks invited sympathy for his victims and put gall in a winy evening."

Covering the behavior of the audience in almost one-third of a page, Joyce Haber reported that every hotel in town was crammed to capacity, every casino was crammed for three days before Sinatra's opening, "and he was at his top—which is something—singing for 75 minutes straight" and receiving five standing ovations. Apart from all the celebrities and stars who jammed the Circus Maximus, there was the New York City secretary on a two-week vacation who intended to see all ten shows of Sinatra's stint. Ms. Haber also reported that although Frank owed Caesars five weeks at a salary of $500,000, the hotel had agreed to pay the half-million for just two weeks.

Caesars Palace spared no expense in glorifying Sinatra's return, casting a special medallion that was presented as a giveaway to celebrities. Moreover the president of the casinotel, Bill Weinberger, threw a midnight supper party in the North Tower Penthouse about which Bill Willard of *Daily Variety* wrote: "Nothing like it has ever been tossed in Vegas history, a celebrity party to make the early saturnalia in Rome look like a quilting bee. . . . "

The following day, the *Los Angeles Times* reported that the Las Vegas D.A.'s office was providing free bodyguards, three of them, during Sinatra's stay in the city. "If this was Pittsburgh," said an assistant D.A., "and the President of U.S. Steel needed extra security, it would be provided, wouldn't it? Well, that's just how important we feel Frank Sinatra is to this town."

In-person, the magic that was Sinatra's was still working its spell.

5. "Pennies From Heaven": The Humanitarian

In May 1976 on a windy day in Las Vegas, Francis Albert Sinatra was awarded an Honorary Doctorate of Humane Letters by the University of Nevada. The honorary degree was bestowed as a mark of recognition for concerts Sinatra had been giving annually in behalf of the university's athletic program, concerts that had raised over $3 million.

"He not only donates his own services, and arranges for the appearance of other artists," said the president of the university, "but he personally absorbs all the costs of musicians, technicians and supporting staff." And in 1976 when the concert raised $680,000, he wrote a check for $20,000 to bring the sum up to $700,000.

Five years earlier the Motion Picture Academy of Arts and Sciences had voted him the Jean Hersholt Humanitarian Award. That year, shortly after accepting the award, he turned a benefit for the Motion Picture and TV Relief

Fund into his "retirement" concert and helped raise over $900,000. In 1972 the Beverly Hills Friars gave him their Humanitarian Award, and the State of Israel, in recognition of his eleemosynary activities, awarded him its Medallion of Valor. The following year he was named Man of the Year by the March of Dimes. In 1979 he received the World Mercy Fund's Premum Vivere Award and the Columbus Citizens Committee Humanitarian Award. In 1980, Variety Clubs International bestowed its Humanitarian of the Year award upon him.

Now, all entertainers devote a portion of their time to benefits and make gratis appearances to help raise money for charitable purposes. What distinguishes Sinatra, dating back to the incipiency of his career and spanning five decades, is the scope, variety, and magnitude of his humanitarian efforts. No one, perhaps not even Sinatra himself, can estimate the massive sums of money he has raised. Associates believe that the total would mount to a nine-digit figure and could be as high as $250 million; they estimate, in addition, that he has personally given away between $5 million and $25 million.

The penchant for giving of himself and his possessions was not an acquired taste. As a skinny, lonely teenager growing up in the tough environs of Hoboken, New Jersey, he took friends to the movies, occasionally bought clothes for less fortunate kids, and sneaked pals into Palisades Park on a pass he secured through his mother, who was a power in Democratic circles. The Hoboken gambit was designed to cope with the area's bullies, and also to win friends.

Shortly after he emerged on the entertainment scene as "an American Phenomenon," in the words of *The New Yorker*, the Voice's feeling for his fellow man took a strong political direction. As an outgrowth of his then-daring espousal of Roosevelt liberalism during FDR's bid for a fourth term, Frank became a crusader for tolerance and brotherhood. Taking time out of his professional activities, he addressed gatherings of high school students in New York City, Philadelphia, Gary, Indiana, and elsewhere in a frontal attack on racial and religious prejudice.

"Sinatra's annual take has diminished," E.J. Kahn, Jr., observed in *The New Yorker* of 1946, "principally because he has lately been making only part-time gainful employment, having chosen to devote a considerable portion of his energies to speechmaking and to entertaining, gratis, on behalf of a number of liberal causes with which he is in articulate sympathy."

Then a solo voice among popular entertainers in his campaign for tolerance, he was warned by his advisers that he was putting his career on the line. He did, in fact, make

powerful enemies, alienating and drawing fire especially from the conservative Hearst press and its columnists. He was attacked before the notorious House Un-American Activities Committee by a home-grown follower of Hitler. Undaunted, he carried his campaign to the point of starring and singing in an antidiscrimination documentary, *The House I Live In*. It won him and Mervyn LeRoy, who produced the short, a Special Oscar from the Motion Picture Academy in 1946.

A *World-Telegram* columnist of the time, Harriet Van Horne, wrote of an interview: "Here was a hard-working young man with a deep sense of his brother's wrong and a social conscience that hasn't been atrophied by money or fame."

That conscience has found expression in facilities that exist at the present time in a number of cities. Not too far from his own compound in Rancho Mirage, California, there are the Tina Sinatra Student Center and the Martin Anthony Sinatra Medical Educational Center, the latter established in memory of his father with contributions of close to $1 million. In Los Angeles the Villa Scalabrini Retirement Center flourishes as a memorial to his mother, with a plaque memorializing Sinatra as a "champion of charity." In Israel the Frank Sinatra International Student Center on Mt. Scopus and the Frank Sinatra Brotherhood Youth in Nazareth both stand as monuments to his munificence.

Merely to enumerate the charities, causes, colleges, hospitals, organizations, educational centers, medical funds, musical facilities, and children's foundations to which he has contributed sums of money or his talents would take pages and pages.

The welfare of children has been of particular concern to Frank, not only kids in this country but all over the world. In the spring of 1961, footing all the expenses, he flew Nelson Riddle and His Orchestra down to Mexico City, where he made appearances from May 5 through May 7. Out of the gratis concerts came a charitable contribution of $50,000 for the Rehabilitation Institute of the city and a tribute in the Congressional Record from Representative James Roosevelt, which read in part: "Sinatra's humane contribution entitles him to applause beyond that given a great entertainer." Repeating the gambit after he had finished filming *The Manchurian Candidate* in the spring of 1962, he augmented his contribution by $25,000.

In April 1962, smarting from a snub by President JFK, who had elected to stay at Bing Crosby's home in Palm Springs instead of his, Sinatra embarked on an international tour of eight foreign cities whose stated purpose was to raise funds for various local children's charities. In Tokyo 8,000 seats for one show were sold out in thirty minutes. In Tel Aviv 80,000 listeners packed a sports stadium to hear him sing. Benefits followed in Athens, Rome, Milan, Paris, London, and, finally, Monte Carlo. Absorbing the expenses of traveling with his staff and a septet led by pianist-conductor Bill Miller—at a cost reportedly of half-a-million dollars to Sinatra—he was able to raise a million dollars. Great Britain's Sunshine Home for Blind Children later received an additional grant when he turned over monetary damages awarded on a successful libel suit brought against an English TV show, that had claimed that the kidnapping of Frank Jr. in 1963 was a staged publicity stunt.

Among the children's charities that benefited from his largesse and artistry into the 1980s were the Thalian Clinic for Children, Friars Foundation for Needy Children, Child Care Center in Watts, Mental Health and Child Abuse Foundation of San Francisco, Britain's National Society for the Prevention of Cruelty to Children, the Reiss-Davis Child Study Center of Denver, St. Jude Children's Ranch in Memphis, and many others. In 1974 he went on an April tour, performing in six American cities for Variety Clubs International. Participating in the "Jerry Lewis Telethon" in 1975, he paid the fees of the thirty musicians who accompanied him and donated $25,000 in the name of his first grandchild, Angela Jennifer Lambert. Later in 1975 he gave gratis concerts in Teheran and Israel for the benefit of Jewish and Arab children.

Recognition of his beneficent efforts in "donating time and money . . . to help children in need" came from

the Italian government in 1979. At a formal ceremony held at the Italian Consulate in Los Angeles, he was invested with the highest honor awarded to a citizen—Grande Ufficiale dell'Ordine al Merito della Republica Italiana.

There are other people around the country whom Sinatra has never met and who can testify to his unsolicited generosity. "From out of the blue," a woman in Gainesville, Florida, told newspapers, "a check for $1,500 from Frank Sinatra arrived for my son." Frank had apparently read in the papers of how her ten-year-old son had lost his left hand in a farming accident and was trying to pay off medical bills by selling bottles, newspapers, and aluminum cans. While performing in the San Francisco area in April 1977, Sinatra learned of a child who had been born heroin-addicted and required extensive hospital care. According to reports Frank paid a visit to the hospital and gave a check for $3,000 to help pay for the treatment. Earlier an elderly Manhattan couple, Sam Labeiko, 85, and Lizi Labeiko, 80, who were about to be evicted from their Lower East Side apartment because of an inability to pay a $10 increase in their monthly rent, found Sinatra's attorney going to bat for them on their legal difficulties.

In 1970, an Indiana police chief, Dan Mitrione, who was serving as a State Department adviser in Uruguay was killed by guerillas. When Sinatra learned that nine children had been left fatherless, he arranged a benefit. Apart from paying for the Count Basie Band and related costs, he invited all the policemen in the Indianapolis area and their wives as well as five hundred servicemen at nearby bases, and paid for their tickets. The widow and the nine children ended up with a fund of $100,000.

In 1976, according to accounts in a hardly friendly paper, Frank donated money to five orphanages in Japan, a children's orthopedic hospital in Hong Kong, a nursery in Athens, a crippled children's hospital in Paris, and Boys' Town in Italy. He was reported to have raised, including a dozen charity benefits, or himself contributed close to $7 million.

Shortly before the assassination attempt on President Ronald Reagan's life in March 1981, he joined Sammy Davis, Jr., in a mission of mercy. Atlanta, Georgia, was then the scene of the mystifying murders of twenty helpless black children. Municipal coffers had been drained by a lengthy investigation, which had until then failed to uncover the perpetrator of the grisly, inexplicable crimes. When Sammy volunteered his services for a benefit, Sinatra offered his collaboration. Coming from different parts of the country, the two flew into the city aboard private jets.

In *THE MANCHURIAN CANDIDATE, 1962.*

Atlanta Civil Center was crowded to the rafters for the concert. Midway through a three-hour performance, singer Roberta Flack and native Georgian Burt Reynolds added their presence. Receipts for the evening approached the $200,000 mark, with $145,000 coming from a sell-out assemblage of 4,600 (who paid from $25 to $1,000 for a seat) and the rest, from corporate donations and other sources. Spurred on by the show of citizen support of the concert and the cause, the Georgia legislature proceeded to vote a matching $200,000 for a continuing investigation by the police.

"I came here to express to the parents of the children brutally murdered," Sinatra said in an onstage statement, "my compassion and love. I weep with them and for them. You have my prayers it should end without further bloodshed." He added: "I will never waver in my contention that justice will prevail against dishonorable deeds. I love you and grieve for you, and pray that all of you will live in the sunshine of an eternity of peaceful tomorrows."

Sensitive about his own lack of formal education—how often has he expressed regret that he was a high school dropout—Sinatra has used his resources and talent to advance educational opportunities for young people. In the mid-sixties, he set up a program at UCLA in which he annually distributes monetary scholarships to ten outstanding students of music, a program that increased to

$10,000 in 1970 and, more recently, was raised by him to $12,500. Among the schools and colleges that have benefited from his bounty are the Los Angeles Music and Arts School, Buckley School of Beverly Hills, School of Fine Arts at New York University, De La Salle High School in New Orleans, University of Santa Clara, and, understandably, Hoboken High, which he left in his junior year.

It is said that in Hollywood, there is no softer touch than Frank. Among those who can bear witness—and received assistance without asking for it—one finds actors George Raft, who had tax problems; Bela Lugosi, who had drug problems; Lee J. Cobb, who had enormous hospital bills; the widow of Mocambo owner Charlie Morrison; restaurateur Mike Romanoff; and arranger-conductor-composer Don Costa, who suddenly required a bypass heart operation. When Judy Garland died Liza Minnelli found a four-figure check in her mailbox for funeral expenses. For the last three years of his life, Swifty Morgan, a hanger-on who had sold jewelry to the stars and had become indigent, had his hotel bills and meals paid for by Sinatra. When singers Sylvia Syms and Bob Eberle faced serious medical problems, it was Frank who came to the rescue. "Over the years," restaurateur Toots Shor told Earl Wilson, "Sinatra has given me $150,000." Actor Martin Gabel, who is himself well-heeled, has told of how he once admired a pair of evening pumps worn by Sinatra—and received six pairs a few days later.

With Judy Garland and her husband Sid Luft at Hollywood's Mocambo.

In addition to facilities that Sinatra has established like the Medical Education Center erected in memory of his father at Palm Springs, quite a number of other hospitals around the country and world have benefited from his largesse. Among these are the Atlantic City Medical Center, Cedars of Lebanon-Mt. Sinai in Los Angeles, Eisenhower Medical Center in Palm Springs, Memorial Sloan-Kettering Cancer Center in New York City, Children's Diabetes Foundation of Denver, Welfare of Blind in Iran, and Lenox Hill Hospital in New York City.

Although raising funds and garnering votes for politicos are hardly to be classed as "humanitarian" activities, they do involve performing without remuneration. Sinatra's contribution in this area dates back to the early days of his career when he ardently supported FDR — and this at a time when entertainers were not supposed to display their political preferences. Years later, in 1959, Sinatra waged a vigorous campaign, using contacts and concerts, to help John F. Kennedy launch his campaign for the presidency. After 1962 when his relationship with JFK, by then president, foundered, he seemed to sit on the political fence for a time.

The renewal of political activity came in 1970, when he abandoned a long-standing tie to the Democratic party and endorsed Ronald Reagan over Jesse Unruh in Reagan's second bid for the governorship of California. When Reagan launched his campaign for the presidency, Sinatra, abetted by Dean Martin, was an early fund-raiser and campaigner, starting with a highly successful concert in Boston.

Since the centennial year, Sinatra has concertized not infrequently, as he did even during the period of his retirement, in behalf of a variety of political figures, most of them on the Republican side of the fence. Among those who have been beneficiaries of his entertainment bounty, one can count Richard Nixon, Henry Kissinger, Spiro Agnew, New York Governor Hugh Carey, and others.

Joseph Cerrell, a Los Angeles Democratic political consultant who worked with Sinatra in 1959, told Robert Lindsey of *The New York Times* News Service that "no other entertainer has more ability to raise money for politicians at events such as $1,000-a-plate concert benefits than Sinatra."

"When he decides to help," Cerrell said, "it doesn't cost you anything. Just a simple phone call to him and he takes care of the whole thing. There aren't any bills for the orchestra, no bills for limousines. He buys his own block of tickets and pays for everything. People don't say no to him. They jump up in the air when he calls. He not only performs but also recruits business friends to perform and offers other kinds of help, such as lending his airplane for campaign trips."

At one of several fund-raisers at which Sinatra performed, Ronald Reagan, told a $1,000-a-plate audience at New York's Waldorf-Astoria: "It isn't every candidate who has a king in his corner."

What baffles Cerrell is that "when you get somebody who's even slightly tainted, people avoid him like the plague. But not Sinatra. In fact, it may add to his mystique." The taint was Sinatra's oft-publicized "friendships" with alleged members of organized crime.

Apart from his fund-raising craft, Sinatra unquestionably appeals to politicians because of his superstar status — something that was well demonstrated when Gotham politicians, including the Mayor and Governor, came to be photographed with him during the New York filming of *The First Deadly Sin*.

As for Sinatra, according to Cerrell, "he's still a little kid from Hoboken who likes to be stroked by Presidents. He does it for his ego. He likes the attention. And I've never heard him ask for anything. . . ." And he has been stroked by Richard Nixon, Gerald Ford, and JFK, as well as Ronald Reagan.

One of the high points of 1977 in the bustling life of New York City came on Wednesday evening, April 27, when Sinatra staged a charity bash of such dimensions that *The New York Times* reported the event in a long story with a six-column wide headline that read "Frank Sinatra Does It His Way — And a Crowd of Celebrities Turns Out for the Party." The crowd included top names in the theater, films, sports, government, society, and big corporate enterprise. The beneficiaries were the Lenox Hill Hospital and the Institute of Sports Medicine.

The evening began with a concert at Carnegie Hall, where Walter Cronkite served as master of ceremonies and Robert Merrill and Sinatra performed. "The scene outside the Hall was bedlam," *The Times* reported, "as celebrity-watchers were unable to identify most of the people stepping out of limousines. This is a hazard faced by the rich who have made their money in fields other than politics, sports, movies and television, and so are written off as 'nobodies' by such crowds."

The "nobodies" included people like the head of Warner Communications, who underwrote a good part of the evening; members of the Ford auto family; owners of Greek shipping liners; the heads of Tiffany's, 57 Varieties, Estee Lauder perfumes, Parnis dresses, and so on.

Among the "somebodies" spotted by the crowd were Claudette Colbert, Bella Abzug in a black picture hat, and Jacqueline Onassis in long white gloves.

Prices for concert tickets ranged from $10 to $250. Eight hundred tickets were sold for sums ranging from $500 to $5,000, and these entitled the holders to attend a supper-dance at the Waldorf-Astoria Hotel, hosted by New York Governor Carey. The Park Avenue entrance to the hotel was closed to the general public, as it had been on only one other occasion—a birthday party for President John F. Kennedy in 1963.

The supper-dance was held in two rooms—the Empire Room, renamed Frank's Place, and the Hilton Room, renamed Ol' Blue Eyes. Frank and his wife, Barbara, headed the list of celebrities in one room, along with Joe Namath, Claudette Colbert, the Iranian ambassador, Phyllis and Robert Wagner, and others. Across the way were Mrs. Onassis, Governor Carey, Robert Sarnoff, Ben Grauer, Howard Cosell, Anna Moffo and her husband, among others.

Both rooms had been transformed into Italian trattorias through the use of red-and-white-check tablecloths, white candles in wine bottles, and knives tied with red bows. Each table was loaded, trattoria-style, with buckets of vegetables, crocks of nuts and dried fruit, tubs of butter and cheese, and sausage and bread piled on boards.

"After several days of interminable negotiations," *The Times* explained, "approval was given [for Sinatra to be photographed] on the understanding that the name of the photographer would be submitted in advance, that each photographer would be conducted to his table separately, and that no more than a minute or two be allocated to each. And no interviews, here, and no further pictures of anyone else in the room in which Frank sat. After these logistics, which would have done credit to General Eisenhower and D-Day planning, photographers were led out to await similar ground rules in the next room."

The money raised for the two facilities, Lenox Hill Hospital and the Institute of Sports Medicine, was a record $750,000.

Even that figure was exceeded by one of two notable benefits in which Sinatra participated two years later. The concert of October 28, 1979, in behalf of the Memorial Sloan-Kettering Cancer Center, was held in Lincoln Center at the Metropolitan Opera House. Although the program included the Met's black diva, Shirley Verrett, as well as operatic baritone Robert Merrill and famous fiddler Itzhak Perlman, there was no doubt, in *Variety*'s words, "who sold the tickets at $100 and up for all that chemotherapy, or why Society with a capital $ was present."

Said benefit cochairwoman, Phyllis (Cerf) Wagner: "It's been amazing. We started planning back in June. On the first day, we sold over $80,000 worth of tickets."

Even though Frank said, "I'm out of my class tonight," the name of the game was "Sinatra at the Met." An enthusiastic audience of 4,000, which shouted "Bravo" at the end of his stint, did not agree. Neither did Beverly Sills, master of ceremonies, who noted the classic dimensions of the evening in her opening remarks: It was the largest pre-sold benefit for charity on record; it was the first time that the director of the New York City Opera (herself) ever appeared on the stage of the Met; and it was also Frankie Boy's first appearance at the Met after four decades of singing—a forty-year journey uptown from the old, defunct Paramount Theatre.

After Sinatra had delivered a dozen songs in his easy, beguiling style, Laurance Rockefeller, benefit chairman, presented him with a white doctor's jacket inscribed, "Francis Sinatra, M.D." Rockefeller kidded: "Probably means Director of Music."

"More likely—multiple drinker," Sinatra countered and added: "Let me know if you need money." Turning to Beverly Sills he said: "A funny thing happened to me on the way to the Paramount. Just think if I'd gone operatic, today it would be Beverly Sills and me. What a team—Bubbles and Troubles!"

Bubbles and Troubles did team up with Robert Merrill, each standing behind a music stand, to sing "What's in the Daily News," one of the showstoppers in the stage and screen musical *Guys and Dolls*. Employing special lyrics, doubtless written for the occasion by the master of special lyrics, Sammy Cahn, and though it was obviously not too well rehearsed, the number brought the house down. It was a memorable ending to a memorable benefit-concert that raised more than $1 million for cancer research, making it, in the words of an official, "one of the most successful benefits in the history of New York City."

The significance of "Sinatra at the Met" went beyond the large sum of money grossed by it. The event was dominated not only by Society, with a capital $, but by Big Business. The list of 20-odd underwriters read like a file of *Fortune* magazine's top 100 corporations. One of the sponsors, as a memorial to her late husband, picked up the tab for the rental of the Met, thereby making the income from ticket sales net, or close to it.

Headlining its lengthy coverage, "*Sinatra at the Met*: $1,100,000 from Beautiful Monied People," *Variety* observed: "The benefit may well serve as a capstan of fundraising technology and of the Sinatra phenomenon."

The pattern of big business involvement, apparent in the Carnegie Hall–Waldorf-Astoria benefit of 1977, was also manifest in a legendary benefit in which Sinatra participated on September 27, 1979, just a month before "Sinatra at the Met." It was then that he sang at the foot of one of the Seven Wonders of the World—the Sphinx and the Pyramids just outside Cairo. Again, the sum of money raised was astronomical. And again, the benefit assumed a significance beyond its immediate humanitarian impulses.

Sinatra's appearance was in behalf of Cairo's Faith and Hope Rehabilitation Center. A favorite charity of Mrs. Jehan Sadat, the wife of Egypt's President Anwar Sadat, the 4,000-bed center was designed to help those suffering from birth defects, brain damage, and ailments considered incurable. Frank favored holding the benefit in the United States. But Mrs. Sadat, concerned with building Egypt's tourism and industry, wanted Sinatra to reverse the Moses syndrome and lead travelers and business back into Egypt. Frank agreed, provided that not less than half-a-million dollars would be realized for the hospital.

The co-chairmen of "Three Extraordinary Days on the Nile" were the Chairman of the Board of Revlon, Inc., Michel Bergerac, and the Chairman of the Board of Pan-American World Airways, William T. Seawell. Pan-American, which did not as yet have ingress into Egypt, provided a charter flight on a 707 for which the cost was $1,700. (Accompanied by Mrs. Sinatra, Jilly Rizzo, and lawyer Mickey Rudin, Sinatra jetted in on a Panama Polar flight from Los Angeles to London where Anwar Sadat's private Gulfstream 2 jet picked him up for the journey to Cairo.)

Other companies that sponsored the event or came for a look-see at Egypt's business potential included Metromedia (John E. Kluge); film producers Joseph E. Levine and David Brown, the latter accompanied by Helen Gurley Brown, editor of *Cosmopolitan*; Peat Marwick & Mitchell, one of the world's largest accounting firms; fashion designer Pierre Balmain; jeweler Nicholas Bulgari; Boeing Corporation; Newhouse Newspapers; and *TV Guide*. It was less a showbiz than a jet set-Dun & Bradstreet crowd of 400, with representatives of brokerage, communications, pharmaceutical, advertising, and banking firms, mingling with princes, dukes, and other titled figures from all over Europe and Asia.

Egyptian workers, it was reported, labored for two months to transform the area in front of the Pyramids into a huge tented ballroom, laying thousands of feet of carpets to cover the sand. Balmain put on a fashion show for the ladies and an entertainment, including bellydancers and a whirling dervish. But the major attraction of the three-day gala was Sinatra, who rose grandly to the occasion and to a beg-off, standing ovation so protracted that he had to explain he had not rehearsed additional material.

"It might have been one of the wealthiest audiences he's ever played for," *Variety* commented. "The jewels of the ladies present conceivably could have paid off Egypt's national debt." In a concluding observation, *Variety* pinpointed the broader impact of Sinatra's contribution: "He did much to develop Las Vegas, and he is now demonstrating the power of entertainers to aid in the development of an entire nation."

An article that appeared in *The New York Times*, subsequent to the Egyptian concert, aroused the ire of the *Los Angeles Herald-Examiner*'s James Bacon, who lead off an article correcting the *Times* story with the sentence: "The more I travel with Frank Sinatra, the more I side with him in his famous battles with the media."

According to the *Times*'s Cairo correspondent, "a well-placed insider" averred that Frank's expenses were paid for him and his retinue. The article also implied that Frank wanted to do a TV special and record album, thereby profiting from Mrs. Sadat's charity benefit.

"Nothing could be further from the truth," Bacon stated flatly. "The trip cost Frank close to $100,000 out of his own pocket" in expenses for himself and his personal retinue and musicians. Bacon broke the figure down in detail.

As for the TV special, Frank had considered it as "a way of underwriting the enormous cost" of bringing almost fifty additional musicians and their equipment from London. When "their expenses were paid by the 30-odd sponsoring corporations of the Gala—all of whom had vested interests in Egypt," the TV special was discarded. "At no time," Bacon wrote, "was a record album even considered."

On February 15, 1980, a Valentine Day's love-in was staged by "Frank, His Friends, and His Food" in behalf of the Desert Hospital in Palm Springs. A home-cooked Sicilian dinner was prepared at Sinatra's nearby Rancho Mirage home and brought to the Canyon Hotel, where the benefit concert was held. It included round, hearth-baked Italian bread flown in at Sinatra's behest and expense from the S. Giordano Bakery in Newark, New Jersey. Among the star entertainers who generously gave of their talent were Rich Little as emcee, Debby Boone, John Denver, comic Pat Henry as well as Frank.

Seated at tables, decorated Valentine-Day style, were luminaries like the Gerald Fords, Walter Annenbergs, Spiro Agnews, Danny Thomases, Marvin Davises of Denver, Glenn Fords, Peter Falks, Dinah Shore, Lucille Ball, and Gene Autry, among others. Guests left the evening's festivities with a tote bag containing mementoes of the event as well as Sinatra's forthcoming album, *Trilogy*.

Despite problems of transportation, occasioned by roads that had been washed away by heavy desert rains, Sinatra succeeded in attracting more than 1,000 guests, each of whom paid $1,500. Two million dollars was raised for the hospital's building fund. An announcement was made that the new five-story addition to the hospital would be named The Sinatra Tower, and Frank left the festivities with a miniature replica of the cornerstone of the building.

Another Palm Springs facility, the Desert Museum, boasts the Frank Sinatra Sculptured Court—the building was donated by Sinatra.

Together with "his illustrious friends, Luciano Pavarotti and George Shearing," as the advertisement read, Sinatra presented *An Evening of Glorious Music* at the Radio City Music Hall in New York City on Sunday evening, January 24, 1982. Seats were priced at $50 and $100. Preferred tickets at $250, $500, $1,250 and $1,500 entitled the holder to admission to a post-performance party at the Rainbow Room. The evening was another benefit for the Memorial Sloan-Kettering Cancer Center, for which Sinatra had already helped raise over $2 million. It brought the total of the money he helped raise for the facility to over $4 million.

Just one week later, on Sunday evening, January 31, Sinatra journeyed to Washington, D.C., where he acted as master of ceremonies at the world premiere of the film *Genocide*, a multi-media documentary on the Holocaust. The showing was at the Eisenhower Theatre of the Kennedy Center for the Performing Arts, for an audience of 1,100 members of Congress, government employees,

With opera great Luciano Pavarotti.

survivors of the concentration camps, and people from the Washington, Baltimore, and Los Angeles Jewish communities.

Thirty months in the making, the film was produced under the auspices of and presented by the Simon Wiesenthal Center, toward the establishment of which Sinatra had given the first sizable donation. The center is located on the campus of Yeshiva University of Los Angeles.

In introducing Simon Wiesenthal, whose dedication and activities have led to the capture of over 1,000 Nazi war criminals, Sinatra said: "I would gladly give up every song I ever sang to rest my head on the pillow of his accomplishments."

To Elizabeth Taylor, who served gratis as co-narrator (with Orson Welles) of the film, Sinatra presented a framed *Genocide* poster. He was himself presented with a poster and accepted one for Orson Welles, who was not present due to illness.

As she received the framed poster, Elizabeth Taylor said: "What happened was real and it could happen again. Some people today think it was fictitious, but it was true and it must never happen again."

At the conclusion of the film, Sinatra said: "At this point, words are more than inadequate. It was a total eclipse of mankind when the countrymen of Bach and Beethoven became the custodians of Auschwitz and Treblinka."

6. "The House I Live In": The Man

As a man, Sinatra is complex, contradictory, and controversial. Although he says that he has grown tired of singing "My Way," he has shaped his career and ordered his life *his* way. Headstrong as well as hot-tempered, he has always said: Don't tell me, suggest.

Aware that the press has greatly contributed to his rise and popularity, and a masterful manipulator of the media, he has, nevertheless, allowed reporters and columnists to involve him in public confrontations that have elicited widespread and unfavorable publicity. The bad boy image has not been helped by his admitted friendships with notorious mobsters.

Yet the startling fact is that neither of these well-publicized aspects of his career has alienated friends in the film capital—Gregory Peck, Cary Grant, Burt Lancaster, Kirk Douglas—or in the country's capital—President Ronald Reagan. Nor has his popularity suffered. On the contrary controversy adds to his marquee value and his following. He is sui generis.

Unswerving in his loyalty to his friends he has been equally considerate, if not solicitous, in his relationships with his ex-wives. Despite his early divorce from the mother of his three children, he has kept a tight rein on them and remained a warm, caring father. Now he is showering grandchildren with affection and outsize gifts.

Ex-wife Nancy Sinatra has said that she has never known a man with a greater capacity for love. He has himself admitted to "an over-acute capacity for sadness," which, he says, his present wife has done much to help him control.

His appeal to the females of the world has not dimmed with time. "I don't care how old he is," Peggy Lipton has said, "He turns me on."

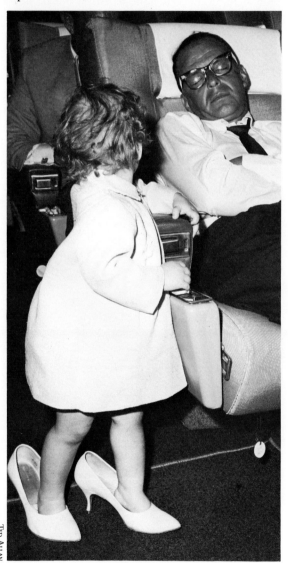

TED ALLAN

In October 1974, shortly after Frank re-entered the world of entertainment, Thomas Thompson, former editor of *Life* and a man who had gotten to know Frank well, respecting him and being respected in turn, wrote an article in *McCall's* titled "Understanding Sinatra." If that gives the impression that Thompson was about to provide the key to the man, the reader was in for a letdown. A key sentence in Thompson's piece read: "I cannot begin to understand this man—indeed, I doubt if he understands himself."

Thompson went on to narrate two incidents that occurred the first time he went to interview Sinatra on the eve of his 50th birthday in 1965. It was in a penthouse suite at the Eden Roc Hotel in Miami Beach, where Frank was then performing. Some time after the interview began Frank slipped out of the room to give some instructions to an aide. Thompson later learned that the aide had arranged for a substantial check to be sent for medical expenses to a child that had been severely burned, a situation that Sinatra had learned about from a small item in a local newspaper. But that evening, after he had imbibed freely, he took a catsup bottle and emptied the red sauce onto an adoring friend's tuxedo and dress shirt. The friend stood there, with the gook dripping down, embarrassed and humiliated, not saying a word, before 40 or 50 people in Sinatra's party. "Frank thought it was hugely funny," Thompson commented, "but I felt pain for the man."

Now, how does one reconcile the two incidents— the one, revealing a person of deep feeling for the suffering of others, and the second, exposing a man of little sensitivity, little kindness, and much arrogance? In attempting to provide a possible clue to such antithetical behavior, Thompson writes: "One key to Frank is that he relishes power. He revels in it more than any public figure I can think of. . . . Perhaps his reasoning is that because he has occupied for so long a time the summit position in show business, this entitles him to sit as an equal at the table of other kings—those of industry, medicine, politics, government. . . . "

It is hardly a secret that Sinatra does view himself as a king among kings. Even when he is "kidding," the ego is apparent: "Welcome to the Palace of the Caesars," he greets the audience at the Circus Maximus showroom, "where resides the noblest Roman of them all—me!" In accepting the Variety Clubs International Humanitarian of the Year Award from Princess Grace (Kelly) of Monaco, he said: "I propose a toast to her Serene Highness Princess Grace and to her royal crown. And to my Crown Royal."

How do other people see him—family, friends, columnists who are or have been close to him?

Columnist James Bacon: "His moods are as varied as his songs. When he's charming Cary Grant could take lessons from him. When he isn't, Muhammad Ali should. . . . Probably the main reason that Frank has people like Jilly and comedian Pat Henry around him much of the time is because Frank doesn't like to be alone. . . . Frank is probably the most complex man in show business. And that, of course, is what makes him Frank. . . ."

TV's Barbara Walters: Writing of the ten men she found most appealing in 1971: "Frank Sinatra because of his old-fashioned courtliness. . . . I can vouch for the fact that he treats women as if they were made of glass. He's as concerned with their comfort and dignity as a Victorian. He has another little-known quality—grace."

Daughter Nancy: "I've never known a man with such a large capacity for love. . . . he never finished school but he's a self-educated man who reads everything. His capacity for loving and sharing is just as great as his capacity for learning. . . . Although Mom and Dad were divorced . . . he was always there [at Christmas]. And he and Mom got along beautifully, as they still do."

Son Frank, Jr.: "They say my father is a difficult man. In some ways, I suppose that's true. But I've known him as a father and our relationship has been wonderful. He does have a temper, yes, but the man has been through a lot in his lifetime. Few people could understand completely the pressures he's faced—and beaten. As his son, I have no complaints. I think he's the greatest. And lots of other people in this town agree with me."

Actress Rosalind Russell: "Frank Sinatra is an American classic. . . . To be Frank's friend is like one of his songs: *All or Nothing at All*. It is a total, unconditional commitment, a never-fraying security blanket. . . . To describe Sinatra in one word I respond without hesitation: *compassionate*. I have never seen him refuse a child anything. . . . There are several Sinatras. Perhaps this is what makes him both fascinating and controversial. He is tempestuous, tender, searching, indefatigable, unexpected. As a father, he is doting, generous, always involved. . . . The perfect host, there is [also] Sinatra the loner, the constant observer, a profoundly sensitive man."

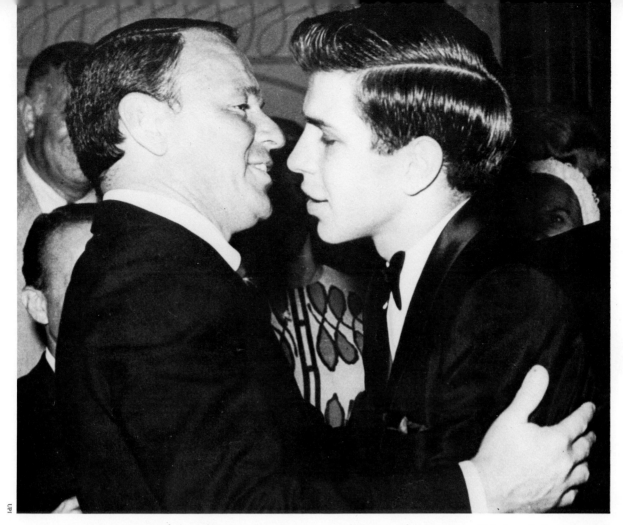

Actor Burt Lancaster: "My feeling about Frank is that he is basically a lonely person. . . . Maybe that is why Frank is always having a big bunch of hangers-on about him. He's a marvellous host. . . . He always has had strong feelings about the rights of people, coming as he does from a background in which Italian people were legislated against in the early days much as blacks and Chicanos are today [1972]. Frank is very, very independent of spirit. . . . He is a man of fierce loyalties. . . . He is a very paternalistic man and worries about his daughters. . . . He is a very stern father — fair-minded but stern. . . . Is Frank a happy man? I don't know. I don't know if it is possible for him to be happy in the sense that we think of happiness. Frank is too sensitive a man, too involved in problems that are personal, and also problems that are related to the conditions in the world, not to be distressed by them. . . . "

Journalist Richard Schickel: "In real life, he is a man of mercurial moods, sudden generosity, and equally sudden temper, of fierce loyalty to friends and implacable hatred."

Former Vice-President Spiro Agnew: "If Frank Sinatra lived to be a hundred, he would never get back even a small portion of the loyalty and kindness he has bestowed on others. I am proud to be his friend."

There is clearly a core of agreement among these selected commentators. What surfaces from their reactions is that Sinatra is a complex man, the complexity deriving from a cluster of contradictions. How many men are not a combination of black-and-white stripes? But Sinatra stands forth as the engaging and beguiling personality he is because these clashing characteristics coexist at such a tense and elevated level. His has grace but he can be vulgar. A compassionate friend, he is an unforgiving enemy. Sensitive to slights, he can be imperiously arrogant. Bookish, well-read, and well-spoken, he can spew forth street expletives like a gutter kid. He is gregarious but a lonely man. A flamboyant extrovert, he can be moody and introverted. Patient and a perfectionist in his work, he can be recklessly intemperate. Generous and kind, he can be surly and ornery. A champion of the little man, he has been known to mistreat little people. The man who says, "Don't tell me. . . suggest," and who has always done things *his* way, is a composite not merely of opposites but of violent and explosive extremes.

Frank, Jr. gets fatherly support as he makes his singing debut at the Flamingo Hotel in Las Vegas, 1963.

Musicians and friends all regard Sinatra as a facile and bright talker whose mind roves over many areas (as a result of wide reading during sleepless nights) and who displays an engaging sense of humor. When he appeared at Caesars Palace in January 1980, the following resolutions for 1980 were part of his show as transcribed by Elliot S. Krane of the *Las Vegas Sun*:

1. Give up drinking all day on February 30.

2. Not get upset with the crummy press unless they deserve it and I will be the judge.

3. Do all I can to keep the Ayatollah Kockamami in good health until I can get him over here and show him on a trip to the Grand Canyon, personally. I talked to Red Eyes [Dean Martin] and he said if the Duke were alive, between the Duke, Red Eyes, and me, we would barbecue him.

4. Boycott Rona Barrett, Chuck Barris, and Iranian oil—all of which give me gas.

5. Pay my income taxes with rubber checks so I can bounce them around April 15 the way the IRS bounces us around the rest of the year.

6. Help little old ladies and Dean Martin cross the street whenever I can.

7. Stop referring to the colored cat who sings "Candy Man" as Smokey, treat him with the dignity he deserves, and refer to him with his given name, "Sambo Davis, Jr."

8. Be kind to dumb animals including all cats, dogs, and reporters from the National Enquirer.

9. Stop losing in the casino unless they stop keeping a closer eye on me.

10. Stop smoking—as in the shower.

11. Help my fellow man even if this means seeing that Don Rickles gets laryngitis the rest of the year.

12. Play more golf and give up using golf carts to conserve power. That way it will give more exercise to my throne-bearers.

13. Do everything I can to help the best man get elected President even if it means digging up Millard Fillmore, Abe Lincoln, or one of those other cats—or Tom Mix.

14. Tell no more Polish jokes. After all they are a wonderful people and it's wrong to make fun of an entire nation just because it takes seven of them to change a light bulb.

15. Do more to help my country and start by sending the President and Congress tubes of Crazy Glue to brush their teeth with.

16. Finally, in 1980 and all the years that follow: I resolve to love you more than ever and to hope for your wishes and dreams during the day every day of the year and to pray for your health and happiness and for your families every night of my life—and I mean that. God Bless You!

As an entertainer, Sinatra possesses that elusive quality known as "charisma." When he struts or saunters onstage, all eyes are drawn magnetically to him, regardless of how many people are with him. Actress Peggy Lipton has said: "I don't care how old he is. He turns me on." To Marlene Dietrich, he was "The Mercedes-Benz of men!" One of "America's most sensuous men," is how columnist Joyce Haber described him. Sex apart, he commands attention among men wherever he is.

Director Stanley Kramer said after the filming of *The Pride and the Passion*: "When Sinatra walks in a room, tension walks in beside him. You don't always know why. But if he's tense, he spreads it."

Others have tried to define, if not deal with, his *intimidating* presence, sensed by at least one writer when Sinatra was just exiting a plane and entering a waiting limousine. Here is how a *Rolling Stone* reporter described his arrival for a concert in 1974: "The door [of the shiny blue-and-white jet] rolls back, and for about five seconds—which is what it takes for him to slip into the limo gunning its engine at his feet—Sinatra can be glimpsed.

"He waves at an idolatrous fan, who is straining to get her Instamatic close, and to a few dozen passersby. That is all. No words. No stopping for pictures. Just a blurred vision of a man dressed in black vanishing into the back of a limo. With squads flashing ahead and behind, the car slides out into the expressway and disappears. The whole thing doesn't last three minutes. *The sense of raw power is frightening.*" (My italics.)

On the occasion of Sinatra's 65th birthday, longtime columnist Pete Hamill adverted to the same impact: "The Sinatra aura," he wrote, "goes beyond talent and craft. He is not simply a fine popular singer. He emanates power and danger. And the reason is simple: you think he is tangled up with the mob."

The reason is not that simple. It doubtless has something to do with what people think. But it also has something, and perhaps more, to do with what he has done. Power? No singer in popular music has maintained a hold on the public for as long as Sinatra. No showman has contributed as much to charity or played as many benefits, and in so many countries. No entertainer has developed friendships with as many figures in high places. No performer has been honored as frequently by as many different organizations.

Power and danger? Is there any other performer who has reacted as violently and unpredictably in public as Frank?

"Write about his guts," the dean of American songwriters, Irving Berlin, told columnist Earl Wilson. "He may have been wrong many times. But he had the guts to stand up for his position, whether it was the government, or a country, or whoever the hell it was!"

From way back, Sinatra has been unafraid to challenge authority, to speak his mind, to insist on doing things his way. He has left rehearsals, terminated agreements—and at least once, after he had arrived to start shooting on a film *(Carousel)*, walked out of a contract to enforce his position.

Not too long ago a photographer told the story of how Sinatra, appearing on an ABC-TV series back in the '50s, had invited him to shoot stills onstage at the old El Capitan Theatre in Hollywood. When the show began taping and the director spotted the photog, he ordered him offstage.

When the photog explained that Sinatra had okayed his shooting, the director said: "I don't give a damn what Mr. Sinatra said. I'm the director and I'm telling you to get off the stage—now!"

As the photog began to leave Sinatra came out of his dressing room, put his arm around the lenser's shoulder, and began walking offstage with him.

"Frank, Frank, where are you going?" the director asked.

"If this place isn't good enough for my friend," he replied, "it's not good enough for me."

After the two had taken several more steps, the director's voice came over the speaker: "OK, Frank, OK. He can stay."

Sinatra has asserted himself in more demonstrative ways. Early in his career, as he became an out-spoken soap-boxer for tolerance and New Deal liberalism, he became the target of a number of Hearst columnists. Another performer would have backed down, terminated his political activities, and/or wooed his critics. Not Sinatra. He traded blow for blow. Eventually, his animus toward Lee Mortimer of the *New York Mirror* led to his taking a poke at the columnist. It was an expensive form of retaliation, setting Sinatra back $25,000 in an out-of-court settlement and legal fees. About the same time he sent Dorothy Kilgallen of the *New York Journal-American*, with whom he had also been feuding, a tombstone.

Sinatra also began using the media available to him for repartee with his detractors. In appearances at the Copa in New York and the Sands in Las Vegas, he would refer to Kilgallen as "the chinless wonder" and compare her face to that of a chipmunk. It was devastating to the woman, who thought of herself as something of a beauty, and she persisted in sniping at him until her death. Sinatra has continued, up to the present, to use his monologues in club and concert appearances to vent his anger against given columnists and newspapers. In recent years he has directed his vitriolic spears at Hollywood columnist-TV commentator Rona Barrett. A number of reviewers have reacted unfavorably to this type of "verbal abuse," feeling that it is an unworthy interruption of the mood created by his music. Audiences seem to accept, if not to expect, it from Sinatra, the battler. It accords with their image of him as a man of independent mind and guts.

His assaults on press people have not, of course, been limited to onstage, teacup comments between song segments. Earl Wilson of the *New York Post* was a longtime friendly columnist when a story with his byline about Sinatra's altercation with a Sands casino executive infuriated the singer. As Joe Hyams was then Sinatra's prime West Coast news outlet, Wilson was his East Coast outlet of information. Nevertheless when Earl showed up at a Sinatra opening at the Fontainebleau in Miami Beach not long afterward, he was barred from entering the showroom. Sinatra had told the management he would not perform if Wilson, who had flown down from New York City, was in the room. It was almost seven years before Frank moved to heal the breach. (When Sammy Davis, Jr., who was a close friend and idolized Frank, made some offhand comments during a radio interview about Sinatra's treatment of little people, which Frank did not like, Sinatra severed his relationship with Sammy and had him written out of a film [*Never So Few*] in which Davis was slated to appear. The breach was healed the following year when Davis appeared on a benefit show for retarded children, emceed by Frank and Dino.)

During the 1970s two confrontations with media people garnered heavy press coverage. In 1973 it was the abrasive, four-lettered epithets with which Frank responded to a provocative query by Maxine Cheshire of *The Washington Post*.

There were no four-letter words in Sinatra's confrontation with the Australian media the following year. But his characterization of press people from the stage where he was performing in Melbourne as "parasites" and "hookers" led to a deadlock—resolved when his lawyer met with Australia's top labor leader—in which the Aussie unions refused to service either his plane or his lodgings.

That there was provocation is as apparent as that Sinatra's reaction was intemperate.

Since these explosive incidents, among others, were extensively aired and rehashed in the media, they seem to embody Sinatra's relationship with the media. This really is not so. For every columnist and reporter with whom he has had run-ins, there are an equal number and more with whom he has cordial relations. It is easy to think of Joe Hyams of the New York *Herald-Tribune*, James Bacon of the *Los Angeles Herald-Examiner*, Joyce Haber and Leonard Feather of the *Los Angeles Times*, Suzy of the New York *Daily News*, Thomas Thompson of *Life*, among others, all media people with whom he has had friendly contact over long periods of time. A much longer list could be set down of freelance writers, including the author of this tome, who have done interviews and written analytical pieces without encountering any unpleasantness.

Thomas Thompson has said: "Reviewing some of the press clippings and magazine articles over the years, I find little to back up Sinatra's claim that he has been mistreated. All in all, Frank has gotten good press."

When he is in a relaxed frame Sinatra himself does not really disagree. Invited to a White House photographers' dinner in April 1977, which he regretted he could not attend, he wrote: "As you may know, I have many good friends in the press who, unfortunately, have thus far refused to identify themselves and go public." Kidding aside, he added: "Having spent the last 40 years in the glare of photographers' flashbulbs, I have suffered through a few bad moments. Let it be known, however, that for the other 90 percent of the time, the press has contributed greatly to what we laughingly refer to as my career and that without its indulgence, I might still be a band singer in Hoboken."

In retrospect it seems clear that Sinatra's occasional intemperate outbursts and use of abusive and unprintable epithets have not really hurt him. Columnists and editors have chided him while some of the more friendly newspaper people have been abashed. But as for the general public, it apparently views his brash and reckless conduct with admiration, approving what seems to it a rare manifestation of self-confidence and courage.

Sinatra's explosive reaction to Maxine Cheshire, as we later learned from Jim Bacon, was prompted by the question "Do you think that your Mafia connections will hurt the chances of your friend Spiro Agnew if he decides to run for the presidency?" Whether he answered "No," or "I doubt it," or "Hardly," or anything at all, he was boxed in by a loaded question to which a reply involved an implicit admission of "Mafia connections."

Bacon went on to say: "As for the Mafia, Frank knows Mafia bosses. So does every other big entertainer who ever worked Las Vegas, Miami Beach, Chicago or New York. The Mafia owns the saloons. Frank, a saloon singer, has to deal with these boys if he wants a hall to perform in. That doesn't mean that Frank is a member of the Mafia or even that he upholds them."

Frank himself told Neil Hickey in a 1977 *TV Guide* interview: "I know a lot of those guys. People have said to me: 'Why do you have friends in the Mob?' I say: 'I was not *friends* with them.' They say: 'Do you know so-and-so?' I say: 'No, but I've met him.' When the Copacabana was open, there wasn't one guy in show business who didn't meet them. Let them buy you a drink. So I've stopped trying to explain that to people. I was having dinner with Rosalind Russell once, and I said: 'Why don't they get off my back about this thing?' She said: 'Forget it. If they had anything to go on, you'd have been indicted years ago.'"

But they have not gotten off his back, and he has had to keep parrying accusations about acquaintanceships with Mafia figures. It all started when a trip to Cuba in 1947 yielded stories of his spending time in the company of Charles "Lucky" Luciano and the Chicago Fischettis, cousins of Al Capone. Later, when a smitten Sinatra was pursuing Ava Gardner, a telegram came to light in which New Jersey mobster Willie Moretti, a neighbor of Frank's, urged him to consider his family responsibilities. Then around 1962, Sinatra was one of a group of entertainers, including Dean Martin, Sammy Davis, Jr., and Eddie Fisher, who apparently appeared without pay at a Sam "Momo" Giancana nightclub just outside Chicago, the Villa Venice, which included an illegal gambling casino. (FBI bugs had picked up an earlier discussion between Giancana and a lieutenant who had suggested killing Sinatra and some of his show business friends because he had failed to get Attorney General Robert Kennedy off their backs, and Giancana had indicated that he had other plans, presumably the appearances at the Villa Venice.) In 1976 and 1977 Sinatra gave concerts at the Westchester Premiere Theater in Tarrytown, New York, which later turned out to be a syndicate swindle that netted prison terms for those involved in skimming and bankrupting the theater. A widely circulated photograph showed Sinatra backstage in the company of a group of Mafiosi, including Carlo Gambino, the New York Godfather, and hit man Jimmy Fratianno, later the source of the book *The Last Mafioso*.

Sinatra was compelled to give up his Nevada gaming license and to sell his shares in two casinos as a result of the presence at one of them of Chicago mobster Sam Giancana, who was listed in the Nevada Black Book of undesirables. Sinatra also became briefly involved as an investor in the Berkshire Downs racetrack, which turned out to be a syndicate undertaking.

Some of these allegations led to a then-unpublicized Justice Department investigation and report, dated August 3, 1962, in which it was stated that Frank had been "in contact with about ten of the best-known gangsters in the country in the late 1950s and early 1960s." Although nothing more substantial than "contact" was alleged, it was this report, ostensibly shown by Attorney General Robert Kennedy to his brother John Fitzgerald Kennedy, that caused the President to bypass the Sinatra compound on a visit to Palm Springs and to lodge briefly instead at the home of Bing Crosby.

Periodically since then various publications have rehashed the allegations of guilt by association, most recently when President-elect Ronald Reagan named Sinatra to stage his Inaugural Gala in 1981. When queried about the allegations Reagan said: "We've heard these things about Frank for years, and we just hope none of them are true." But Reagan had already given evidence of his confidence in Sinatra when Reagan did not object to the singer's including Reagan's name in June 1980 as a reference on Sinatra's application for a new Nevada gaming license.

The bid for a license as a "key employee" had been initiated by Caesars Palace early in 1980 when it undertook to retain Frank as a consultant on entertainment and special event promotions at a salary of $40,000 annually. By March 1980 the Nevada Gaming Control Board voted to conduct a worldwide investigation into Sinatra's associations, finances, and background. On February 11, 1981, in a five-hour session, the three-member panel heard the testimony of a group of character witnesses, including actors Gregory Peck and Kirk Douglas, Los Angeles Sheriff Peter Pitchess, and a number of prominent Nevadans, among them *Las Vegas Sun* publisher Hank Greenspun and Nevada University Chancellor Donald Baepler.

In his appearance before the board Sinatra denied point-by-point all of the allegations that he had ties with organized crime figures. Rejecting the claim that he had played host to Sam Giancana at the Cal-Neva Lodge in 1963 when his license was revoked, he asserted that he was in L.A. at the time that the crime boss stayed at the lodge of which he was then part owner. As for the charge that he appeared gratis at the Villa Venice, his attorneys produced tax reports and contracts to show that he was paid $15,000.

Sinatra denied that Jersey mobster Willie Moretti had used strongarm tactics to get him out of his contract with bandleader Tommy Dorsey. Sinatra denied allegations that he had served as a courier in 1947, delivering $2 million in cash to narcotics crime kingpin Lucky Luciano in Cuba. He denied knowledge of a $9-million bankruptcy fraud, maneuvered by the syndicate at the Westchester Premiere Theatre. When queried about the oft-reprinted photograph of himself and a group of mobsters, he stated that he was a victim of circumstances: It was supposed to be a picture just of himself and Carlo Gambino's granddaughter—and that he had no way of preventing the others from joining in.

"In every instance," as reported in the Las Vegas *Valley Times*, "Sinatra's testimony was backed up by Control Board agents who repeatedly testified that they could find no evidence to back up the allegations."

At the conclusion of the hearing, board chairman Richard Bunker stated: "Every allegation that we looked at and followed through to its ultimate conclusion has failed to bear out what has been carried in the press for the last several years."

The Gaming Control Board voted unanimously to recommend that Sinatra be granted a "key employees' license," stipulating only that it be a 6-month conditional license. But at a two-hour hearing a week later, the parent gaming commission voted 4-to-1 to eliminate the limitation, thereby granting him an unlimited license.

Noting that the six agents investigating the case had not found any substance to the allegations against Sinatra, commission chairman Harry Reid said: "The case against Mr. Sinatra is a figment of newspaper stories."

But what the newspaper stories have done is to create an aura that titillates the public. Instead of hurting his appeal as a performer, the notoriety and allegations have constantly increased Sinatra's power at the box office. Harking back to Pete Hamill's astute observation: "Sinatra is not simply a fine popular singer. He emanates power and danger."

Aura aside, Sinatra's growth as an artist was accompanied by growth as a powerhouse businessman. When disc jockey William B. Williams dubbed Sinatra Chairman of the Board, the title was a toast to his supremacy as a singer. But after a time it had equal relevance to his position as an entrepreneur.

The business impulse had its origin during Frank's days with Tommy Dorsey, who was as sharp a businessman as he was a bandleader and who early set an example as a magnate of interlocking interests in music —publisher, manager, booker, as well as batoneer. A major turning point of Sinatra's career and life came, as we know, in the early '50s, when his loss of following saw him set adrift by the companies that had been promoting and profiting from his talent. Columbia Records, for whom he had sold millions of discs and was to continue selling into "eternity," did not renew its contract. MCA, the giant talent agency that had effortlessly booked him for years, dropped him. And the film companies for whom he had been box-office suddenly had no roles for him. It was then that Sinatra determined he would never again be beholden to anyone for work—and the business tycoon was born.

The turnaround came in 1954, when the Oscar for his role in *From Here to Eternity* transformed him into a hot film property. The years from 1955 into 1957 were crowded with movie-making and starring roles in films like *Suddenly*, *The Man with the Golden Arm*, *Pal Joey*, and others. But Sinatra's eyes were fixed on independent production. By 1956 he was the producer of *Johnny Concho*, a position he took up again in *Sergeants 3* (1962), *Robin and the 7 Hoods* (1964), and *None But the Brave* (1965), adding in *None But the Brave* the chores of director.

In 1957 *Pal Joey* was co-produced by his Essex company, which also co-produced *Sergeants 3* and *Come Blow Your Horn* (1963). In 1959 his own Sincap company produced *A Hole in the Head*, a critically-acclaimed film based on a Broadway comedy whose rights he had acquired earlier. Through the '60s, he organized additional companies like Arcola and Sinatra Enterprises, co-producing films like *Assault on a Queen*, *The Naked Runner*, *Tony Rome*, *The Detective*, and *Lady in Cement*.

By 1961 Frank launched his own record label (Reprise), which he merged three years later with Warner Bros. Records in a deal whereby he retained a one-third interest and received capital gains on a sales price of $10 million. As in the mid-'50s when ABC-TV handed him a check for $3 million for a series of shows, he carried the check given to him by Jack Warner in his billfold for days before depositing it. What a feeling to have that much money in hand, not merely the sense of power but remembering the days when he was happy to get 75¢ from a New Jersey radio station for carfare; the Harry James year when a pot of spaghetti, cooked by his first wife, constituted a feast for the boys in the band; and the tense Ava

Gardner period in the early '50s when she reportedly had to foot some of their bills.

Sinatra's business interests were much broader than his interests in films and records. In the fall of 1961, after spending two months with Frank, British author Robin Douglas-Home indicated that Sinatra's involvement in various projects and enterprises were said to "gross somewhere around $20 million a year." These enterprises, in addition to Essex Productions, the film company, and Reprise, the record company, included four music-publishing corporations, a string of radio stations (with Danny Kaye as his partner), two casinotels in Nevada, and investments in real estate, banks, and loan companies.

The control center for this financial complex was then located in a suite in the City National Bank Building on a knoll of Sunset Bouvelard. "Every month in Suite 512," Douglas-Home reported, "there is a brain-storming session attended by Sinatra and his lieutenants. It starts sharp at 10:30 A.M. and can last late into the evening without a break. Lunch is sent up from Romanoff's and the discussions continue over the buffet. . . ."

What Douglas-Home found extraordinary was "the ease" with which Sinatra was making the transition from king entertainer to business magnate. "He even admits that he is getting as much pleasure from moving pieces around on his business chessboard as he gets from being the principal piece himself."

Sinatra told his British friend: "As a singer I'll only have a few more years to go—as an actor, maybe a few more than that but not many." Obviously, Frank underestimated both his energy and his public acceptance. He added: "I've been performing out front for nearly thirty years now, and frankly I'm getting a bit tired. Now, I want to do more and more behind the scenes, using my head. Finance fascinates me."

Finance not only fascinated Sinatra, it helped him become a multimillionaire. He was not kidding when at the ceremony uniting him and Barbara Marx, as the priest asked the bride, "Do you take this man for richer, for poorer, . . ." he said in an audible aside, "richer, richer."

The prestige and power that come with wealth have made it possible for him to strike out in unexpected ways even in his numerous humanitarian undertakings. When he does a concert for Sloan-Kettering Cancer Research or for a children's hospital in Egypt, not only millionaire benefactors but also some of the country's biggest corporations are ready to give their support. This is so partly because his name carries fiscal as well as artistic weight, partly because he can approach patrons as one millionaire to another —with the result that he has raised sums of money far beyond the wildest dreams of other entertainers and the charities involved. It is no exaggeration to say that he has created a new era in the world of charity.

No one has ever questioned Sinatra's enormous sex appeal. Having begun his career in an amazing surge of female adoration—hysteria far beyond the favorable acceptance of a new singer—he was instantly cast into the role of the romantic lover. When he sang teenagers and matrons alike felt that he was making love to them, a phenomenon that has not been completely dissipated. The romantic image was reinforced by offstage flings and affairs with a long line of beautiful women, mostly actresses, including Marilyn Maxwell, Lana Turner, Lady Beatty, Dorothy Provine, Kim Novak, Jill St. John, Juliet Prowse, and Lauren Bacall.

Unquestionably, his wooing of Ava Gardner while he was still married to Nancy did more to enhance the image than any other attachment. There was a passionate recklessness in his infatuation and, when the marriage crumbled, a painfulness that made lovers the world over suffer with him. (Actor Burt Lancaster, a close friend of Sinatra's, wrote in 1972: "There is no proving that he has ever ceased loving Ava. Certainly, he is always doing favors for her. . . . Yet he also has retained a deep affection and respect for Nancy, his first wife. . . . I think Nancy is still completely in love with him." In 1976 Earl Wilson reported that when Ava saw a life-size picture of Frank in a nightclub, she embraced the Sinatra in the photograph and kissed him full on the lips.)

With Ava.

The union with Mia Farrow in 1966, shorter-lived than his marriage to Ava, revived the romantic image. "He went right politically in the '60s," Thomas Thompson wrote, "and left romantically." Sinatra was past fifty when he married Mia, who was younger than his daughter Nancy. Mia had a brittle mind, a freshness of manner and point of view, as well as innocence and youth. The disparity in years seemed to emphasize Sinatra's continuing search for an overwhelming relationship. That the marriage foundered after only two up-and-down years was hardly surprising. The breakup was not the result of the age disparity but the conflict of outlook and interests as well as Mia's desire for a career when Frank had hoped for a selfless dedication and abiding intimacy.

The romantic image, rooted in his relations with women, drew fire also from his temperament and personality. In a highly publicized career, he stood forth as restless, volatile, unconventional, intemperate, reckless, independent of mind, and emotional—all characteristics that underlined the romantic aura of his singing and flamboyant life-style.

Although the three marriages foundered for different reasons, the core of similarity was in a romanticist's failure to find emotional fulfillment. But the search by the man who has been described as "ever in love with love" continued, as his near-marriage to Lauren Bacall suggested. Temperamentally Sinatra did not seem to change much through the years if one considers his explosive brushes with press people as recently as the late '70s. But the romantic did undergo a change, several changes in fact, when it came to his friendships, his libertarian outlook, and his political associations.

Despite his domineering manner and arrogance, Sinatra is, at bottom, an extremely sensitive man. He has never forgotten (and, perhaps, never quite gotten over) how his father rebuffed him when he refused to go to college and chose, instead, as a high school dropout, to pursue a singing career. Nor did he take lightly the action of

Music Corporation of America of dropping him from the roster of artists they were willing to represent in 1952. But the rejection that cut most deeply was the snub by President John F. Kennedy in 1962—a snub that followed his intensive campaigning for JFK, his marshaling of all his associates to do likewise, his staging of the glorious gala for JFK's inaugural, and his remodeling and adding a wing to his Palm Springs home to accommodate the President on a brief visit. The snub seemed quite unfair to Sinatra, regardless of the reason, and it hurt because JFK had touched the most sensitive nerve in Frank's makeup—his desire for respect.

It was not long afterward that Sinatra began to shed his image as a swinger and to put distance between himself and the rowdy group of entertainers that made up the so-called Clan. He had always been ready to contribute his services for charity and meaningful political events. Now he embarked on an extensive program of humanitarian benefits that has made him the greatest fund-raiser among entertainers.

Francis Albert Sinatra long ago left Hoboken, New Jersey, where he spent the trying, formative years of his life. But Hoboken has never completely left him. Underneath the surface of the rich, literate, world-famous man he has become, there linger feelings generated in him as a lonely, sensitive kid, trying to cope with the coarse, cobblestone cosmos of the tough, riverside city. In Hoboken he grew up as an only child, hungering for the affection and camaraderie of two busy parents; fighting with tough kids for whom his taste in natty clothes was a challenge and his spindly frame an easy mark; being beaten up by police who accused him of stealing a new outfit he wore; and enduring the gibes of an uncle and a father who had been prizefighters and who were trying to teach him the manly art of defense.

Here were born the empathy with the little guy, the resentment of authority, the supersensitivity to slights, the yearning for power, and the sheer gutsiness he has manifested throughout his life. How deeply embedded the

Wedding portrait. Frank and Mia following their wedding at the Sands Hotel, Las Vegas, July 19, 1966.

Hoboken influence remains becomes apparent when a sensitive nerve is touched by anyone, but especially by press people. Like the mild man in TV's "Incredible Hulk," he is transformed in seconds into something he no longer is—a Hoboken kid with a mouthful of street expletives.

From Hoboken, Frank moved in his youth into a cosmos just across the river from the dockside city. Tin Pan Alley, the world of popular music, was not too far removed from Frank's birthplace in manners, morals, and mores. The Alley was a man's world with a macho interest in women, sports, betting, wise-cracking, bookies, booze, gaming, and horseplay. Since the making of a hit song depended not on record spins, as it does today, but on live performances over coast-to-coast radio, the key figure in music business was the songplugger, the man whose tough job it was to persuade bandleaders and singers to perform his plug songs. Sharp dressers, easy talkers, and colorful "characters," the songpluggers used every conceivable gambit to get the plug—cajolery, persuasion, "romance," hype, even including payola with performers who would, in the jargon of the day, "take a hot stove."

From this racy cosmos came Sinatra's first manager, Hank Sanicola, the high-spirited male entourages that were part of his world until he dropped The Clan or Rat Pack, as they were known, as well as the cherry-bomb/raw egg style of partying it up.

Cinematographer Ted Allan has never forgotten a lovely birthday party that Sinatra threw for him during the filming of *Von Ryan's Express,* a party whose liveliness resulted in a hefty bill for damages to the hotel.

"Dessert for my birthday dinner," Allan recalls, "was a huge, round, mouth-watering, chocolate-whipped cream cake—but really huge like the tires on jet planes. My wife and I each had a piece. No one else did. Sinatra arranged for a stunt man to take an unsuspecting chap he did not like and drop him—*kerplonk*—right into the center of

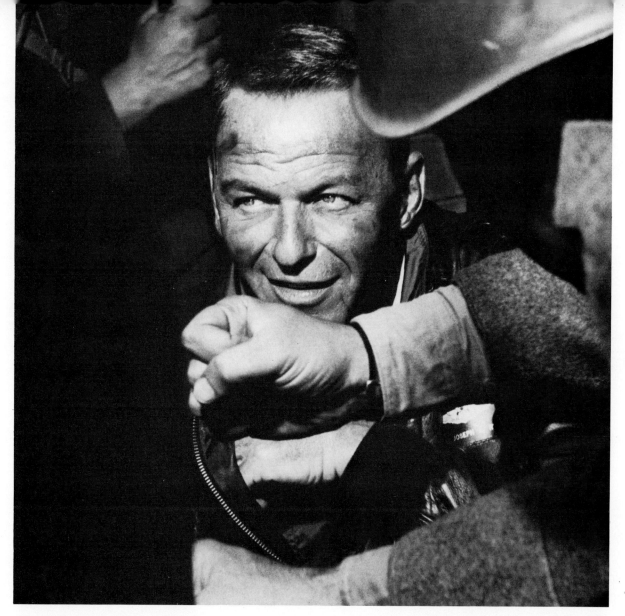

this luscious wheel of pastry. Whipped cream and chocolate frosting went flying all over the place, spattering the diners, the table, the walls and the carpets.

"After dinner, as the party went into high gear, cherry bombs were dropped into the pockets of people, scaring them out of their wits and tearing holes in their jackets — and raw eggs were broken over the heads of some of the celebrants. I was not the recipient of any of this special attention. Sinatra was a perfect gentleman with Farley Focus, as he loved to call me. But the party wore on into the wee hours, and got wilder and rougher."

The kid from Hoboken emerges at times in the monologues he delivers at concerts — monologues for whose "tasteless remarks and racist jokes" he has been taken to task by various reviewers. On one occasion, the embarrassment felt by members of the Count Basie Band over a sick Polish joke brought facial expressions of distress.

In an entirely different vein, the Hoboken kid shows himself in the pride he feels over his association with important people. Despite his displeasure and chagrin over the post-election treatment he received from John Fitzgerald Kennedy, he has had Ted Allan make enlarged copies of small, handwritten notes he received from the late President. Attractively framed, they adorn a wall of his Rancho Mirage home.

In a sense the contradictory qualities constituting the Sinatra persona stem from the superimposition of the world into which he grew on the world from which he came. That, perhaps, is why he can be tough as well as vulnerable, a battler as well as a bleeder, a dedicated family man as well as a perennial lover, a man of culture as well as foul-mouthed, gracious, and courteous but at times unbelievably coarse. By the end of the '60s, the multimillionaire in him had not completely eliminated the kid from Hoboken although the romantic was in full retreat.

In VON RYAN'S EXPRESS, 1965. (left, right)

The
Presidential
Inaugural

JANUARY 19, 1981

IT CAME AS NO SURPRISE WHEN THE NATION'S FORTI-eth President, Ronald Reagan, picked Frank Sinatra, who had switched to the Republicans and was an old Hollywood friend, to produce the show for his inauguration. Sinatra had not only supported Reagan, a frequent visitor to the Sinatra compound in Palm Springs, in his campaign for reelection as the governor of California but had been equally ardent in Reagan's drive to secure the nomination for the presidency on the GOP ticket. With Dino, Frank had launched Reagan's bid for the nomination in November 1979, filling a huge auditorium in Boston.

"I am thrilled," Sinatra said, "overjoyed, humbled and, most of all, honored that I have been chosen for the job twice in my lifetime. And I am especially happy that I will have done it for our two great political parties."

It was inevitable that Frank should think back to a snow-filled night in January 1961 when he had staged the Inaugural Gala for John Fitzgerald Kennedy, with whom he, too, had been friendly.

"I've already started praying," Sinatra said, "that it won't snow like it did last time."

On January 19, 1961, just hours before the JFK gala was set to start, Washington had been inundated by one of the heaviest snowfalls in its history. The blizzard delayed the beginning of the show until almost 11:00 P.M., as special cars were sent out to ferry guests through impassable streets. Since some of the ushers could not reach the Capitol Centre, Frank himself was at the door, checking in celebrities.

The cast assembled by Frank and the show staged by him that snowy night were regarded as one of the all-time great inaugural entertainments. The program included members of the group then known as the Clan: Joey Bishop emceed while Dean Martin, Sammy Davis, Jr., Peter Lawford (JFK's brother-in-law), and Frank Sinatra performed. Other members of a varied cast were Eleanor Roosevelt, Harry Belafonte, Gene Kelly, Ella Fitzgerald, Milton Berle, Nat "King" Cole, Jimmy Durante, Mahalia Jackson, Frederic March (who recited an Abe Lincoln address), Ethel Merman, who was forced to perform in a tweed coat, Bette Davis, who acted without her special gown, and Leonard Bernstein, who conducted in a shirt two sizes too big.

But neither the lateness of the hour nor the lack of proper costumes dimmed the high spirits of the evening. At its close the president-elect said: "We are all indebted to a great friend, Frank Sinatra. . . . Tonight, we saw excellence."

The Democratic party had another reason for feeling indebted to Sinatra. Despite the many people who were prevented from attending by the snowfall, the gala grossed close to $2 million, making JFK the first president to begin his term of office with all campaign debts paid.

With just two months to prepare the Reagan Inaugural Gala, Frank cleared all decks for a full-time work schedule. He had promised Liza Minnelli, who was then having a baby, that he would fill in for a three-night stand (December 8–10) at the Las Vegas Riviera. And he had booked a January 10 date at Radio City Music Hall in behalf of the Memorial Sloan-Kettering Cancer Center— an evening that would raise a staggering $2 million for cancer research. After that, he would be in Washington overseeing the manifold details of assembling and staging the mammoth production at the Capital Center, a sports arena in Landover, Maryland.

To head the cast he chose Johnny Carson as emcee, who opened the show by suggesting to Reagan: "If your movies drew crowds like this"—close to 19,000 attended the gala—"you wouldn't have to get into politics." Carson kidded George Bush as one who "gave up public life to become vice-president." Among the comics who joined in the raillery were Bob Hope and mimic Rich Little. Hope speculated that one advantage of having an actor in the White House was that Reagan would not have to "lie, exaggerate, or cheat—he has an agent to do it." And Rich Little, staging a question-and-answer session as an inquiring reporter, asked: "Mr. Reagan, how are you going to raise defense spending, cut taxes, and balance the budget all at the same time?" and replied in Reagan's voice: "Well, it's very simple. I'm going to keep two sets of books."

It was an evening of song, celebration, and good-humored banter, with an all-star cast that included Ben Vereen, Ethel Merman, Charlton Heston, Grace Bumbry, Debby Boone, Donny and Marie Osmond, Charley Pride, and M-M-M-Mel Tillis. Sinatra was obviously concerned to have all facets of American song represented in the program. Greeted with a standing ovation on his appearance, he closed the show with a familiar group of songs that included a Sammy Cahn parody of "Nancy (With the Laughing Face)," rewritten as a tribute to Nancy Reagan: "I'm so proud that you're First Lady, Nancy / And I'm so pleased that I'm sort of a chum / The next eight years will be fancy / As fancy as they come."

The highlight of the evening came, even if it was not so intended, when Jimmy Stewart wheeled the five-star hero of World War II, General Omar Bradley, 87, and confined to a wheelchair, onto the stage.

Produced at a cost of just under $1 million, the gala lasted for three hours. It was later seen on TV in an abbreviated two-hour version. The Republican Inaugural Committee bought time from ABC-TV and by selling commercial spots hoped to clear at least $6 million. Sinatra had once again demonstrated his savvy as producer. It was a stirring and elegant way for him to start the 1980s, his fifth decade in show business.

7. "September of My Years"

On Sunday, July 11, 1976, at 4:00 P.M. in the declining heat of a one hundred-degree Palm Springs day, Francis Albert Sinatra wed Barbara Blakely Marx. The best man was Freeman Gosden of the famous "Amos 'n Andy" team. The matron of honor was Beatrice Korshak, wife of a well-known Los Angeles attorney. The wedding ceremony was performed on the grounds of the palatial two hundred-acre estate of Walter Annenberg, former ambassador to Great Britain and publisher of *TV Guide*. It was the fourth wedding for Sinatra and the third for Ms. Marx.

Afterward 125 attended a reception at Frank's nearby Rancho Mirage compound. The Ronald Reagans (Reagan felt close enough to Frank to interrupt his campaign for the Presidency to attend the ceremony), Gregory Pecks, and Kirk Douglases, among other notable guests, savored a four-tier wedding cake and watched Frank give his bride six yellow roses and a peacock blue Rolls-Royce. Barbara's gift to her husband was a gray Jaguar.

Not long after Sinatra told an interviewer: "I really have found some kind of wonderful tranquillity. What the hell, it's about time. I'm at a very happy point in life. Barbara is a marvelous woman, a great gal. I have a different kind of life altogether—and two marvelous grandchildren."

After five years of marriage he said: "Barbara is a wonderful woman and takes good care of me. I love her. She reminds me not to stay up late at night and, if we're traveling, to get rest. She sees I eat right. She takes good care of me. I am delighted with her. There's a lot of hoopla in this business when you're single. But there were moments for me when it was all too quiet. In the late night and in the early morning. There was something lacking there. So when Barbara and I were married, I found it a better life."

Unquestionably, Sinatra's fourth marriage at the age of 60 represents a major turn in his life, and one that seems a logical step on a path he had been taking since 1966, when he took a conservative political turn. The direction had actually been set earlier, as early as 1962 when Presi-

dent John F. Kennedy bypassed the Sinatra compound to stay with Bing Crosby.

JFK's alienation was attributed to Mrs. Kennedy's displeasure with the famous, or infamous, Clan—the high-spirited group of entertainers that was supposedly the successor to Humphrey Bogart's iconoclastic Rat Pack and that included Dean Martin, Sammy Davis, Jr., Joey Bishop, and Peter Lawford, JFK's brother-in-law. There had been rumors of wild parties, and Sinatra had, in fact, introduced JFK to a gorgeous gal, Judith Exner, who, it was later revealed, had become the president's occasional bedmate. Regardless of whether Jacqueline Kennedy knew or suspected, it later became known that JFK had put distance between himself and Frank as the result of a Justice Department report whose contents indicated that a number of Sinatra's acquaintances were less-than-desirable citizens.

The JFK snub was a staggering blow to Frank's ego and sense of self-respect. An analytical man, it prompted him to reassess his social position and public image, motivating a turn to activities and friendships more in keeping with his status as a man of wealth, power, and prestige.

But there was another side to Frank's reaction. Long ago his mother had said: "My son is like me. Cross him and he never forgets." It took a bit of time, but Sinatra did not forget. In 1966 the man whose mother had been a power in the Democratic party on a local level and who had himself been a lifelong Democrat announced his support of Republican Ronald Reagan's effort to get himself reelected governor of California. Shocked Democratic friends were not happy. Soon Sinatra was moving in high Republican circles, developing friendships with GOP bigwigs like Kissinger and Vice-President Agnew.

Frank photographed two close friends, Peter Lawford and Marilyn Monroe, at the CalNeva Club. This is possibly one of the last photographs of Marilyn before her death in 1962.

By 1972 the heading on a Jack Anderson column read: "Agnew, Sinatra, Very Close Friends." Noting that they golfed and loafed together frequently at Frank's Rancho Mirage estate, Anderson also indicated that Sinatra insisted on addressing Agnew as "Mr. Vice-President" and that he took umbrage at a Palm Springs golfer who called, "Hey, Agnew!" to the Veep. During the period of his self-chosen retirement, he appeared at a Republican fund-raiser in Baltimore in May 1972 and sang a parody of "The Lady Is a Tramp" ("The Gentleman Is a Champ") to the Vice-President, who was a guest of honor. While there is a bedroom door in Frank's Rancho Mirage home with a plaque that reads, "John F. Kennedy SLEPT HERE November 6th and 7th 1960," and Sinatra treasures a red telephone used by JFK during that visit, the special guesthouse constructed to house the then-President on the visit he bypassed has been named after Spiro Agnew. When Ronald Reagan declared for the presidency in 1980, it came as no surprise that Sinatra became one of his most ardent campaigners and fund-raisers.

By 1974 Thomas Thompson observed: "Sinatra's evolution from a passionate liberal to a querulous conservative is not hard to explain." To Ralph J. Gleason, the pioneer jazz critic and a founder-columnist of *Rolling Stone*, Sinatra's turn was a disappointment and a matter of regret. "He doesn't have to be a nice guy to be a great singer," he wrote. "And he *is* a great singer. And he doesn't owe me or you or anybody a damn thing. But by the same token, I can dig his singing and not dig his style any more nor dig his friends nor his attitudes nor what they imply. . . . I don't believe any more that he is one of us. He is one of *them* now, singing from the other side of the street. . . ."

Sinatra's motivation was discernible in other areas beside the political where, as Thomas Thompson observed, "Reagan's hard-line conservative posture on many social issues was in opposition to Sinatra's liberal persuasions." When he shed his image as a swinger and liberal, Sinatra also shed the sharp clothes, which had once irritated Ava Gardner, and began dressing himself in banker's flannels. His choice of friends veered not only toward Republican influentials but to men like publisher Bennett Cerf, evangelist Billy Graham, and physician Michael De Bakey. "It was as if Frank was determined," Thompson commented, "to cloak himself in respect and dignity enough that any man, even a President, would answer his invitation."

There are a number of Hollywood bigwigs who even conjectured that with the death of John Wayne, Sinatra might succeed the Duke as the kind of American hero he represented. "Sinatra . . . is the only star who can take over the role John Wayne filled," said producer George

Pryce. Sam Wall, a Hollywood publicist, affirmed: "There was a huge vacuum left in Hollywood by the death of John Wayne. . . . Sinatra is the only star left who has that kind of status, that kind of stature. . . . But in order to step into that void, he has to accept the responsibility that goes with respectability. . . ."

Long before John Wayne's death Sinatra had demonstrated that he was cognizant of the responsibility that came with his search for recognition and acceptance in high circles. Appearing before a congressional committee investigating crime in sports in 1972, he thereafter wrote a long, probing letter to *The New York Times,* attacking the proceedings as a "star chamber" trial in which reputations, including his, were besmirched by "gutter hearsay" evidence.

"I wondered," he wrote, "if the people out there in America knew how dangerous the whole proceeding was. My privacy had been robbed from me, I had lost long hours of my life. I was being forced to defend myself in a place that was not even a court of law. . . . If this sort of thing could happen to me, it could happen to anyone, including those who cannot defend themselves properly. . . ."

After the letter was printed in *The New York Times,* he paid to have it run as an advertisement in the *Los Angeles Times,* where it appeared under the title "We Might Call This the Politics of Fantasy." The letter recalled the New Deal years, when Frank had stood forth as a liberal champion of the rights of little people.

But Frank was moving to the right politically, moving further, perhaps, than he intended or planned. "As a man ages," Thompson suggested, "he often grows conservative." The man who was ageless as a showman and still an adventurer as a singer was backpedaling as a politico. In the year of the *Times* missive, actor Burt Lancaster wrote of how he and Frank had become "true friends" because Frank was "a very strong supporter of the American Civil Liberties Union." One of the union's greatest concerns was with the First Amendment and freedom of the press.

However in 1979 Sinatra became concerned with what he termed "the unlimited power of the press" but what others denounced as a "high-domed attack on the First Amendment." Financing the mailing of a tract by a political scientist, Max M. Kampelman, Frank wrote in a covering letter: "I have met and confronted the unlimited Power of the Press. It frightens me as a husband and a parent who is concerned with the well-being and future of his family."

"Sinatra the musician endures," Dan Sullivan wrote in the *Los Angeles Times.* "Sinatra as a defender of the family, a recent persona, has been particularly hard to take." And Jim Bishop, who was generally friendly to Sinatra, castigated the broadside against the press as "infantile venom."

Nevertheless it was true that the family played a larger and larger role in Frank's thinking, and surely in the image he sought to present to the public in the 1970s. In September 1974, just three months after the birth of his first granddaughter, he appeared on the cover of the *Ladies' Home Journal*, happily holding Angela Jennifer Lambert in his arms. Titled "Love Song to My First Granddaughter," the by-lined article was both prayerful and sentimental ("Ol' Blue Eyes Meets Li'l Blue Eyes") and garlanded with photographs of himself coddling the infant; Nancy Jr. holding the baby, surrounded by her mother and Frank's mom; Nancy Sr. dangling Angela in her lap, with Nancy Jr. on the arm of the chair, embracing her mom; and papa Lambert holding the child, with Nancy Jr. and Sinatra in the background.

The family theme was played heavy again when Angela Jennifer had just passed the one-and-one-half-year mark. This time the *Ladies' Home Journal* titled its December 1975 article "Grandpa Sinatra." Mostly an interview with Nancy Jr., Frank's daughter, about her early years with Papa Sinatra, the article once again presented pictures of grandpa with the Lambert family and two poses, one a full page in color, of Sinatra with his grandchild.

By 1981 Frank told Jim Bacon: "I've got a couple of grandchildren and I'm hoping for a couple more. I think my life is quite marvelous. I have good friends and good musicians. People seem to be appreciative of what I'm doing in my work. I don't think I could ask for any one darn thing more. . . . My marriage has played a great part in my life." Shortly before that he also told Jim Bacon: "I have a Sicilian temper, but over the years, I have always admired people with restraint. I guess I've wanted to be like them. I feel now that I have mellowed."

The mellowing process was also advanced by a growing concern, which is quite understandable, with his mortality. "Dying is a pain in the ass," he said one evening on a stage at Harrah's, apropos of nothing. The death of his father of a heart attack in 1969 came as the first of a series of shocks. Even more disturbing was the demise of his mother in a 1977 plane crash. In between these times, a number of close friends passed away: comic Joe E. Lewis, publisher Bennett Cerf, and restaurateur Mike Romanoff.

When the subject began cropping up in his recorded songs—for him, the most acute form of autobiography— it was clear that death had become a real concern to him. Apart from "My Way," with its opening line, "And

now. . . the end is near," the final segment of *Trilogy* was a fantasy about aging and staving off "the cat with the scythe." In the album that followed, *She Shot Me Down*, Sinatra included an obscure Alec Wilder song, "South— to a Warmer Place." In this ballad, cowritten by Loonis McGlohn, the death of a relationship becomes the basis for reflections on mortality. At least one critic, Stephen Holden, felt that Frank's "curtly offhanded tone" suggested that "he has learned to *accept* the conditional nature of things." (My italics.)

The problem is that those of us who grew up with him from the time he was a daring proponent of tolerance and a fighter for the little man do not want him to accept. He is not supposed to follow the normal course of human development—aging, becoming disillusioned, growing conservative. He is supposed to go on fighting, challenging, defying, attacking, rebelling, and snapping the fingers at authority, the establishment, death, the human condition. That's what made him Sinatra as much as his singing artistry. That was part of his charisma, and arrogance is no substitute for guts. No one wants him to deliver "The Best is Yet to Come" as if the best were the least for most people. But how do you avoid that when you are concerned with money and power, being buddy-buddy with the wealthy influentials of Palm Springs and the conservative leaders of government?

Where's the solace? Just thinking of Sinatra the *singer*, Sinatra the actor, Sinatra the showman, above all, Sinatra the *singer*. That's what will endure after his chauffeur-driven pals, all the Reaganites, and even he himself are gone. So put on a record, lean back, and just listen.

And there it is! The unique and impeccable phrasing. The expressive changes of timbre. The sincerity that makes you a believer. In the ballads, the warmth, the vulnerability, the tenderness, the feeling that envelops you. In the up-tempo, rhythmic tunes, the swinging thrust, the buoyancy, and the insouciance.

Mitchell Fink said it in his own way not long ago: "Sinatra is a mirror image of the songs he made famous. His personality—whether you think he's a lovable rogue, or a merry prankster, or a man who hits photographers, or even a Godfather—is merely a by-product of his life in music. The music in Frank Sinatra's life will always come first." Thus stated, and for the moment at least, forget about Sinatra the Living Legend. Put away those harbored thoughts and judgments of his relationship to Ava Gardner, Pvt. Maggio, Jilly, and Ronald Reagan. . . .

Sinatra, the romantic, may be dead and gone as a person. But in his music, he endures. The ineluctable, unconquerable, inescapable romantic endures.

CHRONOLOGY

DECEMBER 12, 1915   Born in coldwater flat, 415 Monroe Street, Hoboken, New Jersey

JANUARY 28, 1931   Graduated from David E. Rue Junior High School of Hoboken

SEPTEMBER 8, 1935   Sings with Hoboken Four at Capitol Theatre. Group wins first prize in Major Bowes Amateur Hour

OCTOBER 1935   Appears in Major Bowes Amateur Hour movie short with Hoboken Four

1937–1938   Sings at Rustic Cabin on Route 9W, Alpine, New Jersey

FEBRUARY 4, 1939   Weds Nancy Barbato at Lady of Sorrows Church, Jersey City

JUNE 30, 1939   First appearance with Harry James Band, Hippodrome Theatre, Baltimore, Maryland

JULY 13, 1939   First record session with Harry James Band. First side: "From the Bottom of My Heart"

AUGUST 31, 1939   Records "All or Nothing at All" with Harry James Band

JANUARY 25, 1940   First appearance with Tommy Dorsey Band, Rockford, Illinois

FEBRUARY 1, 1940   First recording session with Tommy Dorsey Band: "The Sky Fell Down"

MARCH 13, 1940   First appearance at New York Paramount with Tommy Dorsey Band

MAY 23, 1940   Records "I'll Never Smile Again" with Tommy Dorsey Band

JUNE 8, 1940   First child born: Nancy Sandra at Margaret Hague Hospital, Jersey City

MARCH 24, 1941   Appears in film *Las Vegas Nights* (Paramount) with Tommy Dorsey Band

MAY 1941   #1 *Billboard* annual College Music Survey

JANUARY 1942   #1 *Down Beat* poll

JANUARY 19, 1942   First solo recording with Axel Stordahl, arranger-conductor, and Harry Meyerson, A & R man for

Hoboken birthplace. The two-family house at 415 Monroe Street in Hoboken, New Jersey where Francis Albert Sinatra was born December 12, 1915.

Age 6.

Bluebird Records: "The Night We Called It a Day" b/w "Night and Day." Also: "The Song Is You" b/w "Lamplighter's Serenade"

JULY 2, 1942   Last record session with Tommy Dorsey Band: "There Are Such Things" becomes #1 by December 1942

SEPTEMBER 3, 1942   Farewell broadcast with Tommy Dorsey Band

OCTOBER 1942   Leaves Tommy Dorsey

DECEMBER 30, 1942   First solo appearance at New York Paramount as Extra Added Attraction to Benny Goodman and his Orchestra. Film: *Star-Spangled Rhythm*

JANUARY 29, 1943   First appearance on *Your Hit Parade*, a CBS show presenting the top songs of the week in which he succeeded Barry Wood. First song: "Night and Day"

MARCH 11, 1943   First major nightclub booking: The Riobamba, costarring with comic Walter O'Keefe

MAY 1943   Columbia Records rereleases "All or Nothing at All," giving top billing to Sinatra instead of Harry James

JUNE 7, 1943   Cuts first solo sides for Columbia Records, accompanied only by voices because of musicians union ban on recording. First side: "Close to You" released with "You'll Never Know," Academy Award Song of 1943

AUGUST 14, 1943   First appearance at Hollywood Bowl

DECEMBER 18, 1943   *Higher and Higher*, his first speaking role in a full-length feature film, released by RKO Pictures

JANUARY 10, 1944   Franklin Wayne, later known as Frank Jr., born at Margaret Hague Hospital, Jersey City

OCTOBER 12, 1944   Thirty thousand fans cause famous Columbus Day riot at the New York Paramount Theatre

DECEMBER 30, 1944   Last appearance on Lucky Strike

Headlining at the Paramount in New York's Times Square. The line, ten abreast, composed primarily of teenage bobby-soxers, went all the way around the block while police maintain order, 1944.

Your Hit Parade show on CBS. Succeeded by Lawrence Tibbett

SEPTEMBER 12, 1945   Premiere of *Songs by Sinatra*, a CBS radio show that was on the air for two years

APRIL 1946   Voted a Special Academy Award for film short *The House I Live In*

OCTOBER 13, 1947   Frank Sinatra Day celebrated in Hoboken, New Jersey

JUNE 20, 1948   Christina, third child, born at Cedars of Lebanon Hospital, Hollywood

SEPTEMBER 5, 1949   Premiere of *Light Up Time*, a fifteen-minute radio show, sponsored by Lucky Strike, whose *Your Hit Parade* he returned to from 1947 to 1949

FEBRUARY 14, 1950   Nancy, his first wife, announces and files for separation, April 26, 1950

MAY 27, 1950   Television debut as guest star on Bob Hope's *Star-Spangled Revue* on NBC

JULY 1950   First appearance at London Palladium

OCTOBER 7, 1950   Premiere of *The Frank Sinatra Show* on CBS-TV

OCTOBER 30, 1950   Nancy Sinatra secures interlocutory decree of divorce

NOVEMBER 7, 1951   Weds Ava Gardner, Philadelphia, Pennsylvania

SEPTEMBER 17, 1952   Records last side for Columbia Records: "Why Try to Change Me Now" with Percy Faith as arranger-conductor

APRIL 2, 1953   First session at Capitol Records, Axel Stordahl, arranger-conductor of "Lean Baby" and "I'm Walking Behind You"

APRIL 30, 1953   First date with arranger-conductor Nelson Riddle: "I've Got the World on a String" and "Don't Worry 'Bout Me"

OCTOBER 27, 1953   MGM announces separation of Frank and Ava

DECEMBER 9, 1953   Records "Young at Heart," with Nelson Riddle arranging and con-

	ducting, his first hit since leaving Columbia
MARCH 25, 1954	Receives an Oscar as Best Supporting Actor for role in *From Here to Eternity*
MARCH 23, 1955	Records "Learnin' The Blues," arranged and conducted by Nelson Riddle. Climbs to #1 on single charts
AUGUST 15, 1955	Records "Love and Marriage," which he sings in TV production of "Our Town." Arranged and conducted by Nelson Riddle, it climbs to #5 on the charts
JANUARY 15, 1956	*The Man with the Golden Arm* is released. Receives a nomination as Best Actor for his starring role as Frankie Machine
APRIL 9, 1956	Records "Hey! Jealous Lover," a Top Ten hit
JULY 24, 1956	*Johnny Concho*, his first independently produced film, is released by United Artists. Also stars in the film
JULY 5, 1957	Ava Gardner divorces Frank in Mexico
AUGUST 13, 1957	Records "All the Way" by Sammy Cahn and Jimmy Van Heusen, voted the Best Film Song of the Year by the Academy of Motion Picture Arts and Sciences
OCTOBER 18, 1957	Premiere, *The Frank Sinatra Show*, on ABC
MAY 4, 1959	Album cover of *Only the Lonely* by Frank Sinatra receives a Grammy
MAY 8, 1959	Records "High Hopes" by Sammy Cahn and Jimmy Van Heusen, arranged and conducted by Nelson Riddle, the Academy Award Song of 1959
NOVEMBER 29, 1959	Receives a Grammy for Best Vocal Performance, Male, for *Come Dance with Me*. Arranged by Billy May, the album also receives a Grammy for Best Arrangement

DECEMBER 12, 1960	First session at Reprise Records, his own label. First side: "Ring-a-Ding Ding," arranged and conducted by Johnny Mandel
JANUARY 19, 1961	Stages Inaugural Gala for inauguration of John Fitzgerald Kennedy as President of the United States
JANUARY 19, 1962	Announces engagement to actress-dancer Juliet Prowse. Engagement broken on February 22, 1962
OCTOBER 12, 1962	Release of *The Manchurian Candidate* in which he stars
JANUARY 21, 1963	Records "Call Me Irresponsible" by Sammy Cahn and Jimmy Van Heusen, arranged and conducted by Nelson Riddle. Academy Award Song of 1963
FEBRUARY 9, 1963	Frank's parents celebrate their fiftieth wedding anniversary by renewing their vows in St. Augustine's Roman Catholic Church in Union City. Among Frank's gifts: a $60,000 ranch house on Abbott Boulevard in Fort Lee, New Jersey
AUGUST 1963	Sells two-thirds of Reprise Records to Warner Brothers and settles on the lot
OCTOBER 22, 1963	Nevada Gaming Commission revokes Sinatra's gaming license
DECEMBER 7, 1963	Frank Sinatra, Jr. kidnapped at Harrah's Lake Tahoe. Five days later Sinatra pays $240,000 ransom to secure son's release
MAY 10, 1964	Almost drowns in Kauai during filming of *None But the Brave*
JANUARY 1965	Warner Bros. releases *None But the Brave*, produced and directed—his first directorial assignment—by Sinatra, who also stars in the film
JULY 4, 1965	First appearance at Newport Jazz Festival
NOVEMBER 24, 1965	NBC telecast of "Sinatra: A Man and His Music," winner of Emmy, Peabody, and Edison awards

DECEMBER 12, 1965	Party for fiftieth birthday at Beverly Wilshire Hotel
MARCH 15, 1966	*September of My Years*, produced by Sonny Burke, wins a Grammy for Frank as Album of the Year, and "It Was a Very Good Year" nets him a Grammy for Best Vocal Performance, Male
JUNE 1966	"Strangers in the Night" climbs to the top of the charts, his first #1 single in USA as well as Great Britain. Selling over a million to win a Gold Record award, it also makes #1 in Argentina, Austria, Belgium, France, Italy, and Switzerland to become the biggest chartmaker single of his career
JULY 19, 1966	Actress Mia Farrow becomes Mrs. Frank Sinatra No. 3
JANUARY 1967	"That's Life" climbs into the Top Five of pop singles
MARCH 2, 1967	Wins three Grammys: Record of the Year for "Strangers in the Night"; Album of the Year for *Sinatra: A Man and His Music*; and Best Vocal Performance, Male, for "Strangers in the Night"
MARCH 5, 1967	Named National Chairman, American Italian Anti-Defamation League.
APRIL 1967	"Somethin' Stupid," his first recording with daughter Nancy enters the single charts, climbing to #1 in both the USA and Great Britain. Its sales pass the million mark to win a Gold Record from the R.I.A.A.
SEPTEMBER 9, 1967	Altercation with casino boss leads to his cancelling his association with the Sands Hotel in Las Vegas
NOVEMBER 22, 1967	Announces separation from his third wife, Mia Farrow
AUGUST 16, 1968	Mia Farrow secures divorce from Sinatra in Juarez, Mexico
NOVEMBER 26, 1968	Sinatra makes his initial appearance at Caesars Palace in Las Vegas, backed by the Harry James Orchestra

Performing with Sammy Davis, Jr. at an American-Italian Anti-Defamation League rally at Madison Square Garden, October 19, 1967. UPI

JANUARY 29, 1969	Funeral of Anthony Martin Sinatra, Frank's father, dead at 74
MAY 1969	"My Way," recorded on December 30, 1968, makes the charts
JUNE 1969	Made an Honorary Alumnus, University of California at Los Angeles
JANUARY 1970	Ground-breaking ceremony for the Anthony Martin Sinatra Medical Center at Desert Hospital in Palm Springs
JANUARY 15, 1971	Dedication ceremony of Medical Education Center, honoring his father, attended by Vice-President Spiro Agnew and Governor Ronald Reagan
FEBRUARY 5, 1971	Receives Cecil B. De Mille citation at Golden Gloves Awards
APRIL 15, 1971	Receives Jean Hersholt Humanitarian Award from Academy of Motion Picture Arts and Sciences at forty-third Oscar ceremony
JUNE 13, 1971	Following his announcement of retirement, Sinatra makes his "farewell" appearance at the fiftieth anniversary celebration of the Motion Picture and Television Relief Fund, held at the Los Angeles Music Center
NOVEMBER 1, 1972	Receives State of Israel Medallion of Valor Award
APRIL 17, 1973	Sings at White House reception in honor of Italian Prime Minister Giulio Andreotti
NOVEMBER 18, 1973	Returns to the performing scene via *Ol' Blue Eyes Is Back,* Magnavox special on NBC-TV
JANUARY 25, 1974	First 'saloon' appearance since his retirement: Caesars Palace, with Nat Brandwynne Orchestra under the baton of Gordon Jenkins
MAY 22, 1974	Sinatra becomes a grandfather with the birth of his daughter Nancy's first child, Angela Jennifer Lambert

OCTOBER 13, 1974	"Sinatra—The Main Event": Live from Madison Square Garden, ABC telecast. Produced by Jerry Weintraub. Introduced by Howard Cosell. Bill Miller conducts the Woody Herman Thundering Herd
MAY 19, 1975	Sinatra sings at the Sporting Club in Monte Carlo, the first stop in his first European tour since 1962
MAY 1976	Invested with the title, Doctor of Human Letters, by University of Nevada at Las Vegas
JULY 11, 1976	Weds Barbara Marx at the Palm Springs home of Walter Annenberg
NOVEMBER 14, 1976	Named Scopus Laureate of the Year by The American Friends of The Hebrew University of Jerusalem, Kirk Douglas, Chairman of the Sponsors Committee and Gregory Peck, Master of Ceremonies at the Award Dinner and Ball
JANUARY 13, 1977	Funeral of his mother, eighty-two, killed in a plane crash on January 6, 1977
JULY 4, 1977	Receives Freedom Medal from city of Philadelphia
NOVEMBER 2, 1977	Testimonial dinner in mother's memory in Crown Room of Stardust Hotel in Las Vegas
APRIL 3, 1978	Dedication of the Frank Sinatra International Student Center in Jerusalem, Israel
SEPTEMBER 27, 1979	Sings in the shadow of the Sphinx and the Pyramids in behalf of Cairo's Faith and Hope Rehabilitation Center, a favorite charity of the wife of Egypt's president
OCTOBER 28, 1979	"Sinatra at the Met": helps raise $1,100,000 in an appearance at the Metropolitan Opera House in Lincoln Center, in behalf of the Memorial Sloan-Kettering Cancer Center
DECEMBER 12, 1979	Caesars Palace throws a gala party to celebrate Sinatra's fortieth year in show business
JANUARY 3, 1980	*Sinatra, The First 40 Years*, based on

With Barbara.

the Caesars Palace fortieth anniversary party, is telecast over NBC-TV

JANUARY 26, 1980   Appears at Marcãna Stadium in Rio de Janeiro, Brazil, singing to an estimated one hundred seventy thousand people —the largest live audience to hear a solo performer, according to *The Guinness Book of World Records*, 1981 edition

FEBRUARY 2, 1980   Frank Sinatra Chair in Music and Theater Arts established at University of Santa Clara, San Jose, California

APRIL 1980   *Trilogy*, an elegantly packaged three-record set, is released, his first album since 1974. Produced by Sonny Burke, Record One, *The Past* ("Collectibles of the Early Years"), is arranged and conducted by Billy May; Record Two, *The Present* ("Some Very Good Years"), is arranged and conducted by Don Costa; and Record Three, *The Future*, an original cantata by Gordon Jenkins, is conducted by him. Received six Grammy nominations

JANUARY 19, 1981   Produces and stars in the gala for the inauguration of Ronald Reagan as the fortieth President of the United States

JANUARY 31, 1982   Serves as master of ceremonies at the world premiere of *Genocide*, a multimedia documentary on the Holocaust, presented at the Eisenhower Theatre of the Kennedy Center for the Performing Arts in Washington, D.C.

MARCH 25, 1982   Sings at White House reception for Italian President Sandro Pertini, costarring with Perry Como

JUNE 15, 1982   Sinatra is appointed by President Reagan to the President's Commission on the Arts and Humanities

JULY 30, 1982   Sinatra opens at the *new* Universal Amphitheatre with a benefit (all seats $50) for the Jules Stein Eye Institute, the Loyola Marymount University, and the Motion Picture and Television Fund

D I S C O G R A P H Y

Big Band Sinatra
(JULY 13, 1939 — SEPTEMBER 30, 1942)

Harry James' Greatest Hits. (Columbia)
  Vocals by Frank Sinatra, Helen Forrest, Dick Haymes,
  Kitty Kallen
Tommy Dorsey/Sinatra Sessions. (RCA SD 1000)
  A 6-record set containing all the sides Sinatra made
  with Dorsey
This Love of Mine. (RCA LPV 583)
  Frank Sinatra with the Tommy Dorsey Orchestra
Tommy Plays, Frankie Sings. (RCA Victor LPM 1569)
We 3. (RCA Victor LPM 1632)
  Frank Sinatra with Tommy Dorsey, Axel Stordahl

The Columbia Sinatra
(JUNE 7, 1943 — SEPTEMBER 17, 1952)

Frankie. (Columbia CL 606)
The Voice. (Columbia CL 743)
Frank Sinatra Conducts the Music of Alec Wilder.
  (Columbia 884)
That Old Feeling. (Columbia CL 902)
  Orchestra conducted by Axel Stordahl, Hugo
  Winterhalter, Jeff Alexander, Mitchell Ayres
Adventures of the Heart. (Columbia CL 953)
Christmas Dreaming. (Columbia CL 1032)
The Frank Sinatra Story in Music. (Columbia C 2L6)
Put Your Dreams Away. (Columbia CL 1136)
  Orchestra conducted by Axel Stordahl
Love Is a Kick. (Columbia CL 1241)
The Broadway Kick. (Columbia CL 1297)
Come Back to Sorrento. (Columbia CL 1359)
  Orchestra conducted by Axel Stordahl
Reflections. (Columbia CL 1448)
Frank Sinatra's Greatest Hits: The Early Years.
  (Columbia CL 2474)
Frank Sinatra's Greatest Hits: The Early Years. Vol 2.
  (Columbia CL 2572)
  Arranged and conducted by Axel Stordahl
The Essential Frank Sinatra. Vol. 1. (Columbia CL 2739)
The Essential Frank Sinatra. Vol. 2. (Columbia CL 2740)
The Essential Frank Sinatra. Vol. 3. (Columbia CL 2741)
Frank Sinatra in Hollywood, 1943-1949.
  (Columbia CL 2913)
Frank Sinatra, 1943 to 1951. (Columbia KG 31358)

The Capitol Sinatra

(APRIL 2, 1953 — MARCH 6, 1962)

In the Wee Small Hours. (Capitol W 581)
Swing Easy. (Capitol W 587)
   Orchestra conducted by Nelson Riddle
Songs for Swingin' Lovers. (Capitol W 653)
   Arranged and conducted by Nelson Riddle
Frank Sinatra Conducts Tone Poems of Color.
   (Capitol W 735)
High Society. (Capitol W 750)
   Bing Crosby, Grace Kelly, Frank Sinatra
   Arranged by Conrad Salinger, Nelson Riddle,
   Skip Martin. Conducted by Johnny Green
This is Sinatra. (Capitol W 768)
   Orchestra conducted by Nelson Riddle
Close to You. (Capitol W 789)
   Arranged and conducted by Nelson Riddle
A Swingin' Affair. (Capitol W 803)
   Arranged and conducted by Nelson Riddle
Where Are You? (Capitol W 855)
   Orchestra conducted by Gordon Jenkins
Come Fly with Me. (Capitol W 920)
   Orchestra conducted by Billy May
This Is Sinatra, Vol. 2. (Capitol W 982)
   Orchestra conducted by Nelson Riddle
Only the Lonely. (Capitol SW 1053)
   Orchestra conducted by Nelson Riddle
Come Dance with Me. (Capitol W 1069)
   Orchestra conducted by Billy May
Look to Your Heart. (Capitol W 1164)
   Orchestra conducted by Nelson Riddle
No One Cares. (Capitol W 1221)
Nice 'N' Easy. (Capitol W 1417)
   Orchestra conducted by Nelson Riddle
Sinatra's Swingin' Session. (Capitol W 1491)
   Orchestra conducted by Nelson Riddle
All the Way. (Capitol SW 1538)
   Orchestra conducted by Nelson Riddle
Come Swing with Me. (Capitol W 1594)
   Arranged and conducted by Billy May
Point of No Return. (Capitol W 1676)
   Arranged and conducted by Axel Stordahl
Sinatra Sings of Love and Things. (Capitol W 1729)
Sinatra: The Great Years, 1953-1960.
   (Capitol 3 WCO 1762)
   Arranged and conducted by Nelson Riddle,
   Gordon Jenkins, Billy May, Axel Stordahl

*The original caption of this MGM publicity still says, "NEW KING OF VOCALISTS . . .
the idol of the younger set, Frank Sinatra will soon be seen in a new Metro-Goldwyn-Mayer film
which will endear him further in the hearts of his fans." Dated: August 8, 1945.*

Frank Sinatra Sings Rodgers and Hart. (Capitol W 1825)

Tell Her You Love Her. (Capitol [D]T 1919)

Frank Sinatra Sings the Select Johnny Mercer.
  (Capitol W 1984)

The Great Hits of Frank Sinatra. (Capitol T 2036)

London by Night. (Capitol T 20389)
  Orchestra conducted by Gordon Jenkins

My Funny Valentine. (Capitol T 20577)
  Orchestra conducted by Nelson Riddle

Singing and Swinging. (Capitol W 20652)

The Connoisseur's Sinatra. (Capitol T 20734)

For the Sophisticated. (Capitol T 20757)

The Reprise Sinatra
(FEBRUARY 1961 —)

Ring-A-Ding Ding. (Reprise FS 1001)
  Arranged and conducted by Johnny Mandel

Sinatra Swings. (Reprise FS 1002)
  Orchestra conducted by Billy May

I Remember Tommy. (Reprise FS 1003)
  Arranged and conducted by Sy Oliver

Sinatra and Strings. (Reprise FS 1004)
  Orchestra conducted by Don Costa

Sinatra and Swingin' Brass. (Reprise FS 1005)
  Arranged and conducted by Neal Hefti

Great Songs from Great Britain. (Reprise FS 1006)
  Arranged and conducted by Robert Farnon

All Alone. (Reprise FS 1007)
  Arranged and conducted by Gordon Jenkins

Sinatra–Basie: An Historic Musical First.
  (Reprise FS 1008)

The Concert Sinatra. (Reprise FS 1009)
  Arranged and conducted by Nelson Riddle

Sinatra's Sinatra. (Reprise FS 1010)
  Arranged and conducted by Nelson Riddle

*Frank Sinatra Sings Days of Wine and Roses, Moon River
  and other Academy Award Winners.* (Reprise FS 1011)
  Arranged and conducted by Nelson Riddle

Sinatra, Basie/It Might As Well Be Swing. (Reprise FS 1012)
  Arranged and conducted by Quincy Jones

Softly, As I Leave You. (Reprise FS 1013)
  Arranged by Nelson Riddle, Marty Paich, Don Costa,
  Billy May, Ernie Freeman

September of My Years. (Reprise FS 1014)
  Arranged and conducted by Gordon Jenkins

Sinatra '65. (Reprise RS 6167)

My Kind of Broadway. (Reprise FS 1015)

A Man and His Music. (Reprise 2FS 1016)
  Orchestra conducted by Nelson Riddle,
  Gordon Jenkins, Billy May, Sy Oliver,
  Count Basie, Ernie Freeman, Johnny Mandel,
  Don Costa

Strangers in the Night. (Reprise FS 1017)

Moonlight Sinatra. (Reprise FS 1018)
    Arranged and conducted by Nelson Riddle

Sinatra, Basie/Sinatra at the Sands. (Reprise 2FS 1019)

That's Life. (Reprise FS 1020)

Francis Albert Sinatra & Antonio Carlos Jobim.
    (Reprise FS 1021)
    Arranged and conducted by Claus Ogerman

The World We Knew. (Reprise FS 1022)

Frank Sinatra and Frank & Nancy. (Reprise FS 1023)
    Arranged and conducted by Ernie Freeman,
    Billy Strange, Gordon Jenkins, Claus Ogerman

Francis A. & Edward K. (Reprise FS 1024)

Frank Sinatra's Greatest Hits. (Reprise FS 1025, FSK 2274)

The Sinatra Family Wish You a Merry Christmas.
    (Reprise FS 1026)

Cycles. (Reprise FS 1027)
    Arranged and produced by Don Costa

My Way. (Reprise FS 1029)
    Arranged and conducted by Don Costa

A Man Alone. (Reprise FS 1030)
    Arranged and conducted by Don Costa

Watertown. (Reprise FS 1031)
    Arranged and conducted by Joe Scott, Charles Calello

Frank Sinatra's Greatest Hits, Vol. 2.
    (Reprise FS 1032, FSK 2275)

Sinatra & Company. (Reprise FS 1033)
    Arranged by Eumir Deodato and Don Costa;
    conducted by Morris Stoloff

Sinatra's Greatest Hits, Vol 3. (Reprise FS 1034)

Finian's Rainbow. (Reprise FS 2015)

Guys and Dolls. (Reprise FS 2016)

Kiss Me Kate. (Reprise FS 2017)

South Pacific. (Reprise FS 2018)

America, I Hear You Singing. (Reprise FS 2020)

Robin and the Seven Hoods (Sound Track).
    (Reprise FS 2021)

Twelve Songs of Christmas. (Reprise FS 2022)

Frank Sinatra Conducts Music from Pictures and Plays
    (No Vocal). (Reprise R 6045)

Ol' Blue Eyes Is Back. (Reprise FS 2155)

Some Nice Things I've Missed. (Reprise FS 2195)

Sinatra: The Main Event/Live from Madison Square Garden.
    (Reprise FS 2207)
    Orchestra conducted by Bill Miller. Featuring Woody
    Herman and The Thundering Young Herd

Trilogy: Past, Present and Future. (Reprise 3FS 2300)
    Arranged and conducted by Billy May, Don Costa,
    Gordon Jenkins

She Shot Me Down. (Reprise FS 2305)
    Arranged and conducted by Gordon Jenkins,
    Nelson Riddle, Vincent Falcone, Jr.

Kelly sings, Sinatra dances as they play two sailors on leave in ANCHORS AWEIGH, 1945.

F I L M O G R A P H Y

1941   *Las Vegas Nights* (Paramount). Appearing as male vocalist with the Tommy Dorsey Band, Sinatra sang "I'll Never Smile Again."

1942   *Ship Ahoy* (Metro-Goldwyn-Mayer). Appearing as a male vocalist with Tommy Dorsey and His Orchestra, Sinatra sang "The Last Call for Love" and "Poor You."

1943   *Reveille with Beverly* (Columbia). As a name soloist, Sinatra sang "Night and Day."

1943   *Higher and Higher* (RKO). In his first starring role, opposite Michele Morgan, Sinatra sang "I Couldn't Sleep a Wink Last Night," "A Lovely Way to Spend an Evening," "The Music Stopped," "You Belong in a Love Song," and "I Saw You First," all by Jimmy McHugh and Harold Adamson.

1944   *Step Lively* (RKO). Appearing opposite Gloria de Haven, Sinatra sang "Where Does Love Begin?" "Come Out, Come Out, Wherever You Are," "As Long as There's Music," and "Some Other Time," all by Jule Styne and Sammy Cahn.

1945   *Anchors Aweigh* (Metro-Goldwyn-Mayer). Starring opposite Kathryn Grayson and Gene Kelly, Sinatra sang "We Hate to Leave," "What Makes the Sunset?" "The Charm of You," "I Begged Her," and "I Fall in Love Too Easily," all by Jule Styne and Sammy Cahn. Also "Lullaby" by Johannes Brahms.

1945   *The House I Live In** (RKO Radio). Starring in this plea for racial and religious tolerance, Sinatra sang "If You Are But a Dream" (adapted from Anton Rubinstein's "Romance") by Nathan J. Bonx, Jack Fulton, and Moe Jaffe, and "The House I Live In" by Earl Robinson and Lewis Allen.

1946   *Till the Clouds Roll By* (Metro-Goldwyn-Mayer). Appearing as a guest star in this bio pic of composer Jerome Kern, Sinatra sang "Ol' Man River" by Jerome Kern and Oscar Hammerstein II.

1947   *It Happened in Brooklyn* (Metro-Goldwyn-Mayer). Starring opposite Kathryn Grayson, Sinatra sang "Time After Time," "Brooklyn Bridge," "I Believe," "The Song's Gotta Come from the Heart," all by Jule Styne and Sammy Cahn. Also "La Ci Darem Ia Mano" by Mozart and "Black Eyes" in Russian.

1948   *The Miracle of the Bells* (RKO). Playing a dramatic role as a Catholic priest, Sinatra sang one unaccompanied song, "Ever Homeward," by Kasimierz Lubomirski, Jule Styne, and Sammy Cahn.

1948   *The Kissing Bandit* (Metro-Goldwyn-Mayer). Starring opposite Kathryn Grayson, Sinatra sang "What's Wrong with Me?" "If I Steal a Kiss," and "Senorita" by Nacio Herb Brown and Edward Eliscu, and "Siesta" by Nacio Herb Brown and Earl Brent.

1949   *Take Me Out to the Ball Game* (Metro-Goldwyn-Mayer). Starring opposite Esther Williams and Gene Kelly, Sinatra sang six songs: the title tune by Albert von Tilzer and Jack Norworth; "Yes, Indeedy," "O'Brien to Ryan to Goldberg," "The Right Girl for Me," and "It's Fate, Baby, It's Fate" by Roger Edens, Betty Comden, and Adolph Green; and "Strictly U.S.A." by Roger Edens.

1949   *On the Town* (Metro-Goldwyn-Mayer). Starring Gene Kelly, Sinatra sings the title tune, "You're Awful," and "Count on Me" by Roger Edens, Adolph Green, and Betty Comden; and "Come Up to My Place" and "New York, New York" by Leonard Bernstein, Adolph Green, and Betty Comden.

Disguised as a harem dancer for a comedy sequence in ON THE TOWN, 1949.

1951   *Double Dynamite* (RKO Radio). Starring with Jane Russell and Groucho Marx, Sinatra sang only two songs, "Kisses and Tears" and "It's Only Money," both by Jule Styne and Sammy Cahn.

1951   *Meet Danny Wilson* (Universal-International). Starring with Shelley Winters and Alex Nicol, Sinatra sang nine songs: "You're a Sweetheart" by Jimmy McHugh and Harold Adamson; "Lonesome Man Blues" by Sy Oliver; "A Good Man Is Hard to Find" by Eddie Green; "That Old Black Magic" by Harold Arlen and Johnny Mercer; "When You're Smiling" by Mark Fisher, Joe Goodwin, and Larry Shay; "All of Me" by Seymour Simons and Gerald Marks; "I've Got a Crush on You" by George and Ira Gershwin; "How Deep Is the Ocean?" by Irving Berlin; "She's Funny That Way" by Richard Whiting and Neil Morel.

With Groucho in
DOUBLE DYNAMITE, 1951.

1953   *From Here to Eternity*** (Columbia). Sinatra's name appeared fifth in the list of stars, which included Burt Lancaster, Montgomery Clift, Deborah Kerr, and Donna Reed. This film marked the beginning of his career as an actor.

1954   *Suddenly* (Libra Production/United Artists Release). Starred Frank Sinatra, Sterling Hayden, James Gleason, and Nancy Gates.

1955   *Young at Heart* (Arwin Production/Warner Brothers Release). The credits read Doris Day, Frank Sinatra, Gig Young, Ethel Barrymore, and Dorothy Malone. Sinatra sang alone or with Doris Day: the title tune by Johnny Richards and Carolyn Leigh, "Someone to Watch Over Me" by George and Ira Gershwin; "Just One of Those Things" by Cole Porter; "One for My Baby" by Harold Arlen and Johnny Mercer; and "You, My Love" by Mack Gordon and James Van Heusen.

1955   *Not As a Stranger* (Stanley Kramer Production/United Artists Release). The credits read Olivia de Havilland, Robert Mitchum, Frank Sinatra, Gloria Grahame, Broderick Crawford, and Charles Bickford.

1955   *The Tender Trap* (Metro-Goldwyn-Mayer). The credits read Frank Sinatra, Debbie Reynolds, David Wayne, Celeste Holm, Jarma Lewis, Lola Albright, and Carolyn Jones. Sinatra sang the title tune by James Van Heusen and Sammy Cahn.

1955   *Guys and Dolls* (Samuel Goldwyn Production/Metro-Goldwyn-Mayer Release). The stars were Marlon Brando, Jean Simmons, Frank Sinatra, and Vivian Blaine. Among the songs that Sinatra sang alone or with others are: "The Oldest Established (Floating Crap Game in New York)," "Sue Me," the title tune, and "Adelaide," which lyricist-composer Frank Loesser wrote especially for the film.

1955   *The Man with the Golden Arm*** (Carlyle Production/United Artists Release). Frank Sinatra starred with Eleanor Parker and Kim Novak.

1956   *Meet Me in Las Vegas* (Metro-Goldwyn-Mayer). Frank Sinatra made an unbilled guest appearance, along with Debbie Reynolds, Tony Martin, and Vic Damone, in a film that starred Dan Dailey and Cyd Charisse.

In his Academy Award-winning role as Maggio in FROM HERE TO ETERNITY, 1953.

1956 *Johnny Concho* (Kent Production/United Artists Release). The stars were Frank Sinatra, Keenan Wynn, William Conrad, and Phyllis Kirk. Sinatra was also the producer.

1956 *High Society* (Metro-Goldwyn-Mayer). Frank Sinatra starred with Bing Crosby and Grace Kelly, and sang four Cole Porter songs: "Who Wants to Be a Millionaire?" "You're Sensational," "Mind If I Make Love to You?" and "Well, Did You Evah?" the last-mentioned a show-stopping duet with Bing.

1956 *Around the World in 80 Days* (Michael Todd Production/United Artists Release). There are 40 cameos in this film, starring David Niven, Cantinflas, Shirley MacLaine, and Robert Newton. Sinatra appeared briefly as a piano player in a Barbary Coast saloon.

1957 *The Pride and the Passion* (Stanley Kramer Production/United Artists Release). Frank Sinatra starred, together with Cary Grant and Sophia Loren.

1957 *The Joker Is Wild* (A.M.B.L. Production/Paramount Release). Frank Sinatra starred, together with Mitzi Gaynor, Jeanne Crain, and Eddie Albert. Sinatra sang "I Cried for You" by Arthur Freed, Gus Arnheim, and Abe Lyman; "If I Could Be With You" by Jimmy Johnson and Henry Creamer; "Chicago" by Fred Fisher; and "All the Way"**** by James Van Heusen and Sammy Cahn.

1957 *Pal Joey* (Essex-George Sidney Production/Columbia Release). The stars were Rita Hayworth, Frank Sinatra, and Kim Novak. Sinatra sang "I Didn't Know What Time It Was," "There's a Small Hotel," "I Could Write a Book," "The Lady Is a Tramp," "Bewitched, Bothered and Bewildered," and "What Do I Care for a Dame?" all by Richard Rodgers and Lorenz Hart.

1958 *Kings Go Forth* (Frank Ross–Eton Production/United Artists Release). The stars were Frank Sinatra, Tony Curtis, and Natalie Wood.

1958 *Some Came Running* (Metro-Goldwyn-Mayer). Frank Sinatra starred with Dean Martin, Shirley MacLaine, Martha Hyer, and Arthur Kennedy.

1959   *A Hole in the Head* (Sincap Production/United Artists Release). Starred Frank Sinatra, Edward G. Robinson, Eleanor Parker, Carolyn Jones, Thelma Ritter, and Keenan Wynn. Sinatra sang "All My Tomorrows" and "High Hopes," ***** both by James Van Heusen and Sammy Cahn.

1959   *Never So Few* (Canterbury Production/Metro-Goldwyn-Mayer Release). Starred Frank Sinatra, Gina Lollobrigida, Peter Lawford, Steve McQueen, Richard Johnson, Paul Henried, Brian Donlevy, and Dean Jones.

1960   *Can-Can* (Suffolk-Cummings Production/20th Century-Fox Release). Starred Frank Sinatra, Shirley MacLaine, Maurice Chevalier, and Louis Jourdan. Sinatra sang "I Love Paris," "C'est Magnifique," "It's All Right With Me," and "Let's Do It," all by Cole Porter.

High hopes come true for Sinatra with child star Eddie Hodges and director Frank Capra,
during the production of A HOLE IN THE HEAD, 1959.

1960 *Ocean's Eleven* (Dorchester Production/Warner Brothers Release). Starred Frank Sinatra, Dean Martin, Sammy Davis, Jr., Peter Lawford, Angie Dickinson, Richard Conte, Cesar Romero, Patrice Wymore, Joey Bishop, Akim Tamiroff, and Henry Silva.

1960 *Pepe* (G.S. Posa Films International Production/Columbia Release). Frank Sinatra was one of 27 personalities who appeared as guest stars (as themselves) in a film starring Cantinflas, Dan Dailey, and Shirley Jones. All the members of the so-called Clan—Joey Bishop, Sammy Davis, Jr., Peter Lawford, and Dean Martin—also appeared as did Bing Crosby, Tony Curtis, Bobby Darin, and others.

1961 *The Devil at 4 O'Clock* (Columbia). Spencer Tracy and Frank Sinatra were the stars.

1962 *Sergeants 3* (Essex-Claude Production/United Artists Release). The stars were Frank Sinatra, Dean Martin, Sammy Davis, Jr., Peter Lawford, and Joey Bishop.

1962 *The Road to Hong Kong* (Melnor Films Production/United Artists Release). Frank Sinatra and Dean Martin appeared as guest artists (spacemen with little toy propellers on their hats) in this film starring Bing Crosby, Bob Hope, Joan Collins, and Dorothy Lamour.

1963 *The Manchurian Candidate* (M.C. Production/United Artists Release). The stars were Frank Sinatra, Laurence Harvey, Janet Leigh, Angela Lansbury, Henry Silva, James Gregory, and Leslie Parrish.

1963 *Come Blow Your Horn* (Essex-Tandem Production/Paramount Release). Starred Frank Sinatra, Lee J. Cobb, Molly Picon, Barbara Rush, Jill St. John, and Tony Bill.

1963 *The List of Adrian Messenger* (Joel Production/Universal Release). Frank Sinatra was one of 5 stars who appeared in the film in disguise. The stars were George C. Scott, Dana Wynter, and Clive Brook. Sinatra was a gypsy stableman.

1964 *4 for Texas* (Sam Company Production/Warner Brothers Release). The stars were Frank Sinatra, Dean Martin, Anita Ekberg, Ursula Andress, Charles Bronson, and Victor Buono.

In SERGEANTS 3.

ROBIN AND THE 7 HOODS, 1964.

1964 *Robin and the 7 Hoods* (P.C. Production/Warner Brothers Release). Starred Frank Sinatra, Dean Martin, Sammy Davis, Jr., Peter Falk, Barbara Rush, and Victor Buono. Sinatra sang "Style," "Mr. Booze," "Don't Be a Do-Badder," and "My Kind of Town," all by James Van Heusen and Sammy Cahn.

1965 *None But the Brave* (Artanis Production/Warner Brothers Release). Frank Sinatra was producer, director, and star of this World War II melodrama, whose featured players included Clint Walker, Tommy Sands, Brad Dexter, and Tony Bill.

1965 *Von Ryan's Express* (P.R. Production/20th Century-Fox Release). Starred Frank Sinatra and Trevor Howard, with Raffaella Carra, Brad Dexter, Sergio Fantoni, John Leyton, Edward Mulhare, and Wolfgang Preiss as featured players.

1965 *Marriage on the Rocks* (A.C. Production/Warner Brothers Release). Starred Frank Sinatra, Deborah Kerr, and Dean Martin, with Cesar Romero, Hermione Baddeley, Tony Bill, and John McGiver as featured players.

1966 *Cast a Giant Shadow* (Mirisch-Llenroc-Batjac Production/United Artists Release). Sinatra popped in as a soldier-of-fortune pilot into a bio pic of the late Colonel David Marcus, played by Kirk Douglas. Senta Berger starred opposite Douglas, with Angie Dickinson, James Donald, Stathis Giallelis, Luther Adler, Gary Merrill, and Haym Topol as featured players.

In VON RYAN'S EXPRESS, 1965.

1966 *The Oscar* (Greene-Rouse Production/Embassy Release). Frank Sinatra played himself, as did Bob Hope, Merle Oberon, and Nancy Sinatra in a film that starred Stephen Boyd, Elke Sommer, Milton Berle, Eleanor Parker, and Joseph Cotten.

1966 *Assault on a Queen* (Sinatra Enterprises–Seven Arts Production/Paramount Release). Starred Frank Sinatra, Virna Lisi, and Tony Franciosa, with Richard Conte, Alf Kjellin, and Errol John as featured players.

1967 *The Naked Runner* (Sinatra Enterprises Production/Warner Brothers Release). Frank Sinatra starred in a film whose featured players were Peter Vaughan, Derren Nesbitt, Nadia Gray, Toby Robins, and Inger Stratton.

In THE NAKED RUNNER, 1967.

1967   *Tony Rome* (Arcola-Millfield Production/20th Century-Fox Release). Frank Sinatra starred, and the featured players were Jill St. John, Richard Conte, Gena Rowlands, Simon Oakland, Jeffrey Lynn, and Lloyd Bochner.

1968   *The Detective* (Arcola-Millfield Production/20th Century-Fox Release). Frank Sinatra and Lee Remick starred, and the featured players were Ralph Meeker, Jack Klugman, Horace McMahon, Lloyd Bochner, William Windom, Tony Musante, Al Freeman, Jr., Robert Duvall, and Jacqueline Bisset.

1968   *Lady in Cement* (Arcola-Millfield Production/ 20th Century-Fox Release). Frank Sinatra starred, and the featured players were Raquel Welch, Dan Blocker, Richard Conte, Martin Gabel, Lainie Kazan, and Pat Henry.

1970   *Dirty Dingus Magee* (Metro-Goldwyn-Mayer). Starred Frank Sinatra and George Kennedy, with Anne Jackson and Lois Nettleton in featured roles.

1977   *Contract on Cherry Street* (Atlantis Production/ Columbia Release). His first television movie (to be shown abroad as a regular film), *Contract on Cherry Street* was filmed entirely on location in New York City. Starring as a police inspector, Sinatra was supported by Martin Balsam, Jay Black, Verna Bloom, Joe de Santis, Martin Gabel, Harry Guardino, James Luisi, Michael Nouri, Marco St. John, Henry Silva, and Richard Ward.

1980   *The First Deadly Sin* (Artanis–Cinema VII Production/Filmways Release). Serving as Executive Producer with Elliott Kastner, Sinatra starred opposite Faye Dunaway. Costars included James Whitmore, David Dukes, Brenda Vaccaro, Martin Gabel, and Anthony Zerbe.

    * *Received a Special Academy Award.*
  ** *Won an Oscar at the Academy Awards in 1954 as Best Supporting Actor.*
Donna Reed won an Oscar for Best Supporting Actress, and the film won six other Oscars.
 *** *Sinatra was nominated for an Oscar, won by Ernest Borgnine for* Marty.
**** *"All the Way" won an Academy Award as the Best Song of 1957.*
***** *"High Hopes" won an Academy Award as Best Song of 1959.*

25 Favorite Sinatra Recordings

*(Poll Conducted by Solters and
Roskin, April 1, 1980)*

1. "I've Got You Under My Skin" (Cole Porter)
   Arr: Nelson Riddle
   Recorded 1/12/56 (Capitol)

2. "The Lady Is a Tramp" (Rodgers & Hart)
   Arr: Nelson Riddle
   Recorded 11/26/56 (Capitol)

3. "Chicago" (Fred Fisher)
   Arr: Nelson Riddle
   Recorded 8/13/57 (Capitol)

4. "My Way" (Paul Anka, C. Francois,
   J. Revaix, G. Thibault)
   Arr: Don Costa
   Recorded 12/30/68 (Reprise)

5. "Send in the Clowns" (Stephen Sondheim)
   Arr: Don Costa
   Recorded 6/6/73 (Reprise)

6. "Nancy (With the Laughing Face)"
   (Jimmy Van Heusen, Phil Silvers)
   Arr: Alex Stordahl
   Recorded 8/22/45 (Columbia)

7. "Here's That Rainy Day"
   (Jimmy Van Heusen, Johnny Burke)
   Arr: Gordon Jenkins
   Recorded 3/3/59 (Capitol)

8. "All the Way" (Jimmy Van Heusen, Sammy Cahn)
   Arr: Nelson Riddle
   Recorded 8/13/57 (Capitol)

9. "It Was a Very Good Year" (Ervin Drake)
   Arr: Gordon Jenkins
   Recorded 4/22/65 (Reprise)

10. "Night and Day" (Cole Porter)
    Arr: Nelson Riddle
    Recorded 11/26/56 (Capitol)

11. "Come Fly with Me" (Jimmy Van Heusen,
    Sammy Cahn)
    Arr: Billy May
    Recorded 10/8/57 (Capitol)

12. "I Get a Kick Out of You" (Cole Porter)
    Arr: Nelson Riddle
    Recorded 11/6/53 (Capitol)

13. "All or Nothing at All" (Arthur Altman,
    Jack Lawrence)

A rare personal appearance at Macy's department store in New York.

NEAL PETERS COLLECTION

Arr: Andy Gibson
Recorded 9/17/39 (Columbia)

14. "Angel Eyes" (Matt Dennis, Earl Brent)
 Arr: Nelson Riddle
 Recorded 5/29/58 (Capitol)

15. "You Make Me Feel So Young"
 (Joseph Myrow, Mack Gordon)
 Arr: Nelson Riddle
 Recorded 1/9/56 (Capitol)

16. "(In the) Wee Small Hours (Of the Morning)"
 (Dave Mann, Bob Hilliard)
 Arr: Nelson Riddle
 Recorded 2/17/55 (Capitol)

17. "Ol' Man River" (Jerome Kern,
 Oscar Hammerstein II)
 Arr: Alex Stordahl
 Recorded 12/13/44 (Columbia)

18. "All of Me" (Gerald Marks, Seymour Simons)
 Arr: George Siravo
 Recorded 11/17/46 (Columbia)

19. "Witchcraft" (Cy Coleman, Carolyn Leigh)
 Arr: Nelson Riddle
 Recorded 5/20/57 (Capitol)

20. "Put Your Dreams Away" (Stephen Weiss,
 Paul Mann, Ruth Lowe)
 Arr: Axel Stordahl
 Recorded 5/11/45 (Columbia)

21. "One for My Baby" (Harold Arlen,
 Johnny Mercer)
 Arr: Nelson Riddle
 Recorded 6/25/58 (Capitol)

22. "Where or When" (Rodgers & Hart)
 Arr: Axel Stordahl
 Recorded 1/29/45 (Columbia)

23. "Violets for Your Furs" (Matt Dennis, Tom Adair)
 Arr: Nelson Riddle
 Recorded 11/5/53 (Capitol)

24. "Strangers in the Night" (Bert Kaempfert,
 Charles Singleton, Eddie Snyder)
 Arr: Ernie Freeman
 Recorded 4/11/66 (Reprise)

25. "September of My Years" (Jimmy Van Heusen,
 Sammy Cahn)
 Arr: Gordon Jenkins
 Recorded 5/27/65 (Reprise)

ABOUT THE AUTHOR

Arnold Shaw has enjoyed a varied career as a musicologist, composer, and author. His eleven books include *Honkers and Shouters: The Golden Years of Rhythm and Blues*, acclaimed by *Rolling Stone* as "monumental." His 1968 biography, *Sinatra: 20th-Century Romantic* is regarded internationally as a primary source for Sinatra lovers. His books and articles have twice won the prestigious ASCAP–Deems Taylor Award. A former music publishing executive, he worked with such artists as Elvis Presley, Paul Simon, Harry Belafonte, and Johnny Mathis. A songwriter, too, his credits include "Dungaree Doll" and "A Man Called Peter." An academic, he teaches a popular music course at the University of Nevada in Las Vegas where he lives with his wife, Ghita, and daughter, Mindy Sura.

ABOUT THE PHOTOGRAPHER

Ted Allan is the classic Hollywood portrait photographer. His 40-year career began as a commercial artist doing movie displays and progressed to still photography for Charlie Chan and Tarzan movies. Experiments with glamour lighting led to portraits of such stars as Jean Harlow, Carole Lombard, Hedy Lamarr, Spencer Tracy, and Robert Taylor. Seven years as official photographer to Frank Sinatra Enterprises has resulted in the rare collection assembled for this book. With his work appearing at the Museum of Modern Art and in such books as John Kobal's *The Art of the Great Hollywood Portrait Photographers,* Allan is slightly bemused but nonetheless pleased that his 1930's glamour shots should be hailed today as "Art." He lives and works in Hollywood with his wife, Jeanne, his four cats, and Samoyed dogs. Among his prized possessions is an oil painting by Frank Sinatra of New York City at night.